hard to be human

hard to be human

Overcoming Our 5 Cognitive Design Flaws

TED CADSBY

Publisher and acquiring editor: Scott Fraser | Editor: Cy Strom
Cover designer: Laura Boyle | Interior designer: Karen Alexiou
Printer: Marquis Book Printing Inc.

Library and Archives Canada Cataloguing in Publication

Title: Hard to be human : overcoming our five cognitive design flaws / Ted Cadsby.
Names: Cadsby, Ted, author.
Description: Includes bibliographical references and index.
Identifiers: Canadiana (print) 2021022195X | Canadiana (ebook) 20210222557 | ISBN 9781459748842 (softcover) | ISBN 9781459748859 (PDF) | ISBN 9781459748866 (EPUB)
Subjects: LCSH: Cognitive psychology—Popular works. | LCSH: Cognition—Popular works. | LCSH: Brain— Popular works. | LCSH: Thought and thinking.
Classification: LCC BF201 .C33 2021 | DDC 153—dc23

Canada Council for the Arts
Conseil des arts du Canada

We acknowledge the support of the Canada Council for the Arts and the Ontario Arts Council for our publishing program. We also acknowledge the financial support of the Government of Ontario, through the Ontario Book Publishing Tax Credit and Ontario Creates, and the Government of Canada.

Printed and bound in Canada.

Dundurn Press
1382 Queen Street East
Toronto, Ontario, Canada M4L 1C9
dundurn.com, @dundurnpress

To J & M
I’ve got your backs, always.

CONTENTS

INTRODUCTION

Other Animals Have It Easier

You and I are freaks of nature: the only surviving species in the most complex genus of the primate order in the mammalian class of animals. We *Homo sapiens* are a seven-million-year-old hominin experiment that actually began four billion years ago when the first living cells embarked on a trial-and-error path that dead-ended for our Neanderthal cousins and many other human species. We bumbled our way through various obstacle courses that the other humans failed to navigate, and here we are: rudimentary animals with an added layer of mental complexity, off-the-rack primates with souped-up brains. Although, in fairness, "souped-up" doesn't do our grey matter justice.

An elephant's brain is three times as large and has three times as many neurons (257 billion versus our 86 billion). But most of its neurons are crammed into its cerebellum, which navigates its huge body and hard-working trunk, leaving a small portion of neurons for its cerebral cortex — the seat of high-level thinking. We, on the other hand, have three times as many cerebral neurons (some of which make up our unusually large prefrontal cortex — the seat of "super high-level" thinking). No other animal has anywhere close to our cerebral neuronal density, which is the basis of our remarkable cognitive complexity, including the unique form of human consciousness.

As impressive as it is, this cerebral complexity also underlies the human predicament. Tortured by our own minds like no other animal, we expend a lot of mental energy reliving past anguish, anticipating future distress, stewing in self-righteous anger, and reacting to triggers that are products of our overactive imaginations.

If other animals could study us the way we study them, they would be puzzled by our unique ability to inflict misery on ourselves. They would call us out for what we are: oddly paradoxical creatures who long to be happy while creating our own suffering in the form of anxiety, fury, depression, self-pity, and even self-loathing. We worry about things we have no control over. We aspire to goals we lack the discipline to achieve. We whine about not being understood while casting a critical eye on others. We stubbornly defend our entrenched opinions despite ambiguous if not contradictory evidence. Complicating all of this is our struggle to adapt to a complex world that we ourselves created. The paradoxes of being human are stacked high.

While they don't know it, other animals have it easier.

Comparing humans and other animals, the philosopher Arthur Schopenhauer had an interesting perspective on who suffers more. In his 1851 essay "On the Suffering of the World," he argues that there is no contest:

- "Boredom is a form of suffering unknown to brutes … whereas in the case of man it has become a downright scourge."
- Human needs are "much more difficult to satisfy than those of the brute" because "the brute is much more content with mere existence than man."
- "Brutes show real wisdom when compared with us … their quiet, placid enjoyment of the present moment … puts us to shame for the many times we allow our thoughts to make us restless and discontented."
- "Evil presses upon the brute only with its own intrinsic weight; whereas with us the fear of its coming often makes its burden ten times more grievous."

Schopenhauer points out that only humans are haunted by the spectre of their own death. Ultimately, "need and boredom are the two poles of human life" and "suffering in human life [is] out of all proportion to its pleasures." He concludes that we should actually envy other animals, because the human life is characterized by misery "where each of us pays the penalty of existence in his own peculiar way" but "misfortune in general is the rule." He suggests that we humans should address one another as "my fellow sufferer."

Lest you are tempted to dismiss Schopenhauer as comically extreme, he reminds us that most ancient Indian and Greek mythologies put human misery at the centre of their stories, as does the Christian doctrine that "we come into the world with the burden of sin upon us ... having to continually atone for this sin." I would add that the seeming serenity of Buddhism starts from the premise that life is interminable suffering. And that suicide appears to be a unique human affliction: while other animals can inflict harm on themselves and respond to trauma with self-neglect, they do not demonstrate an intent to kill themselves. As science writer Jesse Bering puts it in his book *Suicidal*, "On no occasion has a distraught or ostracized ape ever been seen ... to climb to the highest branch it could find and jump. That's us. We're the ape that jumps." In fact, research indicates that at least 40 percent of us contemplate suicide at some point in our lives, and fully half of that group formulate plans to carry it out.[1] It would appear that it takes the complexity of a human brain to have the sophistication to curtail its own existence. It's hard to sum up the human condition, but physician Russ Harris does a pretty good job: "The psychological processes of a normal human mind are often destructive, and create psychological suffering for us all, sooner or later."[2]

What's Our Problem?

I like the way author Nassim Nicholas Taleb captures our predicament: "Our minds are like inmates, captive to our biology, unless we manage a cunning escape."[3] (Remember these last six words because I'll come back to them.) In fact, our minds have minds of their own. Of the many human paradoxes, this is the central one and the primary source of our unique struggle: we are captive to ourselves. Our well-being depends on a three-pound, electrical meat machine with a long, circuitous history of development that yielded some amazing features but also some troublesome glitches — not "bugs" per se, since the flaws are embedded in the features themselves.

The problem, at a high level: our brains are imperfect in substantive ways that are not obvious to us.

The massively complex information-processing apparatus that is the human brain is a jerry-rigged contraption that evolution built over an extended period by gradually adding new components to an original operating platform. This unimaginably long development process (which is still in progress) has culminated in a peculiar and somewhat sloppy fusion of an "ancient, basic" thinking system (that operates subconsciously) and a "modern, special" one (that is largely conscious). Cognitive scientists typically refer to the older and newer systems as System 1 and System 2, respectively. Each system can be crudely associated with distinct brain areas, but there is significant anatomical overlap between them. And there are a couple of significant kinks in the overall design of this cognitive machinery — features that entail flaws in need of a fix.

There are kinks in the design of our cognitive machinery — features that entail flaws in need of a fix.

First, System 1 does most of the work, but its features were designed to facilitate survival in a different kind of world than the one we live in now. *System 1 design flaws cause us to misperceive reality in significant ways.* The Buddha insisted that human suffering is the result of an illusory view of reality and that the elimination of suffering depends on a deep, meditative acknowledgement of the "facts of existence." We can quibble about what these facts are, but his general insight is piercing: *human suffering is largely a function of misunderstanding how the world (including other people) actually works.*

Second, because System 1 functions largely below the level of our consciousness, its design flaws are concealed from our day-to-day awareness even though they produce conspicuous distress for us. (Decades before Sigmund Freud wrote about the unconscious, our friend Schopenhauer posited that the largest part of our thinking and motivation is hidden from us.) System 1's errors wouldn't be so problematic if we were able to account for them more easily and use System 2's more analytic approach to override them. But the marriage between System 1 and System 2 is not an equitable one: old and new don't always work well together. Our ancient cognitive system — which governs the vast majority of our thinking, feeling, and behaviour — yields little authority to the newer cognitive system, which has the capacity to be better behaved and better adapted to our modern world. Good historical reasons support System 1's dominance — its speed was crucial for survival in the past and still is. But the imbalance between the two thinking systems is outdated: *System 2's backseat role is ill-suited to being human today.*

So it's hard to be human because our extraordinarily complex brains are hard to manage. Much of our incremental suffering, above and beyond what other species endure, arises from (i) System 1 design features that often morph into design flaws, clouding our ability to perceive reality accurately, and (ii) System 2's inability to detect and correct the flaws, constrained as it is by System 1's overbearing nature.

What are the specific design features that become flaws and cause us misery? Five big ones stand out. Are there fixes? Yes, there are fixes — maybe more accurately described as "workarounds," but fixes nonetheless.

Features Become Flaws: The Big Five

System 1's shortcomings induce us to *under*think and *over*react. We think too little and emote too much. We mindlessly take mental shortcuts for problems that require greater cognitive sophistication, and we are taken hostage by emotions whose intensity is disproportionate to their triggers.

We underthink and overreact — we think too little and emote too much.

Underthinking and overreacting are, I believe, the two big precursors to human suffering. But also contributing to our struggle are their opposites: *over*thinking and *under*reacting. We overthink when we obsessively ruminate about trivial things or situations over which we have no control. And we underreact when we neglect the pleasure and serenity available to us in the present moment.

The first step in making it easier to be human is to identify our five big cognitive flaws, emanating from five big design features:

1. **Greedy Reductionism**
   We simplify everything we think about (*design feature*), including the more complicated scenarios in our lives that other animals do not have to contend with (*flaw: chapters 3 and 4*). Our greedy desire to reduce reality means we oversimplify.

2. **Certainty Addiction**
   We are addicted to the feeling of certainty (*design feature*), despite being confronted by ambiguity and uncertainty that do not plague other animals (*flaw: chapters 5 and 6*). We are overconfident.

3. **Emotional Hostage-Taking**
   We react swiftly and strongly to threats (*design feature*), but are prone to overreacting, in part because of the unique human proclivity for excessive, unproductive rumination (*flaw: chapters 7 and 8*). We take ourselves emotionally hostage.

4. **Competing Selves**
   We adapt with flexibility to different people and different situations (*design feature*), but, unlike other animals, we are afflicted with fractured psyches — the competing drives within us that

often clash (*flaw: chapters 9 and 10*). We are burdened by inner conflict.

5. **Misguided Search for Meaning**
   We are constantly trying to make sense of things (*design feature*), but struggle to find overarching meaning in our lives and impending deaths — a conundrum that other animals are not perturbed by (*flaw: chapters 11 and 12*). We are misguided by asking the wrong question about life's meaning.

Our five flaws have become even more problematic in the past century because the modern world is not as friendly to System 1's intuitions as the world lived in for thousands of years by our farming ancestors, and the world lived in for hundreds of thousands of years before that by our hunter-gatherer ancestors. In the savannah desert, and even more recently on the farm, our ancestors could rely on straightforward cues to interpret threats and opportunities; their mental shortcuts and emotional triggers were well matched to the challenges they faced, just as they are for other animals today. But the same cognitive mechanisms are ill-suited to today's complexity, whose important cues are buried and ambiguous. We are socially interconnected in ways that are barely comparable to the small farming communities that 90 percent of us inhabited just a handful of generations ago. Our forebears could not have fathomed the nuances of navigating a fulfilling career path, nor the difficulty of raising kids in a world dominated by social media, nor the existential risk of nuclear war and climate change. They certainly could never have imagined that we'd be walking around with supercomputers in our pockets (aka "phones"), bombarding us with an avalanche of information, and the overwhelming challenge of separating good information from bad in the Age of Big Data. All this change occurred in an evolutionary instant, and our brains haven't kept pace.

It's not that we're always blowing it — we get a lot of things right, or close enough. But, as writer H.G. Wells noted in the 1940s, "hard imaginative thinking has not increased so as to keep pace with the expansion and complications of human societies."[4] More recently,

Taleb has pointed out that human knowledge, because it was developed in a past world that is very different from today's, "does not transfer properly to the complex domain."[5] So I would add to Schopenhauer's extensive list of comparisons: other animals have it easier because their instincts are well matched to their world, an environment similar to the one in which their brains evolved. We no longer live in our "environment of evolutionary adaptedness," so our evolved cognitive shortcuts are often mismatched to our new reality — features become flaws.

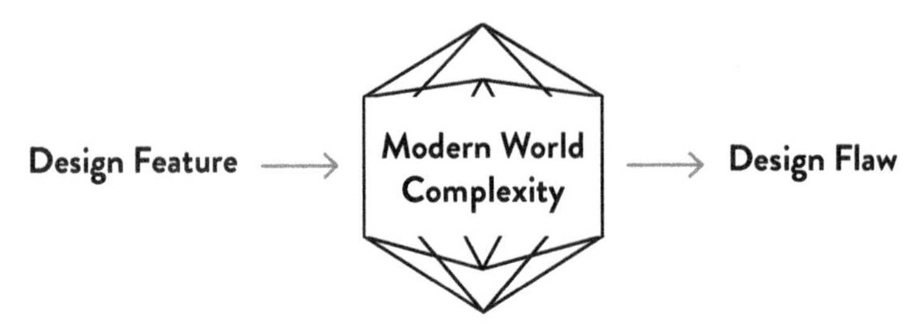

It's hard to be human because human thinking and feeling are often poorly matched to the reality of human life, owing to mental design features that can become flaws, which are accentuated in our modern world.

It's hard to be human because our thinking and feeling are poorly matched to the reality of modern human life.

The human predicament, thankfully, is not hopeless. We just need the "cunning escape" that Taleb alludes to — a way to free ourselves from an ancient brain system that dominates our thinking and feeling. The escape takes some clever manoeuvring because our cerebral deficiencies hide below our day-to-day awareness — they are less obvious than the physical design flaws of our evolved bodies, such as our sore backs, weak knees, vulnerable ankles, and decay-prone teeth. But just as we learn to keep our backs straight when we pick up heavy loads and brush and floss our soft teeth, so too can we learn to overcome our cognitive design flaws. Unlike other animals that are captive to their biology, we are hostage only to the extent that we mindlessly default to our instincts, intuitions, and automatic responses.

What's Our Solution?

The complexity of human consciousness gives us a degree of freedom to be less miserable and better adapted to the twenty-first century, not to mention to be nicer people: to overcome our misguided, misbehaving, and masochistic selves. But this freedom doesn't come easily since, in the spirit of the Buddha, it requires that we first see reality, including other people and even ourselves, more clearly.

The insights of psychology, neuroscience, physics, and philosophy collectively provide a variety of powerful strategies to combat the mental design flaws that make life difficult. These battle plans are the purview of System 2 because they are not intuitive or natural for System 1. In fact, they are anathema to System 1's design (as I will explain in the next chapter). But it's impossible to fully engage System 2 without a concerted effort to climb out of the vortex of System 1–produced thoughts and emotions. We need a place to escape our relentless, automatic thinking; a place we can climb into to get a clearer view. A place I refer to as "The Space Between," for reasons I will explain in chapter 2.

The deeply complex human brain is both the source of unique human suffering and the remedy for the incremental pain we inflict on ourselves.

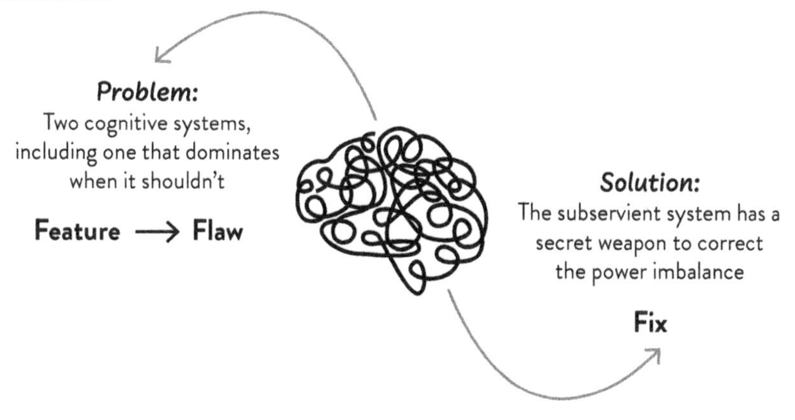

The first step (and focus of chapter 1) is understanding the human predicament as the wobbly marriage between our two thinking systems. The second step (and focus of chapter 2) is exploring the extraordinary solution to this big problem: opening and expanding The Space Between where, by escaping System 1's stronghold, we can empower System 2's ability to implement corrective strategies for each design flaw. The balance of this book examines the five design flaws and practical methods of getting around them.

So I invite you, "fellow sufferer" (as Schopenhauer would have it), to join me in exploring why life is harder than it needs to be. Along the way, I'll share some personal struggles as a means of illustrating the ideas, and I encourage you to reflect on your own dilemmas: we all have histories that can be mined for insights on the challenge of living the human life. I don't pretend to have answers for all that ails us, but I have corralled some of the best ideas of acclaimed thinkers to circumvent the constraints of our default intuitions and their blunt, unproductive responses to the personal and collective challenges we face. The cunning escape from ourselves is available for the taking within each of us, and the payoff is enormous. This is the final and ultimate paradox of *Homo sapiens*: escaping ourselves makes it easier to be human.

It's hard to be human because ...

- *we inflict misery on ourselves,*
- *because our brains are distinctively complex,*
- *such that our cognitive design features are vulnerable to becoming flaws,*
- *especially in an increasingly complex world,*
- *where our thinking and feeling are poorly attuned to the reality of human life;*
- *but there are powerful workarounds for the unruly party in our heads.*

PART 1

the human predicament

CHAPTER 1

Big Cognitive Problem

Man is the most botched of all the animals and the sickliest. – Friedrich Nietzsche

The list of our body's design imperfections is a long one. And the brain is no exception.

In order to move, a body needs a brain. Unlike immobile life forms such as plants and floaters like jellyfish, the brains of travelling animals evolved to navigate their environments. While the human brain may be the most sophisticated "algorithmic compressor" or "Bayesian processor" on the planet, it still expends most of its energy performing an elaborate version of what all animal brains do — getting us through another day and coaxing us to duplicate ourselves along the way.

Given enough time and mutations, Mother Nature's trial-and-error process (aka natural selection) is a competent but highly imperfect engineer. Like all living things, we are a patchwork of bits and pieces that were shaped, reshaped, and added to over time. For example, our throats open into two passages — one leading to the lungs and another to the stomach — which makes us vulnerable to choking when food goes down the wrong tube. The list of our body's imperfections is a long one. And the brain is no exception.

Our two-in-one brain creates trouble for us because the two don't always play well together.

The human brain was cobbled together over millions of years of sculpting and rework, with natural selection gradually adding new mechanisms to old ones. The result is, figuratively speaking, two brains: the "old" one, which operates largely below our conscious awareness, and the "new" one, which evolved more fully over the past one hundred thousand years and is the key to conscious self-awareness. Our unique two-in-one brain is what creates trouble for us, though, because the two don't always play well together. Their interaction is the focus of this chapter, and our two-in-one design is the first of five crucial things to know about the intricate human mind.

Need-to-Know #1: We Have Two Brains in One

The old brain is our ancient automatic-thinking system — the kind most animals are limited to and the basis of our subconscious intuition. The new brain is our modern, effortful-thinking system — the basis of voluntary, conscious deliberation. Some other animals are capable of this second type of thinking but in a much simpler form (such as chimps experimenting with tools). But our kind of effortful thinking is "brand new": its prototype originated in great apes sometime in the past fifteen million years, leading to the first human primates and eventually fully conscious, self-aware, modern humans sometime in the past thirty thousand years.

The distinction between automatic and effortful thinking (referred to as the "dual-process" model of human cognition) is obvious in many examples: eating a meal versus cooking one; walking across a street versus planning a vacation. We're usually not attentive to our mental processes when eating and walking — the thinking is largely subconscious — whereas cooking and planning require some concentrated effort.

While psychologists generally agree on the points of contrast between the two thinking processes, the terms they use to describe each are nowhere near universal, as this very partial list reveals:

AUTOMATIC (ANCIENT)	EFFORTFUL (MODERN)
Intuitive	Analytic
Instinctual	Controlled
Emotional	Rational
Reflexive	Reflective
System 1	System 2

Systems 1 and 2 are the most commonly used descriptors and the terms I will be using.

The fusion of old System 1 and new System 2, while one of Mother Nature's more miraculous achievements, is still a work in progress. System 1, "fast thinking," and System 2, "slow thinking," haven't quite got their act together, largely because the former — the ancient brain system — is a bully.

Need-to-Know #2: System 1 Is a Bully

We are largely at the mercy of our System 1 ancient brain because it orchestrates the vast majority of our thinking and behaviour and because its workings are largely opaque to our conscious awareness. Whereas System 1 chugs along as consistently as our heart beats, System 2 works at its highest potential only sporadically. Despite the impressive accomplishments of System 2 (as in Shakespearean plays and Einsteinian physics), it is slow and inconsistent, easily distracted and readily influenced by external factors such as how much sugar is in our bloodstream and how much sleep we've had. It may not seem like it, but we are very selective in how we focus System 2's effortful attention; we're quite stingy with how much intense concentration we're willing to commit to any particular problem.

How do we decide when to engage our precious effortful thinking? Here's the kicker: the amount of effortful System 2 we invoke is largely determined by automatic System 1, based on its own assessment of whether the effort is worthwhile. As psychologist Daniel Kahneman notes, "When System 1 runs into difficulty, it calls on System 2 to support more detailed and specific processing.... System 2 is mobilized when a question arises for which System 1 does not offer an answer."[1]

This principle is key to understanding how the human mind works. *Effortful thinking is largely at the mercy of the automatic thinking that underlies it.* There is no conscious System 2 without subconscious System 1 preceding it.

First of all, subconscious thinking is always at the party; in fact, it's basically System 1's party. Subconscious System 1 kicks in at between 350 milliseconds and a full ten seconds before conscious awareness of an event.[2] It's why we jump at the sound of a loud bang before we consciously process that it's just a car engine misfiring. The speed of System 1 is what protects us and why we're still here. It's also why we fly off the handle in rage before we catch ourselves and wish we hadn't lashed out.

Second, as the party's de facto host, System 1 decides whether to invite System 2 or not, as per Kahneman's observation above. It's worth repeating: System 1 processing brings into conscious awareness whatever it deems worthy of further deliberation, that is, when it decides it needs System 2's flexible and deliberative strength to help figure things out. If System 1 feels it has everything under control (as in eating and walking), then it won't bother inviting System 2 to the party and wasting precious mental energy.

Third, not only is System 2 late to the party and only there at the invitation of System 1, but System 2, upon arriving, often has great difficulty finding the host! The subconscious thoughts and motivations that give rise to our conscious thinking are often hidden from our awareness and therefore difficult to access and challenge.

System 1 is so powerful — we are so captive to our subconscious, automatic thinking — that psychologists have created a variety of metaphors to describe its dominance:

David Eagleman:	Our consciousness is like a stowaway on a steamship, taking credit for the journey without acknowledging the massive engineering that is actually running the ship.[3]
Jonathan Haidt:	Automatic thinking is the powerful elephant on whose back conscious deliberation rides as an adviser, attempting to cajole the elephant.[4]
Steven Pinker:	The conscious mind is a spin doctor whose job is to create a story that explains the actions the unconscious mind initiates.[5]
Owen Flanagan:	Consciousness is a figurehead president. It has status and putative authority, but it is limited to explaining the real work and output of the subconscious.[6]
Daniel Wegner:	We may feel that we are freely choosing, but subconscious processing is doing the choosing for us and just "letting us know" what it has decided.[7]
Daniel Kahneman:	System 2 is a supporting character who believes itself to be the hero. But System 1 is more influential as the secret author of many of the choices and judgments you make.[8]

Although some psychologists argue that conscious thinking is nothing but the pawn of the powerful cognitive operations that reside below our awareness, the majority are convinced that conscious, effortful thinking can have some influence over the subconscious operations that underlie it. Otherwise, contrary to our everyday experience, any notion of free will would be nonsensical and we would have no ability to change our habits or redirect our goals. But this power over ourselves doesn't come easily because of the bullying. System 1 pushes us to overeat when System 2 tells us not to; to lash out at people when System 2 knows we are escalating conflict; to stay up late watching TV when System 2 knows we need more sleep. And System 1 bulldozes its way through complex problems, hanging "mission accomplished" banners everywhere it ventures before System 2 has had sufficient opportunity to weigh in.

System 1 hangs "mission accomplished" banners wherever it ventures, usually before System 2 weighs in.

In fact, when tackling complex problems, not only is System 2 invited late, at the whim of System 1, which often hides its motives, but the commanding, invisible host can also dismiss System 2 whenever it wants! As soon as System 1 determines that it has things under control, it will eject System 2 from the party by unleashing its weapon of choice: the feeling of knowing.

Need-to-Know #3: System 1 Uses the Feeling of Knowing

System 1 instigates this feeling — and yes, *knowing is a feeling* — the very instant it decides that it doesn't need any more of System 2's help. When System 1 is satisfied, it replaces the discomfort of not knowing with the soothing feeling of knowing. System 1's weaponization of this feeling keeps us "captive to our biology," to use Taleb's terminology. One of the biggest battles we (as in System 2) have to fight against ourselves (as in System 1) is the Need-to-Know — our addiction to certainty. Sugar, alcohol, tobacco, sex — none of these compare to our relentless craving for the feeling of knowing. Chapter 5 examines our certainty addiction in more detail; for now, it's crucial to understand that *our subconscious-thinking system dominates our conscious one with the feeling of knowing.* In turn, this disengages System 2, deterring us from putting further energy into effortful thinking. It's a very efficient process ... except when it doesn't work.

Sugar, alcohol, tobacco, sex — none of these compare to our craving for the feeling of knowing.

Need-to-Know #4: System 1 Lacks Self-Awareness

The partnership between System 1 and System 2 is highly imperfect because the bully in charge — subconscious System 1 — is not always a good judge of its own expertise. It has strong opinions about all matters and fancies itself an expert in most of them, but is largely ignorant of its own deficiencies.

The root of human struggle is that automatic thinking, while crucial for survival, is

- poorly calibrated to the increasing number of complex problems we face,
- not particularly adept at promoting our overall happiness, and
- oblivious to these two weaknesses.

Our brains evolved in a harsh world that was comparatively simple to figure out: there is nothing ambiguous about a charging tiger. A simple view of the world, which we rarely second-guessed, was well matched to the straightforward threats and opportunities that confronted us, many of which demanded fast, decisive responses. Rushing to simple conclusions works not only for dodging predators on the savannah but also for crossing busy street intersections and avoiding dangerous neighbourhoods. System 1's operating style perfectly suits the hundreds of micro-decisions we make every instant where the patterns that define the problems are regular and predictable.

But as we evolved higher levels of conscious processing, we innovated and shared our learnings with others; in an evolutionary instant the complexity in our world ramped up through the agricultural, industrial, and information ages, and now the digital revolution. Today, most of us are living in crowded communities where we are largely anonymous and struggling with complex problems that would have been unintelligible to our not-so-distant ancestors who knew everyone in their tribe. Because System 1 relies on regular, repeated patterns to make reliable predictions, it has a hard time developing expertise in solving complex problems, since no two complex problems are identical. Unbundling the causal factors that define complexity is arduous, time-consuming work — the kind that System 2 was designed for, *when it is invited to do so by System 1.* But System 1 often withholds that invitation because it was designed to conclude as quickly as possible, so it isn't easily deterred by the ambiguity and intricacy of complexity. If it can find a quick-and-dirty answer that *feels right* without having to deeply engage more effortful thinking, System 1 will lock down on conclusions as confidently as if it had deep expertise and perfect knowledge. In our modern world, System 1, in its rush with its first "feels right" conclusions, overestimates its expertise and oversimplifies complexity. Many of the personal and societal challenges we face are not the kind that lend themselves to an exclusive reliance on System 1: just think of your most recent emotional outburst, or the last time you couldn't fall asleep because your mind was spinning about something stupid, or the increasingly polarized, left-right political divide.

Unlike other animals, we make avoidable, "unforced" errors all the time.

Other animals rely almost exclusively on System 1 processing, which works well for them. First, their mental apparatus is well adapted to the environments in which they live (because the dynamics of their world haven't changed much). Second, they don't have to endure the painful conflict that can arise between Systems 1 and 2. For us poor creatures, Systems 1 and 2 often go head-to-head in painful struggles that are uniquely human, such as when we try to resist a second helping of dessert, or when we attempt to curb our spending in order to save money, or when we desperately try to contain our anger when we're seething with fury. These epic conflicts induce frustration, anxiety, and even depression, especially when we succumb to System 1's influence and torture ourselves for giving in: when we fall off a diet, rack up credit card debt, or lash out in anger at those we love. While other animals don't suffer internal conflicts, much human anxiety stems from conflicting goals — a particular design flaw that we will return to in chapters 9 and 10.

Our ancestors did the best they could with the mental apparatus they had. But now, in the twenty-first century, we are making avoidable, "unforced" errors all the time: unforced because we *do* have the capacity to be smarter. Our ability to be smarter is based on a fifth Need-to-Know about the human mind. Both Systems 1 and 2 come in different forms, and there is a particular form of System 2 that underlies "the escape." This form of effortful System 2 thinking goes by the name *metacognition*.

Need-to-Know #5: System 2 Has Its Own Weapon of Choice

Metacognition is an evolutionarily newer form of consciousness and a unique strength of System 2. It is thinking that is directed toward thinking itself, rather than external objects. When we think to ourselves, *How can I control my sugar craving?* or *I wonder why that conversation upset me so much?* we are engaging in metacognition. Separate from thinking and feeling is this process of observing our thinking and feeling.

System 1 is always chugging away behind the scenes, in its many forms of subconscious processing such as instinct, learned skills, emotional reactions, and moral preferences. System 2 also expresses itself in different forms: the kind of effortful concentration used to solve a math problem is different than the kind used for negotiating a raise. But unlike System 1, which is always online, System 2 varies in the degree to which it is used. For routine tasks that System 1 has mastered, we do not need much System 2, which is why our effortful concentration is often shallow, as when we're separating our laundry or driving a familiar route. We invoke more System 2 when we deliberate on a tricky problem or debate someone about a controversial issue. Rarely do we fully engage System 2's capacity for metacognitive self-reflection: rarely do we ask ourselves, *Do I really have enough information to draw a conclusion?* or *Am I considering alternative interpretations of this situation that is upsetting me?* or *Am I taking into account my personal biases?*

While the dominance of System 1 is life-saving, it is also the heart of the human predicament — when it dominates in situations that it is ill-equipped to handle on its own. The good news is that evolution equipped us with our own utility software to tweak the kludge of an operating system that natural selection constructed. The utility software is System 2's metacognition — the ability to evaluate our feelings, desires, and beliefs. While System 1 has the powerful feeling of knowing at its disposal, System 2 has the power of metacognition.

Metacognition is essential to making life easier. But its deepest form doesn't come naturally to us.

Metacognition is a hallmark of being human. While a chimp can engage in some System 2 thinking, including a rudimentary form of self-awareness, only humans can engage in the full spectrum of System 2, including the kind of awareness that enables us to rise above our preferences and ideas in order to scrutinize them. Metacognition is essential to making a human life easier because it enables us to escape the power of System 1 by allowing us to reflect on and counteract System 1's flaws. Metacognition helps us expand our awareness to take into account our five cognitive design flaws and then circumvent them with some solid System 2 thinking.

There's only one problem: before we can implement strategies to combat the flaws, we have to first get System 2 to the party when it hasn't been invited but should have been. In other words, *to escape System 1's dominance and counteract its flaws, we have to initiate the metacognitive process.* But how? Is there a back door to the party that System 2 can sneak into? You bet.

Two things to know about the human mind:

Its awe-inspiring complexity makes its design features susceptible to being design flaws.

There are workarounds for the misery-inducing glitches.

CHAPTER 2

Huge Metacognitive Solution

We no longer derive man from "the spirit" or "the deity," we have placed him back among the animals.... But for all that, he is of course the most interesting. — *Friedrich Nietzsche*

We've got one thing over other animals: a bigger space between.

Charles Darwin was controversial but unequivocal: "The difference in mind between man and the higher animals, great as it is, certainly is one of degree and not of kind."[1] And so the "degree versus kind" debate was launched: whether humans are distinct from all other animals in a more fundamental way than, say, fish are distinct from gorillas. Over a protracted period of time, humans accumulated increasing gradations of cognitive complexity that is many degrees richer than the mental capacities of other animals. Outside of a religious context, I think there is no meaningful difference in the distinction between "difference in kind" and "*huge* difference in degree," so it's not a fruitful debate. Much more interesting is the debate about what exactly differentiates us from other animals: language, hypothetical reasoning, social co-operation, creativity, culture … the list of contenders is almost as long as the comparative psychologists who study these differences.

I already weighed in with my take: *we can think about how we think; they can't.* That's huge. We can remove ourselves from a stream of consciousness, turn our focus onto it, and assess it. Other animals are incapable of this form of extreme, metacognitive self-transcendence. We have many degrees of cognitive control that far surpass them, empowering us with many more degrees of freedom — freedom to choose how we respond to the world. That's really huge. In fact, if it makes any sense to talk about "the hugest idea of all," metacognition has to at least be in the running with ideas like evolution and relativity. If you lean toward the hugest idea being God, or Jesus's crucifixion, or karma, or atman, then how about the second-hugest idea?

Metacognition defines what it means to be human — the burden, the possibility, and even the responsibility. But unlike evolution or relativity, we can't attribute the origin of this huge idea to a single genius because it has been expressed in many ways by many thinkers over millennia. As it happens though, one person encapsulated it more succinctly and more eloquently than anybody ever has. Even then, I want to shorten their observation to make it as pithy as possible. Here's my abbreviated version:

Between stimulus and response there is a space. In that space is our freedom.

Here's the full version: "Between stimulus and response there is a space. In that space is our power to choose our response. In our response lies our growth and our freedom." You may be familiar with this quote given its popularity; one of the ironies about it is that nobody knows who wrote it! It is usually attributed to Holocaust survivor and psychiatrist Viktor Frankl, whose 1946 book, *Man's Search for Meaning*, continues to be a worldwide bestseller. But none of Frankl's written work contains these sentences. Nor did he ever declare them according to the man who popularized the quote. Decades ago, the author Stephen Covey read this quote in a book and jotted it down because he felt it encapsulated a key idea of Frankl's, whom he admired. But Covey was never able to later pinpoint where he read it and who wrote it.[2]

Aside from its mysterious authorship, you might be thinking, *Yeah … I've heard about Frankl and I've heard the quote.* Or even, *I read Frankl's book … we can choose how we respond to things just as he did as a Holocaust survivor. I get it.* But I'm arguing that this idea is so much deeper and more powerful than most people appreciate. Its simplicity and intuitive appeal belie the true complexity and power of cognitive control — the notion that our ultimate freedom lies in our metacognitive ability to pause and reflect before we respond.

Regrettably, the deepest and most profound form of metacognition doesn't come easily to us. So while metacognition gets the limelight and glory, its helpful sidekick is usually underappreciated. But not by the anonymous author, which is why the quote is so compelling. There's no meaningful metacognition without …

THE SPACE BETWEEN.

If I throw something at you unexpectedly, you react immediately and instinctually, either jumping out of the way or shielding yourself from the object. The time between your sensing an incoming object and your response is nearly instant — the space in between the stimulus and your response is negligible. But if I ask you a challenging question that you have to reflect on, such as, "Which of your last two vacations did you enjoy more and why?" you won't react instantly but will take some time to formulate an answer because you'll need to draw on some substantive System 2 thinking to compare and contrast the two holidays. At the most basic level, that time delay to think, between the stimulus of my question and your response to it, is The Space Between.

The Space Between is the temporal zone between stimulus and response — the delay between our awareness of something and our chosen reaction to it.

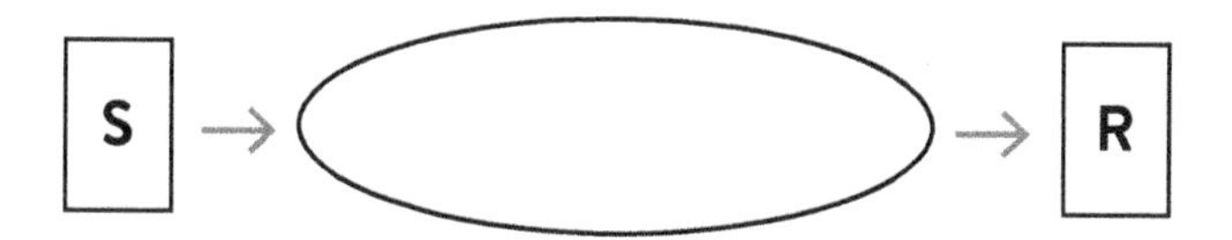

But that's barely interesting. Even a cat will pause and assess before deciding to jump off of a fence. The cat's pause is a space of sorts, but it's not an interesting one because it is involuntary, as is ours most of the time. We automatically slow down with harder problems because System 2 analytical thinking is much slower than instinctual System 1, so just like the cat, we naturally pause before responding.

What *is* interesting is when we consciously and deliberately choose to pause and take time to think — when we say to ourselves, *I'd better not rush to make a decision because I don't trust my gut reaction right now.* This is interesting because comparative psychologists are pretty certain that other animals never *choose* to take time to think, they just instinctually take time when they need it. They don't assess their mental capacity for handling problems; they just slow down without thinking about their need to slow down. They don't engage in the kind of metacognition that humans are capable of when we bring ourselves as thinkers into the scope of our awareness — when we not only contemplate the externalities of a particular scenario, but also reflect on our internal capability of tackling the problem.

Things get even more interesting when we consciously choose not only to insert some additional space for ourselves, but also to use the space to get deeply metacognitive: to really stand back from ourselves and cast a critical inner eye on how we are thinking, feeling, and reacting to a situation. We engage in uniquely human metacognition when we say to ourselves, *I need some space not only to cool off and reflect on this situation, but also to evaluate my own thinking and feeling about it so I can guard against my biases and emotions.* This is the very interesting transition from mindless System 1 thinking to mindful System 2 metacognition, which pulls us as observers into our conscious awareness. It is where we flex our uniquely human cognitive control by opening up the possibility for choices that would otherwise not present themselves.

This unique form of human freedom is only available in The Space Between because only in this space do we have sufficient distance from stimuli to assess them from all angles. And not just a little catlike space, but a big human one. Analyzing our own mental vulnerabilities and flaws does not come naturally to us so we need sufficient room to get a good angle on ourselves. You can't get a good grip on your cognitive frailties if you're not able to remove yourself from them to see the bigger picture of yourself interacting with the world.

In the spirit of the anonymous quote, humans have the ability to insert a much bigger space between stimulus and response than other animals. This bigger space affords us a better view by enabling us to maximize our metacognitive talents to their fullest effect, thereby endowing us with more freedom in our choices. Which makes The Space Between profound, even sublime, and the reason I think it is such a huge idea: *it defines what it means to be human and challenges us to be "more human" in ways that will become apparent throughout this book.*

Unfortunately, we rarely put anything close to as much space between stimulus and response as we are capable of. We therefore forgo much of the freedom that is available to us. The difference between other animals and ourselves and our ultimate potential looks something like this:

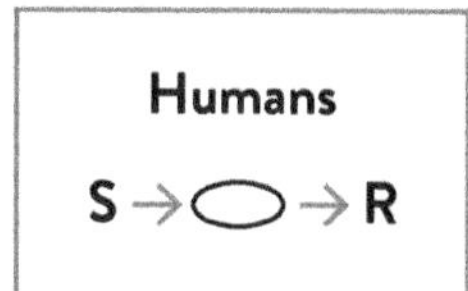

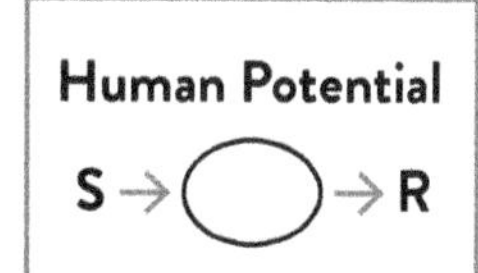

This depiction is too simple for two reasons. First, many animals do hesitate before responding (the cat deciding whether to jump), so to be fair, we should give some of them the benefit of some space, even if it's involuntary. Second, again to be fair to other animals, we humans usually respond instantly to most stimuli; we are only cautious and thoughtful about select stimuli (when System 1 calls out for help). So it's worth refining the comparison to reflect greater granularity:

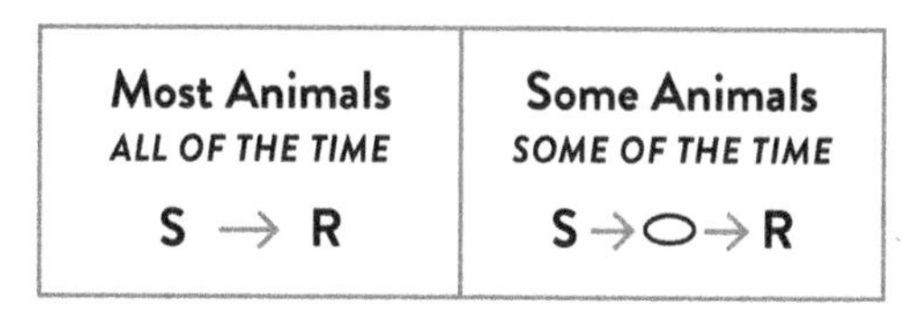

Humans MOST OF THE TIME S → R	Humans SOME OF THE TIME S → R

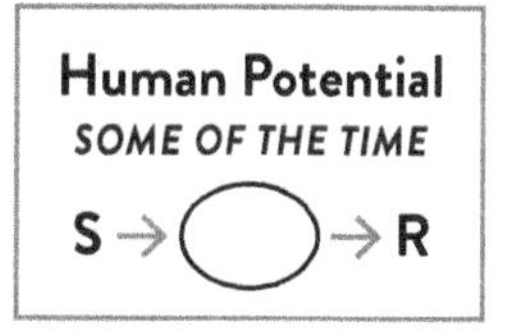

The point is this: *The Space Between differentiates us from other animals and differentiates the most productive and contented humans from the less productive and less happy.* Any and all solutions to the human predicament depend on accessing this space.

The Magic in The Space Between

The Space Between is essential to our well-being for three reasons.

First, we need it to calm our overactive minds. Humans are unique in how obsessively ruminative we can be; much of our spinning "monkey-mind" is not only wasteful but misery inducing. It is the chronic stress that we inflict on ourselves (as opposed to the episodic stress experienced by other animals) that led primatologist Robert Sapolsky to title his book *Why Zebras Don't Get Ulcers.* We can't turn our brains completely off, so we need somewhere to focus our attention when we are spinning out of control. We need The Space Between to quiet our anxiety-inducing machinations.

The Space Between differentiates us from other animals and differentiates the most productive and contented among us from those who are less so.

Second, we need The Space Between to give System 2 a chance to do its special "slow thinking" when it would otherwise not have the opportunity — when System 1's intuitions are poorly matched to the situation but nonetheless dominating. We need the space to give System 2 the chance to expand the mental playground available to us, enabling specific strategies to overcome our cognitive design flaws. The Space Between is the container for developing and implementing these strategies that do not come naturally to System 1 (strategies that will be explored in the "Fix" chapters).

But the space is more than just an empty vessel waiting to be filled with peace-inducing serenity and good ideas. The third need for the space is what I have already identified as the transition from run-of-the-mill, discursive thinking to uniquely human metacognitive observing: the place where we move from a focus on the external world, including other people, to a broader scope of awareness that includes the internal workings of our own mind and the opportunity to make it work better for us. All of the strategies that enhance our cognitive control rely on this metacognitive ability to observe ourselves, which the space facilitates.

The transition from a narrow perspective to a more expansive one, which brings us as thinkers into the frame, is sometimes referred to as "getting behind the waterfall" or "entering the eye of the hurricane," or the proverbial "taking a bird's-eye view." Behind the waterfall, we can observe the torrent of emotion and rumination pouring past us; in the calm centre of the storm, we can watch the mental storms surrounding us; from above, we can inspect the craziness below. We remove ourselves from the deluge of our thoughts and feelings by mentally moving behind (or into the middle of, or far above) them. We unhook ourselves from the chaos in our minds by climbing into The Space Between, where the calm gives us room for more skillful thought that translates into more productive responses. Instead of lashing out at others, making bad situations worse, drowning in indignation or self-pity or obsessiveness, bumbling our way through complex problems by invoking all kinds of unintended consequences ... instead of all these unforced errors, we can climb into The Space Between where we have the opportunity to be smarter — mindful of System 1's traps, judicious in avoiding these design flaws, and skillful in how we respond to the world.

These three benefits are the reason the space is special.

The Magic Inside The Space Between

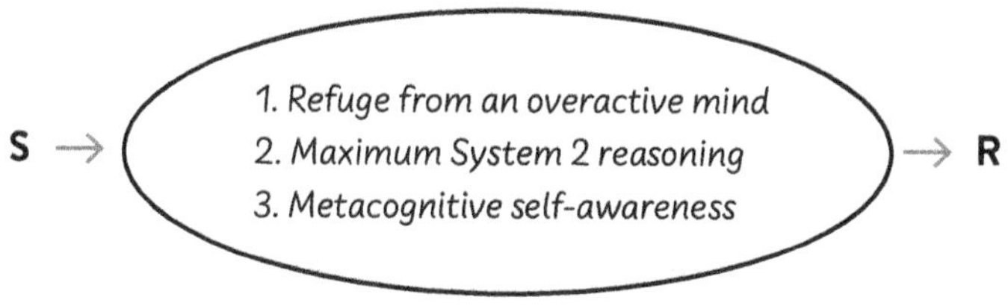

S →
1. Refuge from an overactive mind
2. Maximum System 2 reasoning
3. Metacognitive self-awareness
→ R

The Space Between is the back door to the party of which System 1 is the gatekeeper. But it's not as easy as System 2 just slipping through unnoticed. To outsmart System 1, we have two stealth manoeuvres to carry out. The first is actually inserting The Space Between. That's because System 1 prefers quick cognitive closure with the least cognitive effort: we have to get ourselves behind the waterfall, into the storm's centre, or above the chaos before we can get more System 2 into the party. Once in, the second manoeuvre is to override System 1's commands with more sophisticated cognitive strategies. The first manoeuvre concerns when and how to insert the space. The second manoeuvre is what to do with the space once we've inserted it.

Manoeuvre #1: *Inserting* The Space Between

Inserting the space is a two-step process: we open a space by self-distancing, then we expand that space by investigating the thoughts and feelings we are experiencing. A little metacognition is required for the first step, and more metacognition for the second.

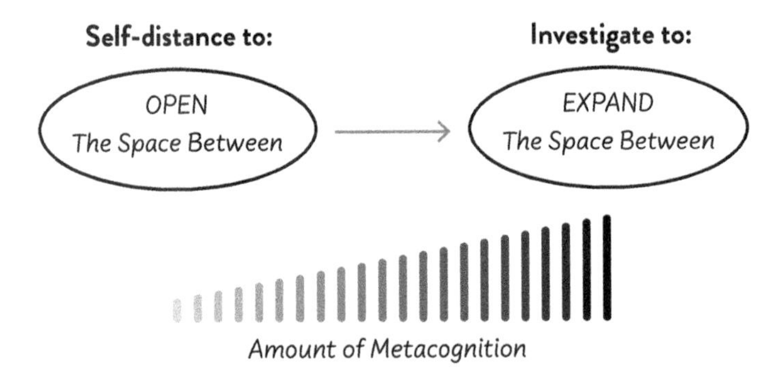

System 2 metacognition allows us to self-distance — to step out of our thoughts and feelings, thereby creating the space needed to observe them. Once we've got our metacognitive foot in the door, we expand the space by turning our attentional spotlight onto our mental churning and emotion. We insert the space by self-distancing, then we expand the space by observing our thoughts and feelings.

There are a variety of ways to self-distance. In addition to the waterfall, hurricane, and bird's-eye approaches to self-distancing, I will review more techniques for opening the space in a section of chapter 8 ("Getting into The Space Between") because it's particularly hard to self-distance when your emotions overwhelm your better judgment — when you're a victim of your own emotional hostage-taking. But a foolproof way to initiate any form of self-distancing is to start by focusing on the breath. Breath focus is the easiest method of opening space; nothing more complicated or fancy than simply paying attention to your inbreaths and outbreaths — the sensations in your stomach and nose as you suck air in and expel it out. Humour me and try it right now:

> Just close your eyes and put all your attention on the sensations in your nose and stomach as you breathe in slowly through your nose, and then even slower out through your nose. Try it two or three times, with longer exhales than inhales.

You just opened up The Space Between. (Or, if you prefer, you just disengaged your sympathetic nervous system and engaged your parasympathetic one.)

Focusing on your breathing is a guaranteed way of slowing your mind down and creating some distance from mental churning — just enough distance to be able to invoke the waterfall, hurricane, or bird's-eye imagery if they are needed, although sometimes focusing on the breath alone is sufficient to open the space. You can even envision your inbreaths as gently and gradually inflating a bubble in your mind — the bubble that is The Space Between.

To go head-to-head with System 1, we need a big space. So once opened, we expand the space by animating our Observing Self, which is the metacognitive part of us that can evaluate the unproductive directions that System 1 pushes us toward, and invoke more System 2 to do the hard work that System 1 doesn't have the patience for. Observing Self is investigative: it brings both curiosity and evaluation to what is happening. It is curious about how we are thinking and feeling about a situation and it evaluates those thoughts and feelings to assess their reasonableness and usefulness in a given situation. If I'm furious with someone for something they said, Observing Self asks, *Are you sure you are interpreting their comment as they intended it to be understood?* And follows that with, *How useful is it for you to be consumed by anger at this point — is the anger leading you to do something productive, or just weighing you down or pushing you to do something destructive?* Humour me one more time and try it right now:

> First, open the space by closing your eyes and focusing on a couple of breaths. Picture yourself in the eye of a storm, where everything around you is busy but you are still and calm. Then move your attentional spotlight to your mind: What thoughts or irritations are trespassing in your calm space — where does your mind want to go if left to its own devices? Are you surprised by what springs into your awareness, seemingly out of nowhere? What is your Observing Self's take on these distractions — are they pleasant diversions or agitating disruptions?

You just expanded The Space Between.

Self-distancing and then animating Observing Self is tricky because we're so used to living IN our thoughts that it's hard for us to get OUTSIDE of them. We have a very passive relationship with our thoughts — we take them at face value without much hesitation or questioning. While we do pause and reflect when we're stumped or puzzled, the insertion and duration of the pause is determined by System 1, which is highly biased in favour of rushed conclusions and strong emotional reactions, often prodding us to melt down or jump to some form of unproductive action. We need System 2 more often than System 1 engages it, and we need it for deeper and longer use than System 1 encourages, which is why we need a bigger space than we're accustomed to creating for ourselves.

We're so used to living IN our thoughts that it's hard for us to get OUTSIDE of them.

After we've inserted a good-sized space, there is still the residual question of *when* exactly we need to insert the space: How do we know when System 1 is out of its depth but unwilling to acknowledge it?

There are two general circumstances when we need the space: when the alarm goes off and when complexity presents itself.

WHEN THE ALARM GOES OFF

The alarm is obvious, but it takes practice to identify and work with it. What is the alarm? Emotional disturbance. Of any kind.

System 1 generates a variety of emotions to motivate us to act in specific ways. A strong negative emotion indicates that System 1 has identified trouble that needs attention. System 1 has a propensity for overreacting, which we can use to our advantage if we're shrewd: a strong negative emotion is a signal (one that most of us miss) that we are being pushed hard in a particular direction that may not be in our best overall interest.

Sitting in a traffic jam with waves of irritability and anxiousness rolling over us, System 1 pushes us to do something when there's absolutely nothing to be done. Or the furious indignation that overwhelms us when someone cuts into our lane and System 1 wants revenge. When we feel irritated, anxious, impatient, jealous, and especially when we feel angry, there is a signal available to us beyond the immediate source of our concern. Emotional disturbance is a signal that requires a special kind of attention — not the usual object-focused kind like *This traffic jam is causing me to be late*, or *This person is infuriating me*. But the self-focused kind: emotional disturbance is an alarm we can use to trigger the need for System 2 metacognitive, self-observation, such as *It's odd that I feel so agitated over something I can't control*, or *I wonder why I am so upset by what that person said?* Noticing our strong emotions is one of the best ways to self-distance and open up a bit of space, which our Observing Self can then expand with its curiosity about how we are thinking and feeling.

The alarm of strong negative emotions awakens us to the need to insert some space:

Overreacting is an unfortunate hallmark of being human that I'll delve into in chapters 7 and 8, including the possibility of meditation as a means of being less captive to System 1's hysteria. For now, I'll point out a gentle criticism of meditation: at its best, it only does half the job. Meditation can be very effective at bringing more System 2 metacognition online, by both calming the mind and inquiring into how negative feelings arise. But meditation doesn't initiate or support a lot of System 2 work; in fact, most forms of meditative practice discourage the kind of analytic System 2 thinking that we need to battle System 1. More on meditation later.

Noticing our strong emotions is one of the best ways to open a bit of space that Observing Self can then expand

---

WHEN WE CONFRONT COMPLEXITY

This one is harder to detect since it is not always accompanied by conspicuous emotional disturbance. When we are tackling a complex problem, we are at high risk of misinterpreting it (and being overconfident in our misguided conclusions, given System 1's profligate use of the feeling of knowing).

"Complexity" is shorthand for "complex system." Everything can be viewed as a system — as the interaction among parts. But some systems are more complex than others: complexity is defined by interactions that are more intricate and harder to decipher than those of simple systems. Consider that a tiger charging you is a fairly straightforward system between you and the tiger: the signals are clear and the outcome is fairly predictable (not a good one for you). In contrast, negotiating with someone over a difficult issue is more challenging because the system of interactions is hard to predict: How rational and reasonable is the other person? How emotional are they about this issue in particular? How much leverage does the other person perceive you have over them? How will they respond to certain moves versus others? There is an element of complexity to all of our personal interactions, since people are more complex than tigers, so the systems between them are much less predictable. Public policy and corporate strategy are complex because of all the moving parts and unintended consequences of our interventions. Our careers, love lives, family dynamics: complex, complex, and complex. Our personal ambitions and needs, as we stumble our way around an often-uncooperative world: complex!

In all of these examples of complexity, the trigger to insert space is rarely a blaring emotional alarm. The signal is more subtle: it is that we are dealing with something that is not straightforward.

Complex Dilemma = Trigger to Insert The Space Between

If the outcomes of what we're dealing with are not highly predictable, it's safe to assume there is a degree of complexity that we need to be cautious about. Hence the need for The Space Between to get more System 2 to the party so we don't jump straight to System 1's first responses, which may be infected by one of the five design flaws. (Chapters 3 and 4 will examine System 1's proclivity to underestimate complexity and therefore underutilize System 2's analytical strength to tackle it.) Unfortunately, we are not conditioned to pick out the scenarios where our strong intuitive gut reactions are misguided, so complexity's signals take some practice in identifying (which I will also cover in the next two chapters).

In summary, manoeuvre #1 is getting effortful thinking to the party so it can counteract System 1's sometimes-flawed thinking. *We get System 2 to the party with the insertion of The Space Between*, which provides a respite from the dominance of System 1. *We open the space by self-distancing and we expand the space by inviting Observing Self to investigate our thinking and feeling.* We need The Space Between when a negative emotional disturbance alerts us to the need for metacognition or when we're dealing with a complex system that is beyond System 1's expertise. In these two cases — emotional disturbance and complexity — we need to separate stimulus and response more forcefully than we've been designed to do. But inserting the space is just the first trick to outmanoeuvre System 1 in the war with ourselves.

Manoeuvre #2: Using The Space Between

The space on its own is helpful to reduce emotional intensity, but once opened and expanded, *it is what we put in the space that makes the difference.* The second manoeuvre is doing something useful after arriving at the party: engaging System 2 to activate less intuitive, more sophisticated strategies for coping than those offered by System 1. This work requires the highest degree of metacognition because it is based on an unflinching confrontation with System 1's flaws. Manoeuvre #2 is the weaponization of System 2 so it can go head-to-head with System 1 when the latter is dominating but underqualified (i.e., when it is bullying) and the former's slower, less rigid approach is better suited to the situation.

We *open* the space by self-distancing; we *expand* the space by investigating; we *use* the space by strategizing to overcome our design flaws.

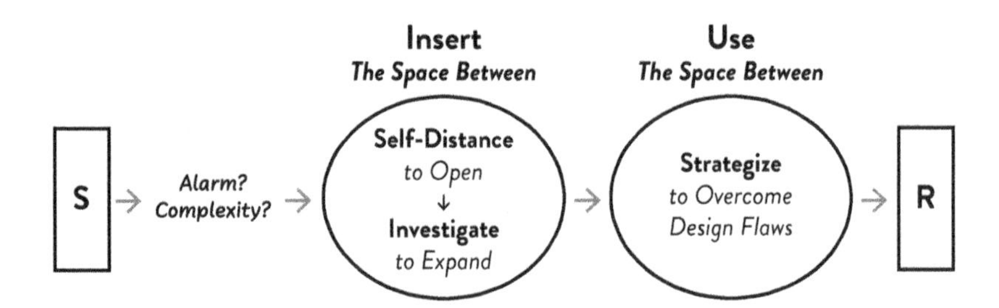

The rest of this book is about the second manoeuvre in the battle with System 1: understanding the enemy (i.e., the five cognitive design flaws that make human life more difficult than other animals') and exploring specific combat strategies. The Space Between is, to use a military term, a "force multiplier": it accentuates the power of System 2 strategies to overcome System 1.

The human version of metacognition is still at the prototype phase: from an evolutionary perspective, we are in the early stages of understanding how we think and how we can manage our thinking better. The best we have (so far) is a somewhat clumsy ability to check our automatic thinking, which requires effort and discipline that do not come easily. This challenge is parallel to the awkward and protracted transition we underwent between knuckle-walking and bipedalism, when we roamed the earth using a version of both. Our ape ancestors didn't stand up one day and marvel at the view that bipedalism afforded. And our more recent ancestors certainly didn't wake up one morning, point to the sky, and spontaneously engage in conversations about the meaning of life. We are (and will always be) works in progress, having not yet mastered the full potential of the intricate but messy brains that natural selection has furnished us with. Engaging System 2 at its fullest capacity — to be "fully human" — is hard work but extraordinarily worthwhile. Even crucial. And only possible inside The Space Between.

One thing to remind yourself every day:
The Space Between is always available when needed.

One question to ask when you're suffering:
Do I need to insert The Space Between to access more System 2 to help me out?

PART 2

a fix for every flaw

CHAPTER 3

FLAW #1: **We're Greedy Reductionists**

The world we live in is vastly different than the world we think we live in. — *Nassim Nicholas Taleb*

It mostly comes down to missing information.

I'm a tidy guy: clean car, organized desk, dirty dishes into the dishwasher right away. I wouldn't say I'm obsessive, but I'm willing to concede that my preference for order over chaos is perhaps a bit more "developed" than average. My daughters were barely teenagers when they confronted me over dinner one night with, "Dad, you are so OCD." I told them that, first, they were misusing the term as it's defined in the *Diagnostic and Statistical Manual of Mental Disorders* and, second, they should contemplate the role that their lax hygiene habits might play in my purported fastidiousness.

I was convinced they were wrong but there was only one way to prove it: I asked a renowned expert at one of Toronto's largest hospitals to assess me, and after two sessions he gave me the rundown. I did not exhibit the symptoms of obsessive compulsive disorder (the inability to manage persistent, unwanted thoughts and acting out compulsions to relieve the tension of these intrusive thoughts). But I didn't get a complete pass either. He described me as a perfectionist, using a clinical term with the unfortunate name of obsessive compulsive personality, or OCP. (In its more extreme form, it has a *D* attached to it, as in OCP Disorder — a condition that prevents people from completing tasks because they can't stop perfecting.) He reassured me that the *D* did not apply to me; apparently, I just like things to be *close to perfect*. When I reported back to my daughters that there was no disorder associated with my fussiness and I was the proud owner of a personality type called OCP, they roared with laughter: "We told you so!" The more I tried to explain that OCP is not the same as OCD, the more they laughed. They may not have appreciated the subtleties of the distinct psychiatric diagnoses, but I still felt vindicated, if only on a technicality.

While I may be a bit more on the fussy side of the spectrum, we all want things to be a certain way. We want life to be fair and not too inconvenient. We want others to appreciate if not admire us. We want right and wrong to be clear and for others to see things the way we do. We want everything to make sense: we want it all to be understandable, sensible, logical, and coherent, and to conform to how we think things ought to work. It's hard to be human because these simple, straightforward expectations are met only half the time (give or take). And we feel we deserve much better than half — we're greedy that way. The world is grotesquely imperfect and brutally unpredictable so you'd think that years of being thwarted and disappointed in a variety of ways would calibrate our expectations, but most of us have difficulty reconciling our demands with what the world offers. We expect the universe to at least be co-operative, if not actually to cater to our needs. But no such contract was ever signed, no verbal agreement was offered; in fact, the universe has never even hinted at caring, let alone compromising.

Our demands are greedy because they are unreasonable; they are unreasonable because they are misguided; they are misguided because, as per Taleb's comment in the epigraph above, we see the world differently than it is. We simplify the complexities and mysteries of the universe to such an extent that we can't help but be disappointed, depressed, and often devastated by the universe's defiance. Author Robert Wright defines this problem as a "Buddhist 'truth.'" As he puts it, "Human beings often fail to see the world clearly, and this can lead them to suffer and to make others suffer."[1]

Our demands are greedy because they are unreasonable; they are unreasonable because we see the world differently than it actually is.

We're greedy in wanting the world to conform to straightforward, intelligible, and fair rules — simple codes that enable us to have complete control over it. That we are greedy simplifiers is one of the most profound features of being human, and the first of four Need-to-Knows.

Need-to-Know #1: We Simplify Everything

We don't just simplify some or most stuff; we simplify *EVERYTHING*. We have no choice but to simplify the tsunami of sensory data that rolls over us moment by moment. We couldn't survive if our brains weren't adept at picking out and interpreting relevant signals, searching for familiar patterns to organize all this data and weave it into stories that make sense to us — stories that cohere with everything we already know. As author Aldous Huxley described it, "To make biological survival possible ... [everything] has to be funneled through the reducing valve of the brain."[2] We reduce the world to something that fits into our minds by transforming it into mentally digestible pieces. The end result is a highly simplified account of reality: a rarefied, reduced representation that usually, but not always, bears some resemblance to the real thing.

If there's nothing else that you take from this entire book, I hope these five words resonate and stick:

To know is to simplify.

There is no knowledge without simplifying. Based on the number of sensory receptor cells connected to our brains, scientists estimate that we process about eleven million bits per second: photons landing on our eyes, air compression waves hitting our eardrums, odorant molecules attaching to our nasal receptors … all converted into electrochemical impulses that our brains are constantly sifting through, separating out useful signals from the huge volume of surrounding noise that is irrelevant, useless data. When we're about to cross the street, the speed and direction of an oncoming car are highly relevant cues to pick out from the noise of other data (such as the brand of the car or how many passengers are inside it). In our simplify-to-know processing, we leave a lot of information at the curb because it's not useful to us.

Of the eleven million bits of data our brains process in any given second, only the tiniest fraction makes it to conscious awareness. The vast majority remain hidden in the depths of System 1 processing. Expanding on his "reducing valve" analogy, Huxley continues, "What comes out at the other end is a measly trickle of the kind of consciousness which will help us to stay alive on the surface of this particular planet."[3] We're consciously aware of only a small fraction of the already small fraction of reality that gets through. That's a lot of simplifying — a lot of information that never gets analyzed.

Having said that, we wouldn't be here if we weren't good at separating signal (useful information) from noise (useless information) and constructing a representation of reality that works for us enough of the time. And we do it super fast. If there are shortcuts, we'll use them. There are and we do, such as these four:

Availability bias:	Relying on information that is immediately available (at the expense of information that is not at our fingertips).
Confirmation bias:	Seeking out evidence that confirms our suspicions (at the expense of contradictory evidence).
Myside bias:	Favouring perspectives that fit with everything else we already believe (at the expense of alternative beliefs).
Representativeness:	Relying on knowledge about one thing to draw conclusions about another seemingly similar thing (at the expense of perceiving differences).

For straightforward problems (such as a tiger charging us), simplifying shortcuts work brilliantly for three reasons:

First:	The information cues are clear and unambiguous (it's not hard to interpret the intention of a charging tiger).
Second:	The patterns are consistent from one problem to another (one charging tiger poses the same threat as another charging tiger).
Third:	The feedback we get from interacting with the problem is "clean" (the tiger's response to being provoked is not random but predictable).

When these three conditions are present, we can develop expertise by relying on shortcuts: System 1 can exploit the clarity and regularity of the signals to develop reliable intuitions. Simplifying expedites speed, and speedy interpretations and responses were necessary for survival in the straightforward but unforgiving world in which our ancestors lived. As long as the patterns are regular and repeated, our shortcuts quickly screen out irrelevant information and focus on making quick sense of the relevant signals.

But, of course, the story doesn't end there.

Simplifying works with familiar patterns that can be assessed quickly and reliably. But where complexity is concerned (e.g., most interpersonal conflict), we are vulnerable to messing up because the three conditions for reliable simplification are not present.

First:	The information cues are buried and unambiguous (your partner might not share their true feelings or share them in an indirect or convoluted way).
Second:	The patterns are varied from one problem to another (no two people respond the same way to the same stimuli and even the same person can respond differently from one occasion to another).

Third:	The feedback we get is "dirty" – muddied by irrelevant or confusing noise (your partner's response may not be directly related to the specific conflict at hand but in the context of having a bad day or your entire relationship history).

System 1 doesn't let a little ambiguity get in the way of a fast answer.

In complex scenarios, many interacting parts are affecting one another in obscured ways: cause and effect are not closely linked together and the cues we need to understand them are buried in noise that masquerades as signal. But because System 1 is always in a hurry to make sense of things, it doesn't let a little ambiguity get in the way of a good answer. And that's when a *design feature* becomes a *design flaw: life-enhancing simplifying becomes life-detracting oversimplifying.* When we confront scenarios that demand more cognitive sophistication than the straightforward problems that System 1 is expert at solving, we are at high risk of converting simplifying to oversimplifying.

Feature Becomes Flaw: Simplifying Becomes Greedy Reductionism

Philosopher Daniel Dennett coined the expression "greedy reductionism" to describe the attempts by scientists and philosophers to reduce complex phenomena to overly simple explanations.[4] Taking Dennett's notion one step further, I am arguing that *we are all greedy reductionists.* The "reducing valve" of our brain is forever condensing reality in order to squeeze meaning out of it; we want that meaning to be tidy and easy to mentally digest.

Sometimes relentless reduction works really well for us — simplifying keeps us alive! Sometimes it's disastrous — when we greedily expect too much from the partial data that we use to weave simple stories. Here's an analogy: Newtonian physics works just fine except when we're operating in conditions that are neither very large nor very small nor very fast. But in these three cases, the error rate of Newton's laws becomes significant and we need more sophisticated models: the unintuitive sciences of general relativity (to account for how large mass objects warp space); quantum mechanics (to account for the peculiar behaviour of subatomic particles); and special relativity (to account for how very fast speeds warp time). Just as Newton's science fails us when the limiting conditions of size and speed are removed, *our default intuitions about the world fail when the limiting conditions of straightforward problems are removed.*

Our first design flaw stems from our failure to differentiate the problems to which simplifying shortcuts are well suited and those to which they are not. When we greedily apply simplifying shortcuts to complexity, we oversimplify.

Reductionism + Complexity = Oversimplifying

If the five most important words in this book are "To know is to simplify," a corollary constitutes another important five words:

There is always missing information.

One of the main ways we oversimplify is by neglecting important signals. This insight, while seemingly obvious, is so far-reaching that it's another Need-to-Know.

Need-to-Know #2: There Is Always Missing Information

The very nature of simplifying is to exclude. Our brain's limited processing power cannot absorb and work on all available data, so everything we contemplate is lacking. At the most basic level, we miss the ultraviolet colours that a cardinal enjoys, the hundreds of scents picked up by a dog's two hundred million scent receptors, the sonar-like hearing of a bat, and the infrared radiation that a rattlesnake relies on. Our equipment doesn't register most of what's happening around us, including the millions of microscopic life forms crawling all over and inside of us. But our limited apparatus is sufficient for our purposes much of the time: we successfully exclude that which is unimportant or unhelpful and focus on the important, useful signals. Most of us develop solid intuitions about how the world works after years of learning about it, so we're fairly expert at quickly picking out the signals we need to make sense of and manage most of the daily challenges we confront. For these run-of-the-mill challenges, we're expert at ignoring information that isn't useful to us. But a lifetime is not nearly long enough to develop expertise in handling every type of problem, especially the kind with patterns that do not repeat themselves with regularity and are therefore hard to master. In our haste to draw conclusions about these kinds of problems, we are vulnerable to missing information. There is always missing information — but here's the point: *The more complex a situation is, the more likely that the missing information is crucial.*

Missing important information is probably nowhere more troublesome than in our interpersonal relationships. As two giants in the field of behavioural economics, Amos Tversky and Daniel Kahneman, write, "The tendency to consider only relatively simple scenarios may have particularly salient effects in situations of conflict. There, one's own moods and plans are more available to one than those of the opponent."[5] This is availability bias in action, where we have immediate access to the details of our own predicaments and feelings but only limited access to the details of other people's — much of the important information about their particular circumstances is missing. The result? We are forever oversimplifying others and the situations they find themselves in, creating and aggravating conflicts with them.

The more complex a situation is, the more likely that the missing information is crucial.

In fact, this "fundamental attribution error" is one of the cornerstones of social psychology: it is a well-researched tendency for us to neglect the information embedded in other people's situations by attributing to them specific personality traits that explain their behaviours. In other words, we interpret the behaviour of others as the *exclusive* signal of their personalities, treating the particular situations that contribute to their behaviours as irrelevant noise even though this missing information is crucial to an accurate understanding of them. For example, if a stranger is rude to us, we interpret his behaviour as stemming from an anti-social disposition: "He's a jerk." The missing information that influences his behaviour — perhaps a stressful argument he just had with his boss — is not readily available to us, so we latch on to his personality as the sole explanation. Unsurprisingly, we are quick to assess our own behaviours much more generously, often attributing them to the nuances of our circumstances, which *are* readily available to us: "I'm not a rude person, I'm just late and having a bad day," or "I only lashed out because I was being provoked." Attribution theory reveals that it is effortless for us to blame others while granting ourselves much more ethical leeway by choosing whether to weigh personality disposition or situation more heavily, depending on what serves our interest ("self-serving bias" means we attribute success to our character but failure to circumstance).

Missing information also makes it too easy for us to "solve" other people's problems more decisively than our own. Because we are only privy to the bare bones of others' predicaments, filtered through the stories they tell us, we jump to hasty conclusions and ill-conceived advice: "Why doesn't she just leave him already?" or "Why doesn't he just get another job if he hates it that much?" The answer to these questions is the same: people don't behave the way we think they should because we don't have all the information they have. The friend who "should just leave her partner" may describe his inconsiderate qualities in detail because they are more likely to elicit sympathy, but deep down would rather be with someone who is a mix of good and bad than be alone. Similarly, someone may figure that the risk of changing jobs outweighs the short-term boredom, but that doesn't stop him from complaining. (Aside from sympathetically listening, our best response in these scenarios is usually to gently probe for the missing information that expands our narrow view of the other person's reality.)

Blaming others — when we perceive them as the straightforward cause of our suffering — is a good example of how we neglect missing information in our greedily simplistic assessment of causality. Cause and effect is our primary model of sense-making, but our intuitive model of causality is very rudimentary, and woefully inadequate when it comes to complex problems. So much so that it's a third Need-to-Know.

Need-to-Know #3: Basic Cause and Effect Doesn't Work for Complexity

"Happy is he who knows the causes of things," wrote the Roman poet Virgil.[6] Our minds establish simple relationships by looking for the single, unidirectional causes that explain the effects we experience: lack of food causes hunger, too many drinks cause inebriation, overexposure causes sunburn. These one-way causal relationships and thousands like them are good enough for coping with straightforward problems.

Straightforward Causality

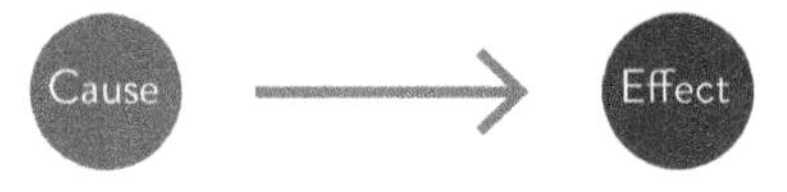

Although we rely on this basic model, it doesn't do a good job of explaining a career path, a company's profits, climate change, the election of a president, or a relationship breakdown. In a world that is increasingly defined by multicausal, multidirectional relationships, our intuitive notion of causality excludes crucial information. We oversimplify causality when we point to our partner's selfishness as the cause of our relationship struggles, or our boss's arrogance as the source of our career frustration, or the government's incompetence as the reason for long emergency room waits, or bankers' greed as the explanation of economic inequality, or religious extremism as the foundation of terrorism.

With complexity, many causal factors interact with one another and all contribute to the effect, which in turn impacts the causes. As I explore in the next chapter, complex situations are defined by elaborate causal chains that are nestled in a series of interactions that reside below the surface of our quick, single-cause interpretations.

Causal Complexity

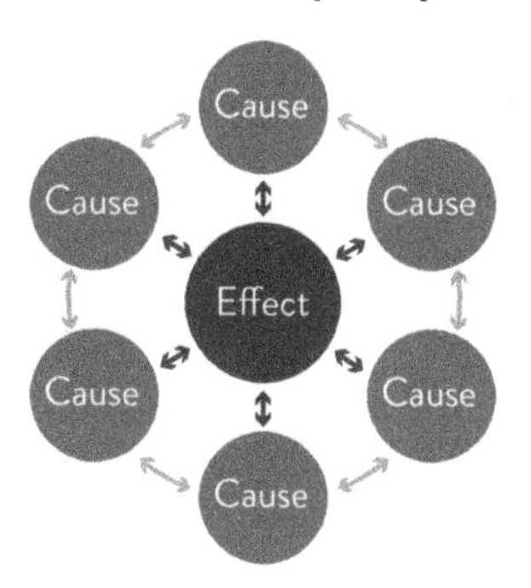

The missing information that reveals the patterns of complexity is contained in these multiple causal factors that are not obvious, and in the interrelationships between these causes, which are even less obvious. Our greedy simplifying of causal relationships stems from our historically life-saving predisposition to work with the first signals that jump out at us. But with modern-day complexity, our preliminary interpretations barely represent the phenomena that we are dealing with, leading us to responses that produce unintended consequences — results that "come out of left field" (in baseball, when a baserunner is sprinting to home plate, they can't see behind their left shoulder so they're vulnerable to a surprise ball being thrown to home plate from left field, just as we are vulnerable to surprises when we rush to simplified conclusions).

With complexity, many causal factors interact with one another and all contribute to the effect, which in turn impacts the causes.

The history of nutrition science is a good example of oversimplifying causal interactions. In 1984, the American National Institutes of Health recommended a reduction in dietary fat intake, kicking off decades of fat-reduced and fat-free products. But obesity statistics rose as food producers dumped enormous amounts of sugar (and salt) into their products to offset the lost flavour from reduced fat. Then the pendulum swung to another simplistic analysis: high-glycemic carbohydrates were linked to fat storage, triggering the explosive popularity of low-carb diets in the 1990s, evolving into today's anti-gluten craze. This chaotic history arose from examining nutrients in isolation. Nutritional scientists are finally acknowledging that a simple model of causality cannot capture how nutrients interact with each other, with other chemical compounds, and with our digestive systems.

The history of genetics is equally revealing. Scientist Francis Galton coined the dichotomy "nature versus nurture" in 1874 when he launched an investigation into which of the two has more influence on our personalities, and the debate has raged ever since. We know today that Galton's simple dichotomy is facile because of how the two interact with one another. In the past two decades, rigorous twin study results have converged to the conclusion that our personalities are an intertwined mix of both genes (nature) and environment (nurture). Identical twins (with the same DNA) raised apart in different homes are more similar in personality than two siblings would typically be (demonstrating strong genetic influence), but they can nonetheless be surprisingly dissimilar (demonstrating strong environmental influence). Genes are more probabilistic than deterministic: the key driver of personality is the interaction between the two, since the environment can influence whether particular genes are activated or not and therefore the extent to which personality traits are fully expressed. We cannot predict personality from genes alone any more than we can predict the outcome of two chefs creating different meals with the exact same ingredients. Geneticists still have a long way to go to understand the interplay between genes and the environment.

These examples are grand versions of the many mundane scenarios on any given day, in which we apply a facile model of causality to everything we think about: every family conflict, every screw-up at work, every relationship meltdown, and every public policy fiasco is the result of a complex web of causal factors that are impossible to diagnose, let alone resolve without unearthing the missing information that is embedded in the complicated interactions. It is because we miss a lot that we are perpetually *underinterpreting* signal (as if it were irrelevant noise). But we're also prone to the reverse: *overinterpreting* noise (as if it were relevant signal). In fact, we have a strong proclivity for perceiving patterns where there is only random noise. Noise is unimportant or useless data; randomness is a subcategory, and the most problematic form of noise for us, because it masquerades as signal when analyzed by a meaning search engine like the human brain. We, unfortunately, are very adept at overinterpreting randomness, which is why it's a fourth Need-to-Know.

Need-to-Know #4: We Interpret Random Noise as Signal

When you are negotiating a raise, the colour of your boss's shirt is irrelevant data — noise. Randomness is also noise but not just because it's useless data: it contains no accessible information at all, useless or otherwise. "Random" essentially means "lacking available information value," and this can be the case for two reasons: the information value is too difficult to access, or there is no information at all. A coin toss represents the first case of inaccessible information, because a multitude of causes produces a head or a tail (the angle and force of the toss, the balance and symmetry of the coin, air friction, etc.), but these interacting causes cannot be measured and integrated to predict the coin's path (which is "computationally uncompressible"). The second case of randomness is more extreme because there are no underlying causal connections, so there is no underlying information to access. This is the feature of quantum mechanics that describes the behaviour of subatomic particles: if the starting position of an electron were known with theoretically perfect precision, its path would still be unpredictable because no causal conditions link its starting position with its ending position. We are limited to describing subatomic particles with wavelike probability distributions, not because we lack more advanced measuring equipment (as in the case of the coin toss, which could in theory be predicted if we could compress all the causal factors into an equation), but because random uncertainty is fundamental to the nature of these particles.

The distinction between the two kinds of randomness — lack of access to the causal chain or a lack of causal chain altogether — is more academically interesting than practical. What does matter, and matters a great deal, is how prone we are to mistaking randomness for signal: we see patterns where there are none; we read meaning into meaninglessness. Randomness is sewn into the fabric of reality and our lives but we underestimate it because System 1 has no tolerance for it.

Because we overinterpret randomness, we see patterns where there are none — we read meaning into meaninglessness.

First, by its very nature, randomness is unpredictable and therefore uncontrollable — but System 1's number-one job is to manage the environment for the benefit of its host's genes, which are on a survival mission. It can't manage the world if it can't understand it, so it doesn't like acquiescing to the unknowable. Second, overinterpreting randomness has been a reliable survival strategy for our entire history. Like all animals, we operate on the basis of a fundamental decision-making principle: *missed threats are more dangerous than false alarms.* Given two possible mistakes we can make, one typically has more downside than the other, which is why we are biased in favour of avoiding the one dangerous mistake even if it means incurring the other less fatal one.

Here's an oft-used example: You hear a rustle in the bush. There are two possible errors that can arise: You can panic when in fact it's just the wind, or you can ignore the rustle when in fact it's a predator. If it's just windblown leaves but you interpret it as a danger signal and start running, that's a false alarm (aka Type I error, or false positive). Your heart races for a bit, but other than wasting energy, the downside to making this mistake is minimal. Now let's say it actually is a predator about to pounce, but you commit the second kind of error: You assume the sound represents no meaningful signal and ignore it. That's a missed threat (aka Type II error, or false negative). You're eaten alive, which could be described as a significant downside to your decision.

The two potential errors are trade-offs: you can't be both overly cautious and carefree at the same time, so you have to choose which error you are more comfortable risking if you're not sure what the rustle is. Natural selection has imbued System 1 with a proclivity to err on the side of caution by assuming there are signals to interpret and respond to, so we're not perpetually underreacting to true threats. Survival depends on this bias: better to be inconvenienced by a Type I false alarm than to be killed by a Type II missed threat; better to risk overinterpreting noise than underinterpreting signal. This "on alert" stance means we perpetually risk overinterpreting noise. The bias, incidentally, makes men prone to reading too much into women's friendly gestures. As a form of wishful thinking, men will sieve through the noise of friendly exchanges to pick out flirtatious signals that don't exist because overinterpreting is a better self-replicating strategy than missing procreation opportunities; all the more reason why men have to be acutely aware of their bias and correct for it.

We are the most pattern-hungry animals on the planet.

Our big brains mean that we are the most pattern-hungry animals on the planet, as confirmed by a number of experiments demonstrating how much worse we are than other animals at overinterpreting. For example, neuroscientist Michael Gazzaniga conducted a series of experiments to compare different species' response rates to random flashes of light.[7] Gazzaniga reported that all animals tend to do better than we do on these random-testing tasks, as do children under the age of four. Older children, teenagers, and adults all try to override the randomness by guessing where a random light will flash, *even when they are told that the flashes are entirely random and unpredictable.* Interestingly, patients with damage to certain parts of the prefrontal cortex have been observed to be less prone to the error of overinterpreting randomness: when it comes to dealing with randomness, it takes a brain lesion to get us to be as smart as a rat!

Our obsessive pattern-seeking is poorly matched with the complexity of today's chaotic world, which throws a lot more random noise at us than we have historically needed to filter out. We overinterpret randomness in myriad ways, largely by ascribing meaning to streaks or clumps of random events: by attributing someone's skill to luck ("Look at his success, he must be brilliant"), by judging a decision on its outcome ("That was a bad choice — just look at the result"), by attributing supernatural forces to random events ("She was destined to get punished by her bad karma"), by drawing unwarranted conclusions ("They must be bad parents given that both their children ended up failing school"), and the list goes on.

Randomness + Pattern-seeking Bias = Overinterpretation

When you combine the pervasive randomness in human life and our design to impart meaning to all data, the result is our tendency to read signal into noise. Our evolutionary default to overinterpret randomness translates into poor strategic choices, ruinous investment decisions, interpersonal misunderstandings, and unnecessary conflict.

Shifting from Simplicity to Complexity

To recap, simplifying is an efficient and effective way to interpret and respond to the world. But we're greedy because we want to simplify *everything*, including the less straightforward stuff, which is why we habitually *over*simplify complexity in two ways. We *under*interpret by missing key information, especially the kind we need to decipher complex causal relationships; we treat important signal as if it were irrelevant noise. And we *over*interpret by attributing meaning to randomness, especially when we read patterns into random streaks of repeated events; we treat useless noise as if it were relevant signal.

Oversimplifying

Underinterpreting Signal	**Overinterpreting Noise**
When we treat signal as noise ↓ ***We miss key information*** *(especially in causal relationships)*	***When we treat noise as signal*** ↓ ***We misconstrue randomness*** *(especially streaks)*

We see separateness where there are systems; we see basic, one-way causal relationships where there are multiple, interacting causal factors; we see patterns where there is randomness. We voraciously compress data into simple stories, thereby losing a lot of key information about how complexity works.

And in System 1's rush to make sense of things, we are typically unaware of how easily we misinterpret complex phenomena. This ignorance accelerates the frequency and depth of our misperceptions about the world and other people, all of which makes life much harder for us.

Our greed for simplicity is paradoxical: *we reduce to make quick sense of the world in order to control it, but we relinquish a lot of control by oversimplifying.*

So what are the fixes to our greedy need to simplify? We find them in a key decision-making theory, which includes three crucial tools, all of which are accessible only in The Space Between.

One thing to understand about the human mind:
It is designed to simplify everything.

One thing to understand about reality:
It is less straightforward than we think because there is always missing information.

CHAPTER 4

FIX #1: Reining in Reductionism

For every problem there is a solution which is simple, clean and wrong. — Henry Louis Mencken

System 1's tools are inadequate for excavating complexity and exhuming the missing information.

Our individual view of reality is a reduced, rarefied version of the real thing. But historically, and even much of the time today, simplifying hasn't been a problem. Our uncorrected intuitions can be completely wrong but it doesn't matter. For most of our history we assumed some basic facts about the world: it is flat, the sun travels around it, heavier objects fall faster than lighter ones, and time passes at the same rate no matter the speed you're moving at. These massive conceptual errors can go unnoticed because they don't impact our daily lives. And much of the time, our intuitions aren't as far off: the difference between the real thing and our conception of it is close enough to support our survival. But when we're dealing with anything that has a bit of complexity stitched into it, our reduction of reality puts us at high risk of oversimplifying in ways that are impactful and can make life hard. We oversimplify in two ways: by *under*interpreting signal (missing crucial information) and by *over*interpreting noise (attributing meaning to randomness). Our intuitive approach to separating signal from noise is unreliable when it comes to intricate causal interactions obscured by randomness.

"Complexity" is shorthand for "complex system." A system is a set of things that are interconnected in some way. The defining feature of any system is the interactions of its parts because the system's behaviour emerges from these interactions. A car engine is a system, as is a dialogue between two people, as is a storm. A system is defined by the boundaries that you choose for it, based on what you're trying to understand: a single cell is a system, as is the human body, as is the relationship between two people, as is the bigger system that encompasses their community and the still bigger system that represents society.

Whereas the parts in a system sometimes follow straightforward rules, the behaviour of the system itself can be complicated; for example, the workings of an individual neuron are straightforward but the network of neurons that make up a human brain is extremely difficult to model. Because System 1 defaults to parsing the world into one-way, simple relationships, we are at risk when we rely exclusively on our default intuitions to dissect complex systems: we tend to focus on discrete parts and neglect the connections between them, and therefore miss the patterns that decode complexity.

The good news is that there is a unifying strategy that combats our proclivity to oversimplify — a model that reins in greedy reductionism by exposing the unintuitive patterns of complexity. This model is systems theory. The practice of employing the theory is systems thinking, which focuses on how things are related to one another. *Systems thinking identifies and dissects the patterns of complexity.*

Because we don't default to a systems-thinking mindset, at least not with any degree of sophistication, we need a heavy dose of System 2, including its metacognitive component, which translates into the need for The Space Between.

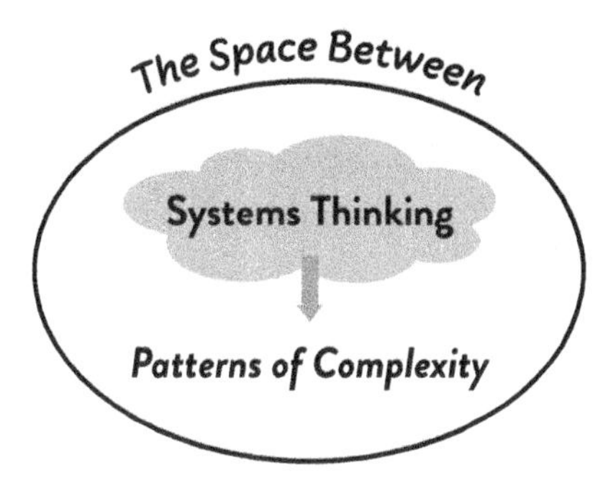

In The Space Between, we have the room to stand back and employ less intuitive, less rushed analysis, including scrutiny of our cognitive weaknesses, all of which are required to leverage the insights and power of systems thinking.

As one of the youngest executives in the bank that I worked for at the time, I built my career by exploiting the insights of systems thinking. And as one of the youngest executives to "retire" from the bank (i.e., lose my job), it was the complexity of systems that did me in, but more on that later in the chapter.

Systems Thinking to the Rescue

Systems thinking reveals that the world we perceive is not so simple. Author Peter Senge describes it this way: "Systems thinking is a discipline for seeing wholes. It is a framework for seeing interrelationships rather than things, for seeing patterns of change rather than static snapshots."[1]

Because a system has its own specific character, the whole is bigger than the sum of its parts. Understanding the whole is the aim of systems thinking. We can respond to complexity more productively and impose less suffering on ourselves and others if we see the whole, by understanding the interactions at play. *Complex systems are defined by the interactions among their parts; systems thinking is a method for revealing and analyzing these interactions.*

Systems thinking is a way of understanding the patterns within complexity — patterns defined by how the parts of a system interact.

How do the parts interact within a complex system? Through feedback loops, the two-way interactions that give life to a complex system. When I stop at a red light, then proceed on the green, it's a simple system of unidirectional causality with no feedback loops, since the traffic light is not impacted by my behaviour. If I then arrive home and am admonished for being late for dinner, to which I respond by slamming the door, following which I am criticized for losing my temper, to which I shout back that dinner was served too early … then we have ourselves an interesting system generated by the informational cues that are being passed back and forth in the feedback loop of belligerent communication. *The key patterns of complexity are contained in feedback loops, which systems thinking is geared toward dissecting.*

Complexity's signals are hard to identify because they are buried, ambiguous, and obscured by randomness; they are not obvious to System 1. We have to climb into The Space Between where the mental agility of System 2 can harness system thinking's tools for excavating complexity's signals — tools that correspond to the Need-to-Knows in chapter 3. We need to bring sophistication to our dissection of causal relationships; we need to neutralize the deceptively streaky nature of randomness; and we need to pose questions that surface missing information.

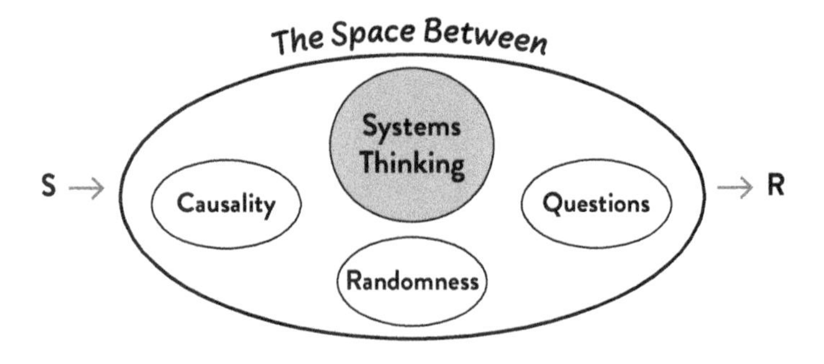

If you don't understand the causal relationships at play, if you don't isolate random noise from signal, and if you fail to ask the right questions, then you are ill-equipped to battle System 1's fumbling interpretation of and response to complex problems. And, therefore, ill-equipped to live productively and happily in the twenty-first century.

Tool #1: Causality — Dissecting the Relationships

Causality in complex systems gives the illusion of being straightforward to a brain relying on shortcuts. It is for this reason that we need to climb into The Space Between, to override our first impressions and dissect complex issues with greater depth and flexibility than System 1 offers. Specifically, there are five features of complex causality that System 1 is insensitive to: distance, direction, non-linearity, emergence, and chaos. Understanding these five properties is crucial because they allow us to better decipher how the causal factors are operating within a complex system; they are the signals that reveal underlying feedback loops. I'll touch on each briefly, leaving the most interesting to the last, before illustrating these properties with a story in which your author is, naturally, the sympathetic hero.

DISTANCE (PROXIMATE VS. ULTIMATE)

Proximate causes are close and usually obvious; ultimate causes are distant and usually hidden. System 1 usually fails to distinguish between them. If our partner comes home and scowls at the dirty dishes and snaps, "Clean this mess up," we are inclined to assume that the dirty dishes are the trigger for the outburst, and they may indeed be the proximate cause. But the more distant, ultimate causal factors (or root causes) are often more relevant, such as frustration at work before coming home or larger concerns about the relationship as a whole. System 1 misses the big picture because it relies on availability bias, which overemphasizes proximate causes. But complex systems are riddled with causal factors that are not readily available. *If we neglect ultimate causes, we misdirect our efforts in managing complexity, leaving us frustrated and defeated.* The trick is to cast a wide net in the search for ultimate causes, not only because they are removed from their immediate effects, but also because the direction of causality can run in many ways.

DIRECTION (NOT ONE-WAY BUT TWO-WAY)

Do chemical reactions in the brain cause depression, or do depressive thoughts trigger chemical reactions? At the risk of unfair stereotyping, neuroscientists generally favour the former interpretation and psychologists generally favour the latter. The dance between thoughts and brain chemistry makes it very difficult to specify causal direction, a problem that cognitive scientists are still grappling with. The best we can assume, as is typical with a complex system, is that causality is multidirectional. (Which is why most mental health professionals advocate both medication and psychotherapy, since the two can be mutually reinforcing in a positive feedback loop.) The key with complex causality is that effects impact their original causes, which in turn impact the effects, often by accentuating them, creating non-linear results.

NON-LINEARITY (NOT CONSTANT BUT EXPONENTIAL)

A non-linear interaction is one where causes produce disproportional effects. It is the grain of sand that causes a sand pile to collapse, the trivial comment that triggers an explosive argument, the viral video that launches a celebrity career, the rumour that torpedoes a stock, and the slow driver that causes a traffic jam. In a lecture on non-linearity, meteorologist Edward Lorenz created the now famous analogy of a butterfly flapping its wings in Brazil, ultimately setting off a tornado in Texas. In 2020 and continuing into 2021, we all experienced the impact of non-linearity firsthand when a microscopic virus leapt from an animal to a human, unleashing a worldwide pandemic that brought the human population to a near standstill. If you don't understand how complex systems create non-linear effects, you are vulnerable to underestimating the impact of seemingly inconsequential causes from which emerge consequential effects.

EMERGENCE (NOT PARTS BUT THE WHOLE)

The fourth feature of complex systems, emergence, is captured in the observation that the whole is bigger than the sum of its parts. The swarm behaviour of a hive emerges from individual bees; innovation emerges from individuals brainstorming together; consciousness emerges from non-conscious neurons; living organisms emerge from non-living compounds; Newtonian properties emerge from a collection of randomly moving quantum particles. It is because of emergence that you cannot understand a complex system by examining its parts in isolation. You cannot determine the behaviour of an ant colony by examining an individual ant, or a company by observing one employee, or a country by scrutinizing one city. When dissecting casual complexity, you have to consider how the system's properties emerge from the parts in often non-linear ways that can also be quite unstable — they can be very chaotic.

CHAOS (NOT STABLE BUT FLUCTUATING)

Complex systems are never stable for long; they tend to move back and forth between perfect order and complete disorder but never reach either extreme. Think of an argument between two lovers: it typically follows a period of stability in the relationship, until some event triggers a conflict, which ignites a heated discussion that can move from terse exchanges to shouting and accusations, followed by relative calm, perhaps some more terse words, and a reconciliation, which holds but remains vulnerable to future instability. Or the stock market, which can gyrate wildly for days in a row and then settle into a narrow trading range before resuming volatility. We spend our lives shuttling between order and disorder. Our lives occupy the middle ground between stability and complete disarray; we are constantly oscillating between the two extremes.

Chaos theory explores the conditions in which certain systems unfold over time in ways that are very difficult to predict accurately, even though there is no fundamental randomness to them: their mystery stems from their sensitivity to imperceptible measurement errors or slight perturbations in the system, both of which can balloon into mammoth forecasting errors. While weather forecasting is the obvious example, my favourite is the chaos reflected in the paths of our individual lives: we can veer far away from our planned paths in shocking, unexpected ways based on the cumulative non-linear effects of seemingly insignificant events, such as the stranger who gets on the elevator with you and ends up being your life partner, or the casual conversation with a neighbour that leads to a new career path. I never wanted or intended to have children, but I fell in love with a woman I met at work who wouldn't move in with me unless I committed to parenthood: the most unexpected, profound, and "thank God I got pushed into this" decision of my life. In the dissection of causality, chaos theory teaches us to be extremely humble in our predictions, to avoid the tempting but facile projection of the current state into the future, and to be agile, because just when you think you've got a handle on complexity you can be sure it will shift on you.

MANAGING CAUSAL COMPLEXITY

There is no surefire method for managing a complex system. But the necessary first step is using The Space Between to step back and engage System 2's metacognitive power to identify and resist System 1's penchant for preserving the separateness of the parts in a system (i.e., neglecting their interrelationships). In the space, System 2 can search out the five properties in order to understand the system and influence it because complex systems are unmanageable if you're not adept at dissecting them.

In The Space Between, System 2 can search out the five properties of complexity that are essential for understanding and influencing it.

In any kind of organization, the higher up you go, the more impacted you are by the challenge of managing complex systems. As a senior banking executive reporting to the president, I was juggling multiple complex systems simultaneously, under pressure to grow revenues while reducing costs and closing down a key product line. Losses on the bank's loans had begun to spike just before I took over, and the decision had been made to no longer offer unsecured loans to our customers until our risk management procedures were improved — a decision that makes sense on paper, and would be endorsed by any financially literate board. But I vehemently protested that while we could reduce our unsecured business, closing it down completely would have a serious impact on our customer relationships. If a client is forced to go to a competitor to get an unsecured loan, their mortgage, deposits, and investments can easily follow. The response to my concern was, to put it mildly (and in printable form), not sympathetic. When you make a lot of bold strategic decisions at the same time, they interact with each other in multidirectional ways that produce exaggerated (non-linear) effects that are sometimes far removed from their immediate causes. For example, the head of the mutual fund division blamed slumping fund sales on lack of training of frontline staff when in fact it was largely attributable to customers taking some of their investment business across the street where they could get easy access to unsecured loans. And the system of interacting causal factors didn't come close to ending there.

When the frontline investment advisers start losing customers who are upset that the unsecured loan they've had for years is no longer available, guess what? The advisers start returning phone calls from recruiters at competitors who are looking to hire them. The non-linear effects of these interacting forces are powerful: Canada's second largest bank becomes Canada's fifth largest.

As I hope is obvious, I am reducing a very complex organizational history to a brief story such that the missing information could fill a stadium. Nonetheless, virtuous and vicious cycles permeate so many aspects of our lives that it behooves us to understand the basics of systems thinking. And if it wasn't hard enough to identify the mechanics of causal relationships, we also face the distraction of random noise that obscures the patterns of complexity.

Tool #2: Randomness — Mindful of the Streaks

If you or I put pen to paper and write down a series of *X*s and *O*s that we think are in a random order (such as *XOXOOXOXXOOO*), we will create a string that a computer program (or really good statistician) will prove is not random. How? Because we switch our *X*s and *O*s too frequently: random series have an unintuitively high number of repetitions (i.e., streaks). Our brains want to switch back and forth between *X*s and *O*s too many times because we don't understand the truly streaky nature of randomness — how random events naturally clump together. ("Poisson clumping," named after the French mathematician, is the statistical way of describing streaks.) Clumping is why "bad luck comes in threes"; why most goals scored in hockey, soccer, and football games occur in one or two periods; why most customers arrive at the checkout counter around the same time, after which there is no lineup; and the list goes on. *Reality clumps!*

This point is crucial and worth repeating: we underestimate streaks because randomness kicks out meaningless patterns and coincidental surprises much more frequently than we expect. Which is why most of us are way off when it comes to guessing the probability of flipping a coin three times and getting a head or a tail each time: 25 percent. What about flipping four heads or four tails in a row in six tosses? Nearly even at 47 percent — unintuitively high for a brain that was designed to extract meaning rather than attribute patterns to random, meaningless coincidence. The probability of two people in a group of twenty-three sharing the same birthday? Much higher than expected at 51 percent. These examples are trivial, but when we attribute meaningful signal to random noise, the quality of our decision-making is severely compromised.

Randomness kicks out coincidental surprises much more frequently than we expect.

The trickiness of differentiating streaks that are meaningful from those that are merely random is probably best exemplified by our proclivity to confuse luck with skill. Lucky streaks are random, whereas skillful ones are non-random, and most outcomes we experience in our lives are a confusing combination of the two. There is some fascinating literature about the role of random luck in the success of movies (so many random factors influence a movie's box office revenues[2]); sports (tennis has the highest skill-to-luck ratio and football has the lowest[3]); business (so-called great companies rarely sustain their success because strategic luck doesn't persist[4]); and investing (extremely hard to tell a lucky stock picker from a skilled one[5]). The research does not deny that superior performance exists in these categories, but that random factors are very difficult to separate from the myriad causes that constitute predictable outperformance. The classic error that System 1 makes when it looks for a signal of skill is to latch onto whatever is easily available and measurable, which are results or outcomes that can be very deceiving to an untrained eye (such as a mutual fund's five-year return). In virtually all realms of our lives, the signal of skill is obscured by the noise of luck; it's just a matter of the *degree* to which embedded randomness is influencing events.

Our struggle with randomness reveals itself when we confuse luck and skill.

There are two ways to separate skill and luck, both of which reduce the risk of overinterpreting random streaks. The first is time, which, as Nassim Nicholas Taleb notes, is the "cleanser of noise."[6] In the short run, skill can be swamped by luck, both good and bad. But over long periods, good and bad luck offset each other, and what remains is the signal of skill. How much time? That depends on the activity. A chess player's skill can be signalled in a single challenging game and is clear in two or three. On the other end of the spectrum is a company executive or CEO's skill, which is typically buried in a lot of noise, both random and non-random, including the decisions of previous management that continue to influence current results, and the lag that occurs between current decisions and future results. Unlike an athlete, a dentist, or an accountant, whose talents are tightly linked to their results over short periods, a company's short-term results do not reflect recent decisions that have long-term impacts, like investing in new technology or discontinuing a product line. In shorter cycles of time (and small samples of data), noise can dominate in the form of deceptive, random streaks where variability does not have a chance to wash out.

What about mutual fund managers? This exact conundrum fascinated me as a young executive responsible for the bank's mutual fund business.

A whole book could be written on this topic (and I wrote two at the time), but the short answer is that there is so much random noise in the performance track record of any investment manager that you need at least twenty years to have a high degree of confidence that you've separated out luck from skill. One of the legends in the investment industry, Bill Miller of Legg Mason Capital, managed to beat the U.S. stock index for fifteen years in a row, but his underperformance in subsequent years eliminated most of the extra gains. In his fourth-quarter report in 2006, he wrote, "There was, of course, a lot of luck involved in the streak."

My professional challenge was to pick out the skilled managers in the hopes that they would outperform competing fund managers. And I hedged my bets by building what was, at that time, the largest index mutual fund business in Canada: index funds don't attempt to outperform anyone or anything; they "merely" replicate the stock index that they are designed to mirror. I put "merely" in quotes because it so happens that index funds have a long history of beating most managers in most years, and the vast majority of managers over long enough periods. My understanding of randomness was a primary factor in catapulting the bank far ahead of its competitors in mutual fund sales, doing wonders for our clients' portfolios, and kick-starting enough career momentum to eventually place me in charge of all the bank's branches in Canada and its international retail businesses. Part two of this career saga isn't quite so glorious; more on that at the end of this chapter.

One final comment on randomness and time: fifty adult working years is not necessarily long enough to scrub out the noise of random clumping in a typical lifespan. Some of us are the beneficiaries of lucky streaks and others are the victims of unlucky streaks, but our stories focus on the talented, hardworking few who rise above the crowd, capturing our imaginations with tales of why they are so successful. The talented, hardworking people who do not get ahead get none of our attention because they are invisible to us. Yet random luck is all that differentiates them: luck determines *which* of the talented, hardworking individuals achieve conspicuous success.

Rather than waiting for time to clean the noise from outcomes, there is a second method of separating noise from signal, a method that was crucial in choosing investment managers: evaluating the process behind the results. Because decisions and outcomes are often not tightly linked, good decisions can yield bad results and bad decisions can yield good results, all because of the influence of random luck. But assessing the decision-making itself, independently of the results it produces, is the cleanest signal we have to evaluate the quality or skill underlying the choices made. To evaluate the effectiveness of a decision, we have to probe the process that generated it: How diligent was the consideration of evidence and perspectives that contradict the going-in assumptions and beliefs? How deep was the exploration of a possible worst-case scenario and how it could come about? Was there a sincere brainstorming of unintended consequences that could arise from the decision? In the case of fund managers, getting into their heads to understand their decision-making process is the only hope of separating the skilled from the lucky if you don't have a twenty-year track record to analyze. Having to constantly interview countless stock pickers, I developed a series of penetrating questions to get a sense of how much skill underpinned their returns.

Questions, in fact, are the best way to reveal the signals hiding within the complexity that pervades our lives.

Tool #3: Questions — More and Better

I can't improve on the philosopher Martin Heidegger's proclamation that "questioning is the piety of thinking."[7] And Voltaire's maxim: "Judge a man by his questions rather than his answers."[8]

If the starting assumption of tackling complexity is that there is always missing information and that this information matters, then the onus is on us to dig for what is hidden. Questions are an essential tool for excavating complexity. But most of us are not skilled question-askers.

First of all, we rarely ask enough questions, because System 1 pushes us to jump to conclusions prematurely. Consider this problem: A fifteen-year-old girl wants to get married right away. What should she consider, and what should she do? Psychologist Paul Baltes and his colleagues use this type of dilemma to research and assess the wisdom of individuals, including empathy, insight, and tolerance for ambiguity.[9] In their model, a response to the problem can be categorized in two ways: a rigid imperative ("She is far too young to be marrying") and a question-oriented response ("What are her circumstances? Is she pregnant, or does she live in a culture that promotes early marriage?"). Wisdom, as defined by Baltes et al., acknowledges complexity through questions that seek out missing information.

Not only do we typically ask too few questions, but we are not very adept in *how* we ask: We don't ask in deep, probing ways that minimize the risk of getting skewed or shallow answers. We gravitate to closed-ended, negative questions ("Why is our relationship so crappy?") that yield much less useful responses than open-ended and constructive questions ("How can we make this relationship work better for us?"). The way we frame our questions shapes the responses we get: if our face, tone, and questions convey a desire for sympathy, we will only receive validation of what others think we want to hear. For example, if a couple has a bitter argument and each partner separately canvasses a personal friend to confide in, each will elicit sympathy and confirmation that the other is in the wrong, because each frames the sequence of events and questions in such a way as to guarantee the sought-after outcome ("I'm not overreacting, right?" or "Can you believe they did that?"). Given System 1's rush to lock down conclusions, our most powerful questions are the ones we rarely get around to asking — the ones that probe for evidence that challenges our initial hunches. System 1's confirmation bias discourages us from asking questions that prove our conclusions wrong, *even though disconfirming evidence is a far more powerful arbiter of truth than corroboration*. System 1 operates with a strong motivation to ask the easy questions (the ones that give us the answers we want and the ones that provoke simple answers) at the expense of hard questions (the ones that challenge us personally and the ones that require more cognitive effort to tackle).

Only in The Space Between can we access the metacognitive power of System 2 to pose essential questions to ourselves that uncover missing information, such as, *Have I really made the effort to investigate the whole system at play here?* And *What is my role in this system — how am I contributing to the dynamics of this situation in ways that are not obvious at first glance?* System 1 doesn't ask those questions of itself. System 2 can ask them, but only if it has the room it needs to operate at full capacity. The trigger of a complex situation — one that has a strong element of unpredictability to it — is our cue to get ourselves into the space so we can take on the missing information quest with a question-asking mindset.

System 1 doesn't ask hard questions of itself but System 2 can ask them … if it has the space it needs to operate at full capacity.

A word on leadership: question asking is, I believe, the sign of a strong leader, no matter the field. High-performing leaders are skilled question-askers because the higher up you go in any organization, the more removed you become from the detailed knowledge of the people closer to the action. In fact, at the very highest levels, in the case of CEOs and board chairs, I believe a large part of their roles ought to be as Chief Conversation Facilitators: good ones foster the kind of deep, challenging conversations that leverage diverse perspectives through incisive questions. Questions uncover missing information that others may be reluctant to disclose for fear of appearing out of step with the majority. A good probe, for example, is "Does anyone have an alternative perspective that we may be missing here?" or "Is anyone concerned that we don't have enough data to make an informed decision?" or "What discomfort or unease is lingering in the discussion that we are not addressing but should?" You don't have to be a CEO or board chair to benefit from this insight, as per Heidegger and Voltaire. Probing, open-ended, and truth-seeking questions are the kind we have to work to come up with because we gravitate to the other kind — the type that are undergirded by preformed opinions. Questions weaken our greedy desire to reduce reality to the quick and tidy stories favoured by System 1. A penetrating question can unlock the missing information that reveals the nature of a complex situation. Or … it can end a career.

One afternoon, all the bank's senior leaders were brought into the main boardroom, where it was announced that the bank would be paying over $2 billion to settle a legal case that originated in the investment banking division. This would wipe out the year's profits. My first thought was the challenge ahead of me to reassure the eighteen thousand retail employees who, through no fault of their own, would be facing much lower year-end bonuses, if any at all. Our competitors were always trying to recruit our best people, and rumours of low bonuses would make us very vulnerable. When the floor was opened for questions, and a heavy silence descended around the massive circular table where we all sat, I turned on the microphone in front of my seat and asked how this news would impact the bonuses of all retail staff, since we would need to communicate something to them immediately after the press release was issued later that day. The response, to put it mildly, was not sympathetic. All it takes is one too many "unhelpful" questions — the Systems Thinking 101 kind that challenge others to think more broadly — before you suddenly find yourself at home struggling to fix your printer jam after years of reflexively asking your assistant to "please call the techies to get my printer fixed."

Was my fate sealed just because I had a bad habit of speaking up at the wrong time with the wrong audience? Yes, in part. Although speaking up with systems-related questions and insights also earned me many promotions. I think my bigger challenge was not successfully recognizing and adapting to predicaments, which I treated like quick-fix problems. It turns out that questions and the other systems thinking tools have their limits.

Coping with Predicaments

"All life is problem solving," according to philosopher Karl Popper.[10] The problem with problem solving is that for us humans, "solving" is not always a realistic goal when it comes to complexity. The reality of complexity is that we often have to settle for the course of action that entails the least unwanted side effects; we have to get comfortable with settling for the best among unsatisfying alternatives. I like economist Thomas Sowell's shrewd explanation of why politicians are more popular than economists: politicians can promise the impossible, whereas economists "keep reminding people that ... there are no 'solutions' but only trade-offs."[11] Solving versus accepting trade-offs is presumably what philosopher Abraham Kaplan had in mind when he explained the difference between problems and predicaments: the former can be solved; the latter can only be coped with.[12] Predicaments are permanent dilemmas that we cannot fix but must continually manage, tweaking our responses as we cope. Many (if not most) of the complex situations in our lives are more predicament-like than problem-like: the challenges in our close relationships, our careers, our child rearing, and our quest to create meaning for ourselves. System 1 abhors ambiguity, so without the broad and patient perspective of System 2, protected in The Space Between, we treat these predicaments as if they were solvable and we make ourselves vulnerable to frustration and suffering.

As a perfectionist "maximizer" who struggles to accept the low bar of merely accepting the first satisfactory solution, I have to work hard to resist the temptation to treat predicaments as problems because I'm prone to burning myself out in a search for flawless solutions when none exist. As a young executive managing discrete businesses that I could get my hands around, I could directly impact the systems within my sphere of influence, as these systems were well defined and tractable — problems that had solutions. But later in my career, managing thousands of employees and a firehose of daily emergencies, not to mention edicts from above that didn't always seem (to me) to reflect an acknowledgement of the intricacy of complex systems, put me face to face with a massive, unwieldy predicament. I failed to recognize what I was dealing with — a situation that requires a high tolerance for imperfection, limited control, and progress that is very gradual at best. I was sprinting in a marathon. If you get frustrated and single-minded about imposing your perfect solutions on the world, you're inevitably going to push back on the people who promoted you. Depending on the tact with which you present your opposing views, and their appetite for hearing alternative perspectives, your next step is more likely out than up.

Predicaments aren't solvable; they're only manageable. After two divorces (and, by my count, six marriage therapists), I have also come to realize that romantic partnerships have a strong element of predicament to them because there are always some irresolvable differences that can only be managed sensitively and empathetically. Same for raising two daughters: a lot of situations arise that can't be fixed but merely worked through. When you realize that some of life's problems are unsolvable predicaments, you make life much easier for yourself (and others).

It would be easier to be human in the twenty-first century if all our problems were of the straightforward variety that lend themselves to single solutions. Wish it were so. Life is easier if you accept the wisdom of Carl Jung, who, when reflecting on his work near the end of his life, confessed, "I had learned that all the greatest and most important problems of life are fundamentally insoluble."[13] More lyrically, in his poem "The Grand Wagon," the thirteenth-century writer Rumi made a similar point: "Beyond right and wrong, there is an empty field. I'll meet you there."

Which is a perfect segue to the second cognitive design flaw.

One thing to remind yourself every day:
It's all about the systems.

One question to ask when you're tackling complexity:
What information is hiding in the system that would enable me to understand and influence it better?

CHAPTER 5

FLAW #2: We're Addicted to Certainty

The gratification of curiosity rather frees us from uneasiness than confers pleasure; we are more pained by ignorance than delighted by instruction. — *Samuel Johnson*

Knowing is one of our most powerful feelings, yet virtually invisible to us.

Samuel Johnson's insight in the above epigraph, while perhaps hard to decipher on a first read, undergirds the main idea of this chapter. The eighteenth-century writer's point is that when we solve a problem and thereby "gratify our curiosity," it is not so much pleasure we feel as the elimination of the uncomfortable tension of not knowing. The "pain of ignorance" is a powerful force: it's why we are addicted to certainty.

It turns out that Design Flaw #1, oversimplifying, has a sibling — a related but distinct flaw. It's one thing to simplify everything, but it's another to assume our simplified conclusions are accurate. The sibling of oversimplifying is overconfidence. We figure things out at lightning speed and much of the time our confidence in our fast assessments is warranted, especially for the straightforward issues we have developed expertise in handling. But our cognitive design also makes us extremely vulnerable to overconfidence, especially for the more complex dilemmas we encounter. Overconfidence stems from Design Flaw #2, our inbuilt addiction to certainty, which pushes us hard to conclude as quickly as possible — often prematurely.

To combat this addiction, and in the same vein as tackling oversimplification, there are four Need-to-Knows about our minds that must be acknowledged. And the first is how stingy we can be in expending mental effort. We are selective in choosing what to deliberate about and once we arrive at a solution that feels right, we are reluctant to expend further energy to check our thinking or contemplate alternative perspectives. Psychologists use the term *cognitive miserliness* to describe how frugal we are in expending conscious concentration.

We are frugal with how much conscious concentration we are willing to expend — just enough but no more.

Need-to-Know #1: We Are Cognitive Misers

One of my favourite experiments illustrating cognitive miserliness is conducted by psychologist Shane Frederick, who uses a simple math problem to demonstrate mental laziness.[1] A bat and ball together cost $1.10; on its own, the bat costs $1.00 more than the ball. How much does the ball cost? Most people quickly land on ten cents as the answer. But if the ball costs ten cents and the bat costs $1.00 more than the ball, then the ball and bat together add up to $1.20 (ten cents plus $1.10), which is ten cents too much. The right answer to the question is five cents (if the ball costs five cents and the bat is $1.00 more than the ball, then five cents plus $1.05 adds up to the $1.10 total).

What is fascinating about this simple question is not that most people get it wrong (mental math is not the forte of most of us), but that few of us check our initial math to see if it adds up to the total $1.10. Why do most people not take a few seconds to double-check their work? For the same reason that most of us choose an escalator over stairs, or a seat on the bus over standing: energy conservation.

Cognitive miserliness translates into defaulting to the simplest explanation we come up with to explain anything. As psychologist Keith Stanovich describes it, we are "strongly disposed to deal only with the most easily constructed cognitive model."[2] And then we leave it at that, full stop, without revisiting our conclusions unless we are forced to. Once we think we've got things figured out, we consider our work to be done — we stop the search for explanation. Our decision-making procedure is to "satisfice," a term coined by psychologist Herbert Simon (combining "satisfy" and "suffice").[3] To satisfice is to accept the first satisfactory alternative we come up with. Satisficing preserves cognitive energy and saves time in making decisions. We cannot interview every potential mate on the planet before picking one; we cannot try every possible job; we cannot test drive every possible car; we cannot tour every house that is for sale. In all of these examples, we go with the best solution we can find after a limited search. And we satisfice when we are making sense of our experience, drawing conclusions about the world and other people by landing on the first reasonable explanation.

Need-to-Know #2: We Conclude by Satisficing

The whole satisficing process is a System 1 specialty: largely subconscious, it occurs rapidly and ends when we conceive of an explanation that is satisfactory and sufficient, at which point we lock down this interpretation as our conclusion. Satisficing is a brilliant strategy for survival in a simple but threatening environment because simple visual cues are reliable enough to facilitate quick, satisficed decisions about the straightforward challenges that have historically confronted us. Our ancestors' first satisfactory explanations were reliable the vast majority of time, which is why natural selection preserved satisficing as a primary sense-making principle. Even today, satisficing serves most of our day-to-day decision-making because it is the best way to make fast decisions about straightforward challenges where a high level of confidence in our initial conclusions is warranted.

Satisficing (accepting the first satisfactory alternative) is a design feature we rely on to conserve mental energy and to react quickly.

While all of us rely on satisficing, some psychologists like to categorize people as either satisficers or maximizers.[4] The vast majority are the former, but a select few fall into the latter category. Satisficers are okay with "good enough," whereas maximizers aim for perfection. As a seasoned perfectionist (as per my daughters' observations in chapter 3), I can tell you that being a maximizer can be exhausting, but you satisficers miss the intense high of making a "perfect" decision (or is it the intense tension release from finally deciding?). I'm the guy who exasperates real estate agents (and ex-wives) with an endless search for the perfect home. Friends have confided that they dread the first fifteen minutes at restaurants with me because of the torrent of questions I inevitably have about the menu. There's a reason why more than one date has asked me, "Is this a date or an interview?" (In fact, the invention of online dating was thrilling to me as a maximizer because the app allows the user to screen many romantic options in a quest for perfection, albeit at the risk of extending the search indefinitely … until you're on your deathbed with only your daughters at your side, chastising you for being too picky.)

In chapter 3, I outlined some of the strong biases that we all operate with. These biases facilitate our hurry to conclude and influence the explanations we consider to be satisfactory and sufficient — biases that usher certain ideas to the front of the line. Ideas are advantaged if they meet one or more of these criteria:

- They are based on information that is immediately available to us ("availability bias").
- They can easily be supported with confirming evidence ("confirmation bias").
- They fit with everything else we already believe ("myside bias").

In our rush to conclude with minimal cognitive effort, we grab whatever information we can access as quickly as possible and favour evidence that supports our initial hypotheses. The most readily available information, besides our immediate sensory experience, is our pre-existing beliefs: myside bias refers to the degree to which our existing beliefs influence our interpretations of new experience. As psychologist Daniel Kahneman cleverly describes it, "In the competition with the inside view, the outside view doesn't stand a chance."[5] Myside bias skews our view of the world by constantly building and reinforcing the belief systems we have already adopted, discouraging us from exploring arguments that contradict our beliefs. Ideas that don't fit what we already know are severely disadvantaged. Most such ideas, like flying cows or talking trees, are disadvantaged for good reason: they do not conform to our experience. But what about ideas that aren't as obviously preposterous but happen to not fit an individual's particular belief set? These challenging ideas are usually rejected because they can't be integrated into our belief systems without a lot of energy-demanding cognitive rework, which miserly brains aren't enthusiastic about. Consider how skeptically we treat unflattering news about our preferred politicians yet how enthusiastically we endorse critical stories about their opponents.

The three biases operate within the vast, automatic processing of System 1 subconscious thinking: as our minds search for possible ways of interpreting incoming data, satisficing limits our consideration to what is easily available, easily confirmable, and fits with our pre-established beliefs. These biases are the reason that psychologists describe us as being more like lawyers arguing for one side of a case than like judges gathering all of the relevant information and making a dispassionate assessment.

A key element of satisficing is how definitive it is — the "coming to a full stop" feature of concluding. It is difficult to dislodge a conclusion that has been satisficed because at that point, we experience the state of knowing — one of the most powerful feelings we have. We don't tend to think of knowing as a feeling, but like all feelings, it arises from System 1 automatically. We cut our finger, we feel pain; we lose a loved one, we feel sad; we figure something out, we feel "knowing." As neuroscientist

Robert Burton describes it, "The feelings of knowing … aren't deliberate" but are "mental sensations that happen to us."[6]

Need-to-Know #3: Knowing Is a Feeling

Some psychologists refer to this knowing feeling as "the feeling of rightness," and it's a strong and pervasive one because we abhor not understanding something that is relevant to us. As psychiatrist Irvin Yalom puts it, "When any situation or set of stimuli defies patterning, we experience dysphoria [a high level of unease], which persists until we fit the situation into a recognizable pattern."[7] We are designed to feel very uncomfortable when something does not make sense to us because discomfort motivates us to figure things out, whether it be a mysterious rustle in the bush, the confusing betrayal of a friend, or the promotion that we didn't get. Not knowing is an "out-of-control" state that we are psychologically motivated to eliminate. Our neuroendocrine system is geared toward this very objective: our sympathetic nervous system secretes stress hormones (cortisol and adrenalin) that activate our alertness responses, putting us on edge until we feel that we have regained control. A lot of our suffering originates from our deep need for control, so much so that I would fine-tune the Buddha's second noble truth — that suffering arises from craving — by suggesting that suffering arises from *craving control.*

We are designed to abhor lack of control, which is why the feeling of knowing is so comforting — it signals that we're in control.

Just as calm is restored in us when our tires regain traction in a car skid and we resume steering, so it is restored when our minds get traction on aspects of the world that require understanding and prediction. We replace the tension of not knowing with the calm of knowing, which puts our mental state back in balance; the feeling of knowing is our internal signal that we have restored control. It is because the discomfort of not knowing is so poignant that we crave the feeling of knowing. And the faster we can relieve the discomfort and bask in the warmth of knowing, the better.

Need-to-Know #4: We Rush to Certainty

Rushing to certainty is conducive to survival: an indecisive caveman is a dead one. We can't afford the time to second-guess ourselves in life-and-death situations. *Quickly generated confidence in definitive conclusions is the life-saving reason we rush to certainty, via the emotional incentive to terminate the discomfort of not knowing.* Satisficing stops the search for explanation upon arriving at the first reasonable one by eliminating the discomfort of not knowing with certainty. We love certainty because it's comfortable — much more desirable than the discomfort of not knowing. Our rush to enjoy the feeling of knowing, which concludes the satisficing process, is a brilliant survival strategy when the scenarios we confront are straightforward enough to accommodate our first intuitions about what is going on and what to do.

But satisficing is not so brilliant if the scenarios embed a hint of complexity, because in these scenarios, our proclivity for simplifying means we're vulnerable to overlooking key information that is hidden (i.e., not easily available, not easily confirmable, not conforming to our prior beliefs). When we confront scenarios that demand more cognitive flexibility, satisficing transforms from a design feature to a design flaw.

Feature Becomes Flaw: Satisficing Becomes Certainty Addiction

We want answers; we need answers; we are programmed to find answers. And we want to know as quickly as possible. We rush to certainty because our need for certainty is like any addiction — a method to escape suffering. In the case of certainty addiction, it is the tension of not knowing that we are trying to squelch. The confident feeling of knowing is a vast improvement over the out-of-control feeling of not knowing. But unlike other addictions, certainty addiction serves an important purpose. For the myriad straightforward problems in our lives, the first reasonable interpretation we lock down is often the best, or at least good enough to get the job done: our confidence is justified. If we abandon certainty altogether, we would second-guess ourselves to the point of analysis paralysis.

Our addiction to certainty serves an important survival purpose, which makes it impossible to give up entirely.

But the best understanding of complex problems rarely emerges from satisficed explanations. The "stop mechanism" of satisficing — the confident feeling of knowing that feeds our addiction — is usually premature in the realm of complexity because our first good enough conclusions are usually based on oversimplified assessments, driven by greedy reductionism. Unless there is obvious and undeniable evidence that triggers us to revisit our initial satisficed conclusions, our addiction to certainty deters our miserly minds from expending further effort in searching for counter-examples to our hypotheses and alternative explanations that better approximate truth. Certainty robs us of deeper and more productive understanding. When satisficing meets complexity, the result is misplaced certainty in our conclusions — overconfidence.

Satisficing + Complexity = Overconfidence

With complexity, our rush to conclude forces a higher error rate because of the trade-off between speed and accuracy: the faster we draw conclusions, the less time there is to uncover missing information, consider alternative interpretations, and critically assess our intuitions. When we're looking for a house or a job, we know that we are satisficing based on having surveyed a limited sample of houses or jobs. But, and this is key, when we satisfice our interpretations of a complex world, we're oblivious to the fact that we have surveyed a small sample of possible explanations. Whether we are dealing with most forms of interpersonal conflict, sorting out the internet's firehose of information and opinion, supporting our kids in coping with a baffling and sometimes cruel social media landscape, mapping out corporate strategy, or assessing government policy, our challenges are not the look-and-solve kind that we excel at resolving quickly. But we confidently plow ahead without differentiating problems we have expertise in solving from those we do not. We ride a wave of confidence based on natural selection's training to be blissfully inattentive to our cognitive weaknesses, ignorant of our logical flaws, irrational quirks, faulty memories, and countless biases, none of which posed much of a problem for us in the evolutionary environment from whence we came.

Overconfidence is aided and abetted by the "illusion of explanatory depth," a term coined by two psychologists to describe the tendency of people to "feel they understand the world in far greater detail, coherence and depth than they really do."[8] They point to two drivers of this illusion by noting that we are "novice scientists" and "novice epistemologists": our knowledge of most phenomena is shallow and our appreciation of our cognitive limitations is underdeveloped. The combination of being cognitively unsophisticated and unaware of it doesn't present too much difficulty for other animals since they live in a world where their skills are matched to their surroundings. Not so much us, in the case of complex systems with which we are now enmeshed.

Once we *feel* like we understand something, no matter how superficial our understanding is, we go about our business with the unwarranted confidence that we've got everything figured out. In fact, the less we know, the more confident we're inclined to be! The illusion of explanatory depth is the source of the "Dunning-Kruger effect," named after the two psychologists who documented this bias, which refers to the inverse relationship between confidence and knowledge.[9] The deeper we go in trying to understand something, the more we uncover ambiguities, contradictions, and further questions; whereas if we keep our knowledge shallow and superficial, it's easy to gloss over complexity (and we are Olympic medallists when it comes to confidently glossing over complexity). As Charles Darwin aptly observed, "Ignorance more frequently begets confidence than does knowledge."[10]

A paradox: sound bites and tweets exhort us not only to endorse oversimplified solutions to increasingly complex problems but also to have supreme confidence in our opinions on these matters. Today's twenty-four-hour news cycle and exploding social media platforms are pruning reality at the same time that social, economic, political, and industrial complexity is exploding. A prediction: the illusion of explanatory depth will become even more pronounced as we continue to organize information into simple cause-effect bundles that belie the complicated causal chains that define wickedly complex problems.

Our addiction to certainty and the overconfidence it breeds doesn't just derail smart decision-making, it routinely threatens our most treasured assets — our relationships. We latch onto convictions that inflame our passions and embolden our disputes with other people, convinced of their folly and the error of their ways. Certainty addiction poisons our interactions with others.

Certainty addiction threatens our most treasured assets — our relationships with others.

So how do we resist the addiction to certainty that pushes us to premature closure?

Shifting from Final Verdict to Scientific Method

Overconfidence arises from automaticity: when System 1 operates without conscious supervision. Our challenge, therefore, is to keep System 2 thinking engaged longer. We fight our addiction to certainty with System 2–generated self-regulation, not unlike the self-control we impose on ourselves to avoid overeating, overspending, and lashing out every time we are in conflict.

But self-regulating our addiction to certainty is distinctly tricky for two reasons I've already mentioned. First, we're rarely aware that we need to self-regulate — as long as we *feel* knowing, we believe that all is good, despite our vulnerability to Dunning-Kruger overconfidence. Second, we can't go cold turkey on certainty the way we can on cigarettes, alcohol, or chocolate cake, because we need satisficing and the feeling of certainty it imparts for all the straightforward decisions we need to make throughout the day. So we have our work cut out for us.

Only in The Space Between can we harness Systems 2's metacognitive power to be cautious about those situations in which an early feeling of knowing is likely to be misplaced — where our quick, intuitive judgments lead us down the wrong path. Only in the space can we harness System 2's metacognitive power, to be mindful of Daniel Kahneman's admonition that the confidence we feel in our judgments is not necessarily a reflection of a deep, reasoned evaluation of the probability that our conclusions are correct so much as it is a feeling that reflects how well our ideas cohere with other ideas we believe.[11] Or as Robert Burton puts it, "felt knowledge" is not the same as knowledge that results from testable observations: "'I am sure' is a mental sensation, not a testable conclusion."[12]

Up to this point, I've neglected Friedrich Nietzsche's book *Twilight of the Idols*, which he wrote in the summer of 1888, four months before being institutionalized for a mental illness from which he never recovered. Many of the ideas in this chapter were captured in *Twilight* long before they were recognized and researched by academics. Prefiguring Herbert Simon's concept of satisficing by nearly seven decades, Nietzsche wrote, "The first interpretation that explains the unknown in familiar terms feels so good that one 'accepts it as true.'" Explaining why we do this, Nietzsche wrote, "With the unknown, one is confronted with danger, discomfort, and care; the first instinct is to abolish these painful states ... any explanation is better than none." And, "To extract something familiar from something unknown relieves, comforts, and satisfies us." Long before the terms *availability bias* and *myside bias* were coined, he wrote, "One searches [for] that which has most quickly and most frequently abolished the feeling of the strange, new, and hitherto unexperienced in the past — our most habitual explanations."[13] Nietzsche is known for his irreverent philosophy, but he was also a penetrating psychologist. I mention him now, not as an afterthought, but as a segue to the next chapter because he not only summarizes our addiction to certainty, but offers a prescription for it.

Only in the space can we push ourselves to be both better scientists (in tackling complex problems) and better epistemologists (in accounting for our mental frailties). How? By breaking our addiction to certainty when it doesn't serve us. How? By exploiting a key scientific principle and three essential tools that arise from using it. In other words, by following Nietzsche's lead.

One thing to know about the human mind:
It is designed to lock down quickly on definitive conclusions.

One thing to know about reality:
It usually doesn't conform to our first impressions of it.

CHAPTER 6

FIX #2: Breaking Our Addiction

Truth is the kind of error without which a certain species could not live. — Friedrich Nietzsche

In the realm of complexity, dogma is for dogs.

The above epigraph is brilliant: it relates our notion of truth to our addiction to certainty in only fourteen words! Nietzsche wrote many pithy observations about truth and certainty, including, "Convictions are more dangerous enemies of truth than lies," and "Truths are illusions about which one has forgotten that this is what they are."[1] He took aim at truth by arguing that we treat our ideas about the world as ultimate representations of reality rather than inventions we have created. We don't have to fully endorse Nietzsche's attack on truth to appreciate his point that there is something suspicious about it, given that everything we know is only available to us through the filter of our individual perspectives. As he put it, "If we could only perceive things now as a bird, now as a worm, now as a plant ... then nature would be grasped only as a creation which is subjective in the highest degree."[2]

I moved to an out-of-area school in grade 7 and was on the lookout for new friends. What drew me to Warren was his mysterious ritual of proudly walking out of the classroom every morning when the national anthem began. As we rushed from gym to the next class one afternoon, I chased after him to ask about his morning routine — and so began a three-year friendship that doubled as my initiation into the study of metaphysics.

If you are familiar with the beliefs and practices of Jehovah's Witnesses, you know what I did not — that devotion to country is anathema to the all-encompassing devotion one ought to have to God, hence the refusal to sing the national anthem. Warren introduced me to a labyrinthine belief system that was absolutely fascinating to a young teenager brought up in a secular household. You may also know that an objective shared by all Witnesses is to proselytize for the purpose of converting people (hence the door-knocking). Warren never lost patience with my endless questions about his religion, in part because he was playing a long game: I was a big catch for a thirteen-year-old Witness to single-handedly reel in. For my part, I was completely engrossed in our endless discussions and arguments, most of which were bookends on either side of intense video game competitions at his house after school.

Ultimately (and ironically), our numerous conversations cemented my atheism. The more he tried to persuade me, the more convinced I was that there was no rational route to God. And I found the notion of faith highly problematic. Over and over again I asked Warren why a benevolent God would deny knowledge of Himself to those who, like me, lacked faith. Warren's answer was always the same — that I wasn't truly open to knowing Him. Eventually Warren and his family became increasingly impatient with my reluctance to attend one of their church sessions and we drifted apart. We remained friendly until he quit school in grade 12 to become a full-time employee of the Jehovah's Witness publication business that produces the religion's materials.

Part of my fascination with Warren was my bewilderment that someone like him — universally recognized by all teachers and students as the smartest person in our grade and probably the school — could believe all the seemingly incoherent things he espoused, including how imminent the impending Armageddon was. I was determined to figure out where the intellectual common ground was between us; I was truly troubled by the vast gulf in our belief systems. How could Warren have such immovable views that were, to my mind, self-evidently false? How could two reasonable people have such monolithic certainty in their own belief systems, yet be in complete contradiction with one another? We couldn't both be right despite both being certain. Or maybe my notion of certainty was too rigid.

We think of truth as a faultless description of reality and when we find it we know it. The "we know it" part is highly problematic for all kinds of reasons, including Nietzsche's point that we can't jump out of our human brains to confirm a legitimate correspondence between our perceptions and the world as it "really is." But leaving aside the intricacies of existential and postmodern epistemology, there is a remedy for the problem of "truth" as we usually think of it, an antidote that alleviates the symptoms of our addiction to certainty.

Scientists rely on a more flexible version of truth than we naturally default to — they do not pursue certainty.

Scientists employ a more flexible conception of truth than the thorny version that System 1 defaults to. Our intuitive notion of *truth as certainty* is not what scientists pursue. Rather, they seek out ideas that are corroborated by evidence and therefore likely to describe some aspect of reality with a high probability of accuracy — "inference to the best explanation." (A similar form of truth is reflected in law, where the standard to confirm guilt in civil cases is "preponderance of evidence" or "balance of probabilities," and the higher standard used for criminal cases is guilt "beyond a reasonable doubt.")

The scientific form of truth is more useful for our complex, twenty-first-century world. It is *truth as provisional*: truth describes a belief that is considered an accurate representation of reality, but not a permanent condition of accuracy since it can be overturned or updated at any time with additional information or insight. Nietzsche described it this way: "The mostly strongly believed a priori 'truths' are for me provisional assumptions."[3]

Just as Systems Thinking is the high-level antidote to the oversimplifying of greedy reductionism, provisional truth is the high-level antidote to the overconfidence of unwarranted certainty.

A Strategy to Avoid Overconfidence

One of my favourite parables is recounted by Indian philosopher Jiddu Krishnamurti in a speech he delivered in 1929:[4]

> The devil and a friend of his were walking down the street when they saw ahead of them a man stoop down and pick up something from the ground, look at it, and put it in his pocket. The friend said to the devil, "What did that man pick up?" "He picked up a piece of the Truth," replied the devil. "That is very bad business for you then," said his friend. "Oh, not at all," the devil replied. "I am going to let him organize it."

Great story, not unlike the equally great Stones song, "Sympathy for the Devil," where the devil points out that what puzzles us is the nature of his game. We are forever sorting out pieces of reality, searching for the truth about our various and sundry predicaments. Siddhartha Gautama, the Buddha, pointed to our misguided effort to fit the world into tidy, conceptual frameworks as a primary source of our suffering. One way around "the devil's curse" is to surrender to the insight that we simply can't get everything conceptually organized. For example, those scientists and philosophers referred to as "mysterians" believe that we will never be able to understand how consciousness or other mysteries occur. Psychologist Steven Pinker makes this point by arguing, "Our thoroughgoing perplexity about the enigmas of consciousness, self, will and knowledge may come from a mismatch between the very nature of these problems and the computational apparatus that natural selection has fitted us with."[5]

As it currently stands, we are a long way from a "Theory of Everything" that reconciles quantum mechanics and general relativity (which are incompatible at the subatomic level); half-a-century's worth of various string theories has still not generated a solution. We are also a long way from solving the "hard problem of consciousness" (how a "felt experience" arises from purely physical, non-conscious particles) and we may never solve this riddle satisfactorily. As psychiatrist Iain McGilchrist points out, "It would be extraordinary if we just happened to have arrived at such a summit of evolution that our brains allow us to understand and be aware of all that exists." He argues that certainty is "a useful illusion," and although it may appear to us that we have the ability to understand all that there is, "If a squirrel could reflect, it would imagine that it understood everything, too — it couldn't conceive of the kind of understanding it didn't have."[6]

Putting aside the question of whether we're just as delusional as reflective squirrels, the notion of truth as provisional accommodates complex phenomena to a much greater extent than our day-to-day version of truth as final verdict. By conceiving of truth as provisional, we instill caution into our conclusions by acknowledging that we rarely have all the facts — there is always missing information! Provisional truth provides a counterweight to satisficing by nudging us to keep the hunt for missing information open rather than locking down premature conclusions. Provisional truth doesn't preclude us from having well-formed beliefs; it just means that what we think of as fact should be construed, as biologist Stephen Jay Gould described it, as "confirmed to such a degree that it would be perverse to withhold provisional assent."[7]

Provisional truth counters satisficing because it nudges us to keep the hunt for missing information open.

Neuroscientist Antonio Damasio describes the goal of science as "improved provisional approximations."[8] Science proceeds by constantly revising and refining insight, and Damasio's description is a powerful way of defining how we should interpret the non-straightforward situations in our lives, especially those that involve other people. We can't possibly understand the complete perspectives of others, especially since they themselves don't always know why they feel or behave certain ways. We can only aim for best approximations of their motivations, which are always subject to correction.

Provisional truth is the umbrella strategy that encompasses specific tools for combatting our addiction to certainty. Just as Systems Thinking has many implications from which I chose three specific tools to combat greedy reductionism, so too does provisional truth have multiple ramifications, three of which I feel are the most important: probabilistic thinking, skepticism, and humility. Once again, we do not default to these tools naturally, notwithstanding how crucial they are for tackling complexity. So once again, we need to climb into The Space Between to access them. When we're feeling pretty sure of ourselves but aware that we're immersed in some form of complexity, we take a few breaths to step back and open the space, then animate Observing Self to expand the space by contemplating our high risk of overconfidence. Then and only then do we have the room to ramp up System 2's use of provisional truth's tools.

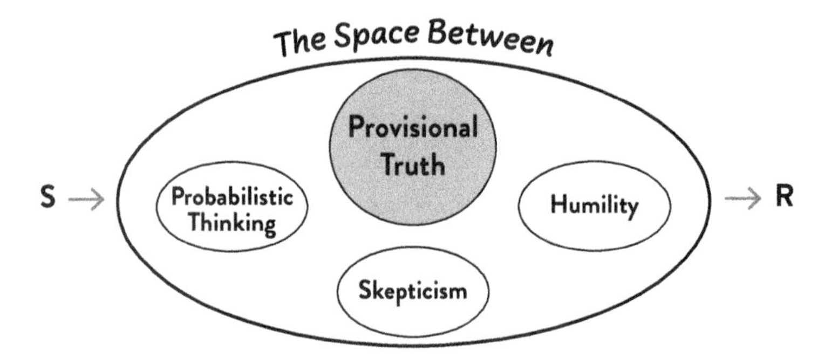

These three tools arm us in the battle against certainty addiction; they mitigate the overconfidence that follows the premature lockdown of satisficed conclusions.

Because provisional truth is never final, it requires a commitment to assessing the likelihood of our being right. So provisional truth has a corollary, which is captured in the first tool.

Tool #1: Probabilistic Thinking (Because It's Rarely Either-Or)

System 1 loves to dichotomize, breaking up the world into two categories: a belief is true or false; the neighbour is a good person or a bad one; the boss is supportive or disempowering; the governing party is competent or corrupt. Tidy bifurcations have been historically survival-enhancing: either an animal is dangerous or not; either the berries are sweet or bitter; either your fellow hunter-gatherer is trustworthy or unreliable. It's not that we never think in probabilities; it's that our intuitive sense of probability is fairly unsophisticated and tends toward dichotomizing between "very likely" and "unlikely." For example, when a weather forecast indicates a 20 percent chance of rain, we tend to be surprised when it rains because we think of it as unlikely instead of understanding what the forecast means: every five times that the atmospheric conditions are identical to those in the forecast, it will rain once. Today's world does not lend itself to simple true-false dichotomies. System 1's rudimentary version of either-or just doesn't work with causal complexity. We need a more sophisticated and nuanced way of assessing things: *probabilistic thinking.*

System 1's rudimentary version of true or false doesn't work in today's world of causal complexity.

Decision theorists distinguish two kinds of probability: objective and subjective. Each does a different job. Objective probability is a method of statistically summarizing the observations of repeatable events, as in the probability of new drivers getting into accidents in their first year of driving. But for one-off situations or ones for which there is a limited history of repeated observations, we need subjective probability, which reflects a level of confidence in a particular belief. It can be numerical, as in "I have a 30 percent confidence level in this belief," but it doesn't need to be this specific. At the very least, it behooves us to categorize our convictions into five degrees of confidence between the two extremes of impossible and certain.

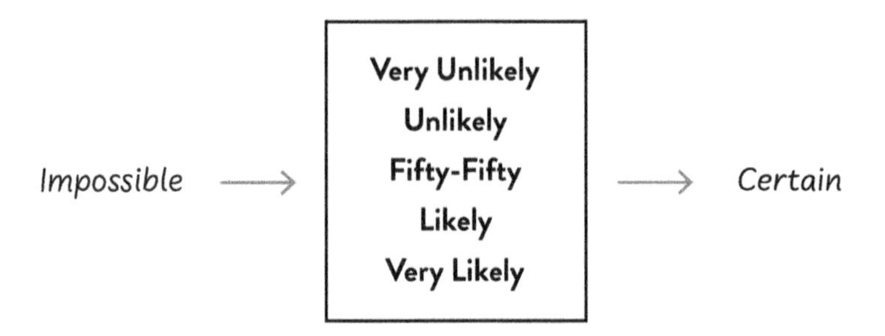

I really like how psychologist Philip Tetlock defines probabilistic thinking as a way to "judge using many grades of maybe."[9] His research analyzes the rare individuals who can consistently predict events with a better than random frequency (whom he calls "superforecasters"), and reveals that "the more a forecaster embraced probabilistic thinking, the more accurate she was."

Probabilistic thinking fosters the kind of metacognition that encourages us to separate ourselves from our beliefs in order to reflect on the likelihood of their correctness as well as the likelihood of alternative interpretations. It encourages us to suspend our judgment when we assess the likelihood of our correctness being only marginally higher than fifty-fifty. It slows down our thinking to ensure we are not rushing to certainty. And when it works really well, probabilistic thinking encourages us to make more frequent use of expressions such as "I'm not sure," "perhaps," "I need more information," and "I'm not yet comfortable rendering a judgment." There is no greater discipline we can impose on our thinking than fairly assessing the probability of our correctness with a sufficient degree of granularity — either by assigning a percentage probability to it or by using the five classifications I outlined above. And because wise, probabilistic thinkers are acutely aware of the biases and errors humans are prone to, they infuse their probability assessments with a heavy dose of the next two tools of provisional truth.

Tool #2:
Skepticism (Because "Probably Not")

Other animals (and here I'm of course referring to animals in their natural state) can afford to be single-minded because they live in a world that resembles the one in which they evolved. But in the realm of complexity, dogma is for dogs.

Skepticism doesn't mean having a permanently suspended mindset that never draws conclusions. It doesn't put all beliefs in the same category. Rather, skepticism decelerates the System 1 lockdown process that otherwise catapults beliefs to the elite status of certainty. Skepticism is complementary to probabilistic thinking because it nudges us to be honest and realistic in how we assign probabilities to our conclusions. It does this by proportioning our confidence to the actual evidence rather than our first intuitions, and by taking into account our biases and other cognitive limitations. Most importantly, skepticism counterbalances our insatiable lust for speedy, tidy answers.

The final word on anything complex is rarely final. "Probably not" and its more diplomatic version, "could be," are useful mantras for reminding ourselves that early conclusions regarding complexity are provisional because there is always missing information. "Probably not" also reinforces the notion that even once we have rigorously tested our assumptions and explored alternative explanations, we are still restricted to statements of probability rather than certainty. We are limited to darker and lighter shades of grey rather than black and white.

Skepticism decelerates System 1's rush to catapult beliefs to the elite status of certainty.

Skepticism doesn't come easily to us, since we are programmed to jump to definitive conclusions quickly and we have constructed our world to suit that purpose — an artificially constructed habitat that shuns shades of grey. Our educational system is geared toward getting the one right answer within the time allotted; students are rarely (if ever) challenged with ill-defined problems characterized by insufficient relevant information but lots of distracting noise — in other words, the kind of problems that represent real-life complexity. And long after graduating from the true-false world of institutional education, our main source of information is the media, which operates on the basis of being succinct, dramatic, and, above all else, definitive.

In fact, we are shockingly gullible when it comes to things we're told by sources we consider to be credible: we rarely contemplate the probability of correctness of claims that appear legitimate, even though any good scientist knows to be deeply skeptical about preliminary research that hasn't been replicated many times by different researchers. When epidemiologist John Ioannidis analyzed the most frequently cited research studies in the medical field, all published in the most reputable journals, he discovered that 41 percent of the studies made claims that, when retested, proved to be either patently false or grossly exaggerated.[10] That number doubled to 80 percent when he broadened the sample to include less-known research and journals. He and his colleagues concluded that the majority of research culminates in claims that are more likely to be false than true. This disappointing revelation is the result of many factors that are endemic to the "publish or perish" imperative in academia, as well as the fact that research funding and publishing opportunities cluster around new and interesting research rather than less intriguing work that merely confirms or refutes prior claims. A startling number of research claims never get challenged (or the challenges are not widely reported since the initial claims become old news very quickly). "Replication failure" is a widespread problem, especially in the social sciences like psychology, where an experiment can be reported as revealing a discovery or new insight on the evening news, long before it has been replicated and confirmed by other scientists (and, as per Ioannidis, many claims fail to replicate when rigorously tested). Preliminary research that hasn't yet been reproduced and validated is catnip for the media, always in search of newsworthy headlines.

I once worked for a smart, Harvard-educated executive who enjoyed challenging my penchant for alternative perspectives with his favourite expression, "Ted, the numbers don't lie." In one late-night meeting, I was exasperated and snapped back, "Of course the numbers lie! Numbers lie because they rarely tell the whole story; they lie because they are compiled by people who lie, purposefully and inadvertently." My studious response didn't improve the conversation (seems like a pattern for me and bosses, if you're keeping track). I could fill a book with examples of lying numbers (and dedicate it to him), including the "hard numbers" like audited financial statements and research study results, not to mention the half-baked statistics hyped by the media during the Covid-19 pandemic (including "excess deaths" attributable to the virus that ranged from 20 percent of reported deaths to as high as 300 percent).

I'll limit myself to one detailed example. A reputable economist published extensive statistical analysis demonstrating that looser gun laws *decrease* the incidence of crime (supporting the theory that you won't rob or attack someone if you think they might be concealing a weapon). He and his co-author went as far as asserting that U.S. states that prohibit the carrying of concealed weapons were generating an additional 1,570 murders and over 60,000 assaults every year.[11] (The National Rifle Association enthusiastically endorsed the study's results, as well as the economist's subsequent book *More Guns, Less Crime.*) But along came another reputable economist who analyzed the data and discovered that the original results were skewed by the rise of crack cocaine trafficking in big cities, which ushered in a wave of crime that was unrelated to the tighter gun laws in these cities. When the numbers were normalized for rising drug-related crimes and compared to states with looser gun laws, the results showed the exact opposite — restrictive gun laws correlated with *lower* crime rates.[12] Each side is still embroiled in a politically charged dispute about the other's statistical methodology. Point is, numbers lie.

They lie because they don't reflect missing information, which is precisely why initial "discoveries" are often overturned when they fail subsequent replication tests. It is extremely difficult to uncover legitimate causal relationships: events can be correlated for many reasons other than direct causation (like tight gun laws and rising urban crime rates). Sometimes the relationship is mere coincidence, and often there are hidden "confounding variables" that have not been accounted for (like increased crack usage). My favourite example of lying numbers and causal confusion is fictional, but it cleverly demonstrates what scientific research usually looks like, especially the headline-grabbing kind. This example, courtesy of Professors Hillel Einhorn and Robin Hogarth, is a hypothetical experiment intended to reveal the correlation between intercourse and pregnancy.[13]

In this imaginary scenario, the fictional observer has no theory to explain how babies are made. They simply record their findings in a sample of two hundred observations.

	Pregnant	*Not Pregnant*
Intercourse	20	80
No Intercourse	5	95

The results suggest that pregnancy may be related to intercourse or perhaps some underlying cause that triggers both intercourse and pregnancy. But there is no consistent and direct connection between them because intercourse does not usually produce pregnancy. In five cases, pregnancy is induced without intercourse, so the latter is definitively not a necessary condition of the former. If the research were published, the headline would read, "Intercourse Unlikely Cause of Pregnancy."

That five experimental subjects purportedly got pregnant without intercourse is typical of research: people forget, they lie, and the experimenters make mistakes.

This example is revealing because it resembles most preliminary research results: the data are usually confusing and difficult to interpret reliably. The fact that five subjects purportedly did not have intercourse but did get pregnant is typical of any study: people forget, they lie, and the experimenters make mistakes when tabulating the numbers. So five impossible scenarios can easily be reported as legitimate even if they are just misleading noise. This example seems preposterous only because we know the truth about pregnancy, but it is very typical of how science proceeds and why preliminary results are rarely final, no matter how definitely they are presented.

The scientific method is the best and only viable method of building and deepening knowledge. The point is that if the deliberate and structured methodology of science is prone to error and misleading results, imagine how weakly supported many of the claims are that we are exposed to in daily life. Provisional truth necessitates a degree of skepticism when it comes to complexity, including skepticism turned inward, toward ourselves.

Tool #3: Humility (Skepticism Directed at Ourselves)

In his poem "The Second Coming," W.B. Yeats wrote, "The best lack all conviction, while the worst / Are full of passionate intensity." Nassim Nicholas Taleb describes our frailties in a characteristically indelicate way, writing that "we are a bunch of idiots who know nothing and are mistake prone, but happen to be endowed with the rare privilege of knowing it."[14] I would point out that this "rare privilege" of knowing how dumb we can be is usually in the form of criticizing other people: we rarely apply the same degree of scrutiny to ourselves as we do to others. The illusion of explanatory depth and its offshoot, the Dunning-Kruger effect, promote the feeling of knowing that emboldens System 1's rush to certainty, at the high risk of overconfidence. Which is why humility is such a crucial tool: we need to bring the same skepticism that is useful in evaluating the claims of others to our own assumptions and grand conclusions.

Humility is foundational to probabilistic thinking: If our estimate of being right is to be useful, it must reflect our biases, shortcuts, and recurring mental missteps. You can't assign a reasonable probability to a belief or prediction if you don't account for the reasons you could be wrong. And with anything that has even a hint of complexity, we know we are going to be at least partially wrong because we never have the whole story (there's always missing information). Taleb is fond of repeating that it isn't the forecast that matters so much as the *forecast error* that we ascribe to it.[15] Why? Because quantifying forecast error imposes humility on us; lack of humility breeds overconfidence, which hampers mental agility and hinders better understanding and better solutions. When we reflect on the possibility of misconstruing other people and complex situations, and actually quantify the likelihood of being wrong, we open our minds to alternative interpretations that could be more accurate and to ways of interacting with the world that could be more productive. And we improve our ability to adapt to unfolding events that do not conform to our predictions.

Explanations and predictions are a dime a dozen; how often do you hear someone estimating the error probability that underlies their thinking?

Management professor Chris Argyris coined the term "double-loop learning" to describe the extra step in problem solving that we usually miss.[16] We're fairly adept at single-loop learning: when we interact with the system that defines a problem, we generate feedback from the interaction that improves our understanding of how that system operates. Double-loop learning is deeper because it starts with single-loop learning but goes one step further: the second loop uses the feedback to adjust how we actually think about the problem. The second loop is metacognitive because it requires that we self-examine — that we consider the biases and shortcuts that influence our assumptions about the problem.

Self-examination is what distinguishes Tetlock's "superforecasters": "Our analyses have consistently found commitment to self-improvement to be the strongest predictor of performance." And, "The degree to which one is committed to belief updating and self-improvement … is roughly three times as powerful a predictor as its closest rival, intelligence."[17] "The best indicator of the quality of people's judgments," he says, is metacognition: "soul-searching, Socratic commitment to thinking about how they think."[18]

Tetlock contrasts different people's thinking habits by categorizing them into two different styles, both of which have merit. "Hedgehogs" are narrow and deep in their thinking. "Foxes" are broader but not as deep — they integrate a variety of information sources to form their opinions. Hedgehogs stick to their beliefs and assign higher probabilities to being right. Foxes are less definitive, more likely to change their minds, and more humble in assessing the likely accuracy of their forecasts. Granted, this dichotomy is simplistic, since we can be more hedgehog-like or more fox-like depending on the situation, but it's worth pausing for a second, to ask yourself:

Am I a hedgehog or a fox?

Hedgehogs are very confident in their expertise and are almost three times as likely to take more extreme positions (such as describing future unknown events as either inevitable or impossible). Foxes are more comfortable with ambiguity and do not feel compelled to espouse grand theories or definitive views: they are more balanced between self-criticism and self-defence. Tetlock's work demonstrates that foxes are consistently more accurate forecasters than hedgehogs, who are "less suited for tracking the trajectories of complex, evolving social systems." The irony is that hedgehogs make great media pundits since most of us don't have the patience for cautious forecasts and nuanced explanations; foxes do not make for good TV, even though their interpretations and predictions of world events are better calibrated to reality.

My buddy Warren was a hedgehog — he had deep knowledge of the Bible and his worldview was unshakable, as was his forecast that Armageddon was imminent. Nothing could convince him otherwise. But before proudly portraying myself as a wise and humble fox, I have to acknowledge that I was equally adamant that theistic narratives were incoherent and that atheism was the only viable worldview. I've since softened my cosmological perspective a little (psychedelics tend to do that to a person — more in chapter 9). I'd like to think that I'm more of a double-loop learner now than I was in grade 7.

Complex Thinking for Complex Problems

Our long evolution as a species has nudged us toward being overconfident because natural selection trained our ancestors to disregard the difference between the world outside our heads and the one we depict inside it. These two worlds — actual and perceived — were not that far apart in the straightforward environment that hundreds of generations of our ancestors evolved in. But the gap between the two has widened. Iain McGilchrist puts it nicely: "It is like comparing a world in all its richness with a useful map of that world, which leaves almost everything out, except the strategic essentials. We have become like people who have mistaken the map for the thing itself."[19] I would add that today we even miss some of the "strategic essentials." It's easy for us to forget that the depiction in our heads never maps onto the actual world perfectly (not even closely sometimes). Each of us produces, directs, and stars in a play performed in the theatre of our own mind, and we are completely oblivious to the fact that we are the one and only one audience member for this play. We default to assuming that the play we are watching is the one everyone else is privy to. But others are absorbed in their own private plays. The key to humility, and to resisting our addiction to certainty, is keeping the discrepancy — between the real world and our internal play about it — foremost in our conscious awareness, mindful that the two can diverge quite widely if we aren't careful.

We assume everyone is watching the same play as we are, but others are absorbed in their own private dramas.

The powerful force of knowing pulls our ideas in one direction to a final destination (a single "basin of attraction," to use the language of complexity science). Breaking our addiction to certainty requires us to explore other possible resting points (other basins) without getting prematurely stuck in the first one that satisficing offers up. We can do this only by treating truth as provisional. As Tetlock describes it, "For superforecasters, beliefs are hypotheses to be tested, not treasures to be guarded." Provisional truth is defined by the probability we attach to our beliefs, and best approached with a healthy degree of skepticism and an even bigger helping of humility.

Systems thinking and provisional truth constitute the foundation of complex thinking.

In The Space Between, we can avail ourselves of System 2's flexible analytic strengths and its metacognitive superpower to harness the tools of systems thinking and provisional truth, thereby applying complex thinking to complex problems. In The Space Between, we can leverage systems thinking to be more sophisticated scientists (improved single-loop learners), at the same time as embracing provisional truth to be more sophisticated epistemologists (capable double-loop learners).

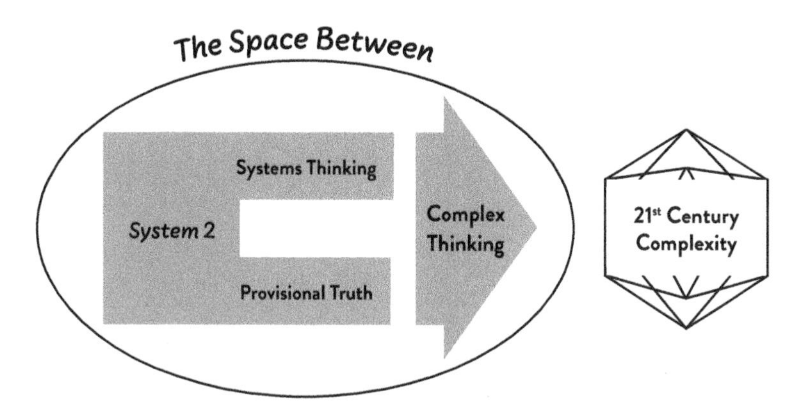

I'd like to think that since my passionate debates with Warren about God, I've matured into a more sophisticated scientist and epistemologist, if only because I'm more humble. Which is why I'll close this chapter with my favourite quote from Taleb — both a brilliant thinker and an avowed Christian. Twelve words to live by: "To be sophisticated you need to accept that you are not so."[20]

One thing to remind yourself every day:
You're at least partially wrong most of the time (in part because you rarely have all the information).

One question to ask when you feel certain:
What is the percentage probability that am I wrong? (And the number cannot be lower than 10 percent!)

CHAPTER 7

FLAW #3: We Hold Ourselves Emotionally Hostage

The mere addition of thought ... exposes [every human] to such violent emotions, to so many storms of passion, so much convulsion of feeling that what he has suffered ... may be read in the lines on his face. – Arthur Schopenhauer

Compared with other animals, we are emotional hysterics.

If you polled philosophers to find out who was the most pessimistic writer of all time, the response would be unanimous: Arthur Schopenhauer, whom I featured in the introduction. It's easy to be depressing, but to be gloomy in a deeply psychological, articulate, and holistic way takes prodigious intelligence and creativity: it is for good reason that Schopenhauer had considerable influence on Freud, Nietzsche, and Wagner, among others.

Schopenhauer claimed, as per the uplifting epigraph above, that much of our emotional suffering stems from "the mere addition of thought," which transports us through mental time travel to a past filled with regret and indignation, and a future coloured by worry and fear. For the non-human animal, "because its consciousness is limited to the present moment … the actual pleasure of the moment comes to it whole and unimpaired."[1] While many other animals experience emotion to varying degrees, we humans are uniquely susceptible to emotional turmoil that is triggered by the inventions of our own minds. As Robert Sapolsky points out, all animals are designed to cope with short-term crises, but humans worry chronically about *anticipated* stressors — not immediate physical threats but manufactured psychological ones. Channelling his inner Schopenhauer, he writes, "We can experience wildly strong emotions (provoking our bodies into an accompanying uproar) linked to mere thoughts."[2]

On a bright autumn Saturday afternoon, I was walking home across a bridge above a ravine — a thoroughfare that was busy with car traffic but few pedestrians. Striding along, I noticed something on the other side of the bridge that took me a moment to make sense of: a man was standing on the outside of the bridge's protecting wall, with his back to the road and his arms behind him, clutching the bridge wall as he leaned precariously over the precipice. When I realized that the man was seconds away from jumping, I dashed through the traffic to the other side, shouting, "Stop, stop. Wait!" As I came up behind him, he turned his head and looked at me with a face that was devoid of expression but revealed layers of underlying pain and suffering. I pleaded, "I can help you. I know what it's like and I'll get you help and it will be okay. You have to trust me. Come back over the wall." He looked below, and again at me, and swung one leg back over the wall to straddle it. He was now sitting on the wall with one leg on each side of it, and shouted at me, "You don't get it. You don't fucking get it!" I gingerly pulled out my phone, avoiding any sudden movements. "Look, I'll call an ambulance and stay with you and we'll get you to a hospital so you can heal. Come onto the sidewalk. Trust me, please." He glared at me as he swung his other leg over toward me and jumped onto the sidewalk. He was now furious and threatening. Leaning into me, he screamed even louder, "You don't fucking get it! You don't get it. You don't get it," before abruptly turning and walking away. I called 911, reported the incident, and insisted they send support to take him to a hospital, all the while following him down the street. He kept turning around to see if I was on his trail so I kept my distance. The emergency operator advised that based on my description and the direction he was heading, the police would be able to track him down and it was safer to stop following. Shaken up, I hurried home, late for a cocktail party.

Thirty minutes later my phone rang: the police wanted me to return to the bridge so they could ask a few questions. When I arrived, my heart instantly sank. There was an ambulance, many fire trucks, and police cruisers. Beneath the bridge in the ravine, a tarp covered a body with one arm and one leg jutting out from beneath it. A crowd had gathered, but nobody had witnessed the actual jump (someone had phoned it in from their car). I was the last person to have spoken to him.

The next morning, I walked down into the ravine and sat on the rock where his body had landed. I told him I was sorry I had abandoned him and that I wish I had done more.

I eventually tracked down the detective overseeing the case and, unsurprisingly, he was unwilling to share any details about the man. But he promised to pass on my offer to his family — they could call me if they wanted to hear about my exchange with him on the bridge. They never called. Part of my reason for reaching out was selfish: I wanted to understand who this man was and why he was so distraught. What kind of Schopenhauerian suffering was he inflicted with? What kind of emotion caused him to take his own life, even after my initial but illusory success in deterring him? I suppose I also wanted to ease the guilt I felt: he came back and jumped because I had left to go to a party.

The emotion that motivated him to take his life was forcibly destructive. The horror of seeing his lifeless body below the bridge and the feeling of guilt that I could have prevented it have stayed with me. Emotions are powerful forces. Sometimes too powerful.

The Emotional Brain

We need emotion because it's the physiological arousal that motivates us to act, without which our reaction times and survival would be severely compromised. Emotion is the product of System 1 processing, the neurochemical reactions that originate in subcortical brain structures (loosely, the limbic system) that evolved long before our higher brain functions developed. Our kludge of a brain houses the basic mammalian emotional system, plus a whole lot of extra neuronal circuitry that complicates things. Of the many complications, there are three in particular that contribute to uniquely human turmoil.

First, as Schopenhauer pointed out, the amazing flexibility of our brains enables us to jump out of the present moment to deliberate on the past and contemplate the future, giving us no end of opportunities to find things to be upset about. As Stephen Batchelor describes it, "The mind flings us into tawdry and tiresome elaborations of past and future."[3] Two psychologists titled their research paper "A Wandering Mind Is an Unhappy Mind" to convey two key findings:[4] First, our minds wander a lot — on average about 47 percent of the time. Second, and the kicker, mind-wandering tends to make us unhappy. So we are happiest when we are *not* daydreaming, yet daydreaming is what we do about half the time we're awake (talk about a design flaw!). *We are the species that ruminates*, causing us no end of uniquely human suffering. It's as if the cognitive miserliness that I discussed in chapter 5 applies only to immediate problems, for which System 1 pushes us to conclude ASAP without overtaxing System 2. But *when immediate problems are solved to our satisfaction, our minds go looking for something to occupy them*, searching out other problems (past or potential) to mull over. Our minds never quit — they just keep churning out the thoughts (about one billion in a lifetime, according to physicist Frank Wilczek's estimate[5]). If only there were an off- or kill-switch we could flip to take a break. (There is, which we'll get to in the next chapter.) And when we feel we've been wronged, watch out! Our minds are like magnets that attract self-righteous grievances, which we fiercely cling to, swirling them around and around in a relentless, obsessive spin of debilitating vertigo. That's our "special thing" as humans and a pernicious design flaw.

Our minds are magnets that attract grievances that we swirl around in an obsessive spin of debilitating vertigo.

Second, we have the unique ability to ruminate on suffering itself, thereby adding a second layer of pain on top of the original suffering. Other animals aren't "smart enough" to double their anguish. The Buddha famously labelled this feat as the "second arrow" problem. He described the plight of the "uninstructed person" who laments their suffering as being shot with two arrows: the first is the initial pain and the second is the distraught reaction to the first. The "instructed person," in contrast, only suffers the initial pain: they do not indulge in self-pity but merely accept the first pain as it is, without adding additional suffering to it. Most of us are in the "uninstructed" category: we're highly prone to catastrophizing unpleasantness. As psychologist Daniel Kahneman points out, when bad things happen, it is not our default to consider "how much worse things could have been."[6] We usually opt for wallowing by layering on what therapist Russell Harris describes as "dirty discomfort" on top of the natural, "clean discomfort" that is unavoidable in our lives: "We can have anger about our anxiety, anxiety about our anger, depression about our depression, or guilt about our guilt."[7]

Third, our emotional system is poorly adapted to life in a complex, modern environment. We are designed to be very sensitive to risks because this particular bias keeps us alive and it worked extremely well in the harsh environment in which we evolved. The speed of System 1, combined with its risk sensitivity, means that we generate strong emotional reactions to anything problematic, including minor inconveniences and situations over which we have limited or no control (as in the proverbial traffic jam). Worrying about the next day's presentation can foster the same stress hormones as the smell of a predator in the wind. Indulging in sanctimonious fury at a perceived insult in a text message can trigger the same physical response as an aggressor stealing our limited food supply. The bluntness of our emotional system is not well suited to our busy, socially complex lives, riddled as they are with every conceivable complication and frustration: *we react to noise as if it were signal.* And as the busyness of our interconnected, hyper-complex lives increases, so does the noise that taunts us.

The bluntness of our emotional system is poorly suited to the complexity of life today: we perpetually treat noise as signal.

All three unique human challenges are provoked and amplified by an underlying emotional mechanism: negativity bias. This mechanism influences how we interpret and respond to the world, and is the one and only Need-to-Know about our proclivity to overreact.

Need-to-Know: Negativity Bias

One of the most important insights to arise from cognitive psychology in the past few decades was foreshadowed by our genius friend Schopenhauer nearly two centuries ago when he observed that "we generally find pleasure to be not nearly so pleasant as we expected and pain very much more painful."[8] Positive and negative emotions are not mirror images of each other. Negative emotions are "more" than positive ones:

- Pain is more painful than pleasure is pleasurable.[9]
- Failures sting more than successes feel great.[10]
- Losses upset us more than gains excite us.[11]
- Criticisms have more impact than compliments.[12]
- We weigh negative traits in others more heavily than positive traits.[13]
- Strong negative emotions persist longer than strong positive ones.[14]
- Pain comes in many flavours, pleasure in but a few: there are 67 percent more words for negative feelings than positive ones.[15]

Negative emotions are more negative than positive ones are positive (about double the intensity).

As a rule of thumb, behavioural economists consider negative emotions to be roughly two times as strong as positive ones. Now, it must be said that for most of us, neutral to mildly positive emotions win the *frequency* contest by dominating our moods much of the time. This is referred to as the "positivity offset," which keeps us on an even keel most of the time. But negative emotions win the *intensity* contest by a significant margin, and last longer than positive ones. A kind word is appreciated but fleeting compared to a harsh word that stings and lingers throughout the day. This imbalance is the source of our negativity bias: our neutral-to-mildly-positive moods are punctuated with sharp twinges of negativity that can persevere. In other words:

There is a strong evolutionary underpinning for negativity bias because danger can never be fully eliminated, whereas pleasure is only useful to the point of satiation. The marginal value of eating and sex declines rapidly once we have had our fill, but the marginal risk of danger never declines because it's omnipresent: pleasure has an upper limit whereas danger has no bounds. There is a second imbalance between the two: a missed meal or sexual encounter can be replaced later, but falling off a cliff or being eaten by a tiger is a one-time event. This asymmetry between risk and reward is precisely why our operating system skews toward a greater sensitivity to pain than pleasure.

In fact, negativity bias is structured into our biology: the brain's amygdala works with rough, barely processed data to detect risk or danger. It has a direct connection to the brain stem, so as soon as it detects the *possibility* of trouble, it triggers a fight-or-flight response in the brain stem before our conscious mind sorts out what's happening. The amygdala is a key feature of System 1, designed to err on the side of interpreting danger and eliciting strong negative reactions in order to protect us, as any good survival-enhancing design ought to do. But negativity bias entails a crucial trade-off; there's a price to pay for avoiding the risk of underreacting to real threats. And in many situations, the price is steep — a design feature morphs into a design flaw.

Making a decision in any condition of uncertainty entails a trade-off between the risk of two possible errors — a false positive (false alarm) and a false negative (missed threat). In chapter 3, I described how this trade-off relates to *over*interpreting randomness (risking a false positive), which has been a historically safer bet than *under*interpreting it (risking a false negative). It's safer to assume the rustle in the bush is a predator and not just the wind; otherwise, your downside risk is that your very last words will be, "Silly me for invoking a false negative." As emphasized in chapter 3, missed threats are more dangerous than false alarms, and the price we pay for reducing the risk of the former is increasing the risk of the latter.

The exact same trade-off is in play with negativity bias, which is just a by-product of our design bias of overinterpreting in order to avoid false negatives. *System 1 is designed to err on the side of assuming bad things in order to reduce the chance of underreacting to real threats.* It can only avoid the risk of false negatives by increasing the risk of false positives (i.e., reacting to false alarms). Negativity bias comes at a cost. And that cost is emotional overreaction.

Feature Becomes Flaw: Negativity Bias Becomes Hostage-Taking

Negative emotions are crucial for survival, just as reductionism and satisficing are (as per chapters 3 and 5). But like all the cognitive design flaws, too much of a good thing is injurious. Negative emotions protect us, but being hostage to them is not conducive to our well-being. When simplifying and satisficing are overextended, they become oversimplifying and overconfidence. *When negativity bias is overextended, it becomes overreaction.* And our big, complex brains are better at overreacting than any other animal's.

It's an unfortunate fact about being human: *the intensity and duration of our negative emotional reactions are often disproportionate to the threats that trigger them.* We both amplify our negative feelings and hold on to them long past their usefulness. We are quick to invoke fear or furor at the slightest *perceived* danger or offence. The fear that motivates us to leap out of the way of a speeding car and the furor that provokes us to defend ourselves against a physical attack are both productive emotional reactions; not so much the fear of being late for a meeting that triggers reckless driving or the furor of a misinterpreted comment that induces us to lash out at a loved one. Not to mention the anxiety of exam writing, job interviewing, or speech giving. Or the irritation of standing in a long line, the stress of losing keys, the worry of boarding a plane. None of these emotional reactions is useful. They are overreactions that burn a lot of emotional calories in the service of destructive and often self-sabotaging behaviour.

Negativity bias exaggerates the impact of the three human vulnerabilities I listed at the beginning of this chapter: mental time travel, the second arrow, and the mismatch between System 1's neurophysiology and the world we now live in. The result is that we can be excessively exasperated, envious, embarrassed, and enraged.

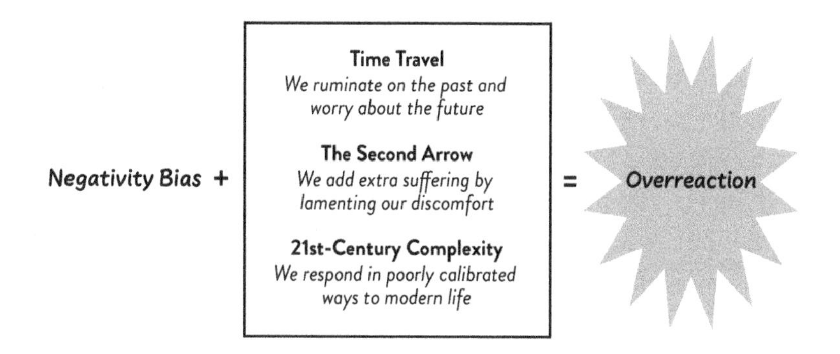

We surrender a lot of control to our negative emotions: they float up within us, without permission, and take us hostage. Emotional overreaction is self-sabotage — a hostage-taking in which we are both perpetrator and victim. *Tilting* is a term used by poker players to describe emotional reactions that interfere with their ability to play the game well. I think *tilting* has a much wider application: negativity bias–induced overreaction interferes with our ability to play the game of life productively and satisfyingly.

We surrender a lot of control to our negative emotions: they float up within us, without permission, and take us hostage.

We may have limited control over the crazy thoughts that bubble up within our goofy brains and the crazy emotions that spring from them as a result, but we do have some control over the intensity and duration of our emotions. Most importantly, we have control over what *to do* with our emotions. We can't stop them from arising, but we don't have to be captive to them.

Shifting from Captive to in Control

Emotions are *triggered* by lower brain functions (subcortical activity), which initiate the emotional response. But emotions are *moderated* by higher brain functions (prefrontal cortex activity), which allow us to subdue our emotional reactions. Our design accelerates emotional reaction, but it also provides us with an emotional brake. The human brake is much more developed than other animals' for two reasons. First, we have much bigger prefrontal cortexes, offering us a higher level of "executive functioning" to evaluate our emotional reactions (i.e., metacognition) and influence them. Second, this influence is enhanced by having many more cortico-amygdala connections, meaning our higher-level cortical areas are more tightly connected to the lower-level subcortical structures, allowing us more executive intervention over our emotional processing once it has been triggered. "Neocortical in-puts have become incorporated into subcortical function to a greater degree than in nonhuman animals," according to psychologist Kent Berridge, who points out, "Human evolution has changed only [this] one major aspect of the organization of emotional core processes within the [mammalian] brain."[16] System 2 thinking equips us with the ability to assess our emotions for their usefulness, and then take whatever next steps befit the assessment. We can intervene like no other animal, to deter negativity-biased System 1 from dominating when it prods us to overreact. Sounds easy; of course, it's anything but.

It takes a fair amount of cognitive discipline to manage the overreactions generated by negativity bias. This discipline is available only in The Space Between because only in the space can we kick-start the process of self-control with System 2's metacognitive power, and then persevere with System 2's analytic prowess. Only in the space can we subdue System 1's histrionics by arming ourselves with tools to escape emotional hostage-taking. And there are indeed some very impressive tools on offer, including that elusive kill-switch I mentioned earlier.

One thing to know about the human mind:
It is designed to overreact because false negatives are riskier than false positives.

One thing to know about reality:
It's usually not as threatening or problematic as it can first appear.

CHAPTER 8

FIX #3: Freeing the Hostage

Thus is feeling; thus is the arising of feeling; and thus is the disappearance of feeling. — Gautama Buddha, as quoted in the Satipatthana Sutta

Only in The Space Between can bad stuff matter less (and good stuff matter more).

The Buddha's point above is that a wise monk is observant of how emotions come and go, understanding their fleeting nature. This insight is more profound than it first appears, but I'll get to that in the one and only Need-to-Know of this chapter. According to Buddhist tradition, we achieve nirvana when we extinguish the painful cycle of rebirths that we are trapped in. Contemporary secular Buddhists have adopted a less mystical view of nirvana, describing it as the freedom to release ourselves from obsessive rumination and emotional turmoil. Nirvana, in this latter view, is not a permanent state of enlightenment but the moment-by-moment opportunity to free our minds from negative thought patterns. I find this version of nirvana appealing because it has immediate utility, and is more empowering and optimistic than philosopher David Hume's famous dictum, "Reason is the slave of the passions; it can only serve and obey them."[1] Despite my passion for Hume, I think he overstated our helplessness. In fact, as a younger man, I wish I had been aware of the emotion-regulation strategies in this chapter, which would have saved me suffering on many occasions, including one in particular.

When I lecture university business students, I usually offer this gratuitous advice: "If you want to do well in your careers, don't do stupid shit." The undergraduates nod and the MBAs look blank, waiting for an explanation. I don't know if this is because the younger students know exactly what I mean or are just being polite before I explain myself. The most outstanding career trajectories can be instantly derailed by emotion-fused, dumb-ass choices. I've seen it — many times, mostly men, including me. I was one of the lucky ones who learned the lesson at the very start of my career, without paying as high a price as I could have.

On the way home from work one night, I stopped at a mall to purchase a CD (long before iPods or streaming music). I told the music store clerk that I was looking for a song I had heard in a car commercial but didn't know the name of. He didn't know the ad so I offered to sing the song to help him identify it. I launched into the best rendition I could while the clerk smirked and said he wanted to get his manager's input. He seemed just a little too amused when he returned with a smiley-faced manager who implored me to sing for them. The two stood with their arms crossed as I resumed humming before they looked at each other and broke out laughing, at which point I stopped despite their pleas to continue. My face must have conveyed the fury that was welling up inside me for being mocked, because the manager giggled and said, "Okay, buddy, I think you're looking for 'I'm a Believer,'" and pointed to an aisle.

I found the CD but was still seething with rage at being humiliated and figured that if I unloaded on them, they would just get a bigger laugh. Adrenalin coursing through my body and System 1 drunk on vengeance, I popped the CD into my pocket and left without paying. I got fifteen feet out of the store when I felt a hand on my shoulder. "Buddy, you'll have to come back to the store with me." It was the manager, who escorted me to a back room where we were joined by two mall security guards (it must have been a slow night). They had already called the police, and as we all waited for them to arrive, the store manager put the misappropriated CD into a portable player and cranked the volume on the now ruined-for-me-forever song, much to everyone's amusement except mine.

I was ultimately let off with a warning, but the incident took a heavy toll on me — I was horrified that my anger had moved me to break the law. Nobody in my professional circle was ever aware of my rage-fuelled stupidity, although it could have been otherwise. Hence my teachable moment: don't do stupid shit. The corollary to this motto is more specific: learn how to manage your emotions — especially the hot ones.

Emotional hostage-taking is characterized by self-immersion — when we are narrowly and intensely absorbed by inner turmoil. In contrast, when we proactively self-distance and open up The Space Between, we move out of the clutches of System 1 and into the calmer hands of System 2. We can then harness the full metacognitive potential of Observing Self, who is patiently waiting for us in the space, ready to help us self-interrogate, as a step toward self-regulation.

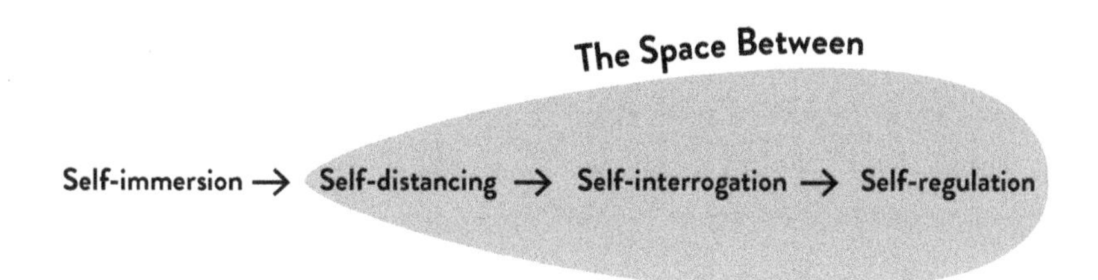

Unfortunately, opening up and climbing into The Space Between is never more difficult than when we have been taken emotionally hostage. Transitioning from self-immersion to self-distancing requires a concerted effort, so before we get into specific emotion-management tools, let's briefly revisit how to escape System 1's control.

Getting into The Space Between: Four Techniques

As I described in chapter 2, a reliable starting point for opening up the space is, has always been, and always will be … the breath. Focusing on and controlling our breathing is always available to us and is a proven strategy for opening up space. It can be as simple as just following the breath, in and out, at least three times over at least twenty-five seconds (sometimes that's all it takes to trigger "the relaxation response"). Or it can be more elaborate, by focusing on a particular sensation associated with each breath, such as your stomach rising and falling or the air flowing past the tips of your nostrils. If I'm experiencing a strong negative emotion, I take a deep breath in and then slowly exhale with a gentle sigh, focusing on the inbreath and the sigh of the outbreath (minimum three times but often more to really stabilize). Focusing on our deep breaths is about as surefire a way to initiate self-distancing as there is. *Observing our deep breathing is the kill-switch for emotional overload.* It is virtually impossible to be really emotional at the same time that you are focusing on the sensations of deep breathing.

At some point today or tomorrow, when you're feeling anxious, annoyed, or antsy, try to prove me wrong. You won't. Not to say the emotions won't come flooding back when you stop (which is what the balance of this chapter is geared toward handling), but as long as you're taking deep breaths and paying close attention to them, you've unhooked from emotional overload and given yourself freedom to choose your response.

The kill-switch for emotional overload is available any time: deep breaths.

The following four techniques are designed to self-distance even further, as follow-ups to an initial breath focus or as standalone tricks that can be initiated without a preceding breath exercise. I have found these four to be useful complements to breathing; some will resonate more than others for different people.

Waterfall (or hurricane or 10,000 feet): Some people find it helpful to visualize themselves standing in a crevice behind a waterfall. The water pouring in front contains the perceptions, thoughts, and feelings that seek to monopolize our attention. An alternative visualization is being at the centre of a hurricane, around which are swirling the same images of negative thoughts and feelings. Yet another is to picture yourself far up in the sky, looking down at the drama below, which looks tiny and insignificant from 10,000 feet up (all that running around and fretting about pretty much nothing). I use all three but favour the waterfall because I like the image of standing safely behind the deluge of my overcharged thoughts as they stream past me.

Mara (at the door): It is written that when the Buddha was tempted to give in to his emotions or desires, he declared, "I see you, Mara." *Mara* is the Pali term for the devil; the Buddha would call out the demon for interfering with his meditative practice. By calmly identifying the devil, he strengthened his resolve to seek enlightenment. You can use this metaphor to say, "I see you, Mara," when you feel agitated or, "I'm watching out for you, Mara," when you're entering a potentially stressful situation. The key is to follow the Buddha's lead in gently and playfully accepting the presence of difficulty, frustration, and all the daily inconveniences that relentlessly tempt System 1 to blow a fuse.

Opportunity (lucky me): This is an acknowledgement that we have the chance to exert mastery over ourselves: "I've just been handed a gift — a chance to practise my self-mastery skills. Lucky me!" As flaky as it sounds, it's quite empowering to view being hijacked by our emotions as a chance to flex our System 2 muscles, pushing ourselves to focus our attention on formulating a skillful response that will make our future self proud.

This is it (right now): This insight is one of the most profound yet neglected perspectives we are capable of. It is a centrepiece of Western-style mindfulness, with roots in the ancient Buddhist emphasis on the sacredness of the present moment, distinct from our remembered past and our imagined futures. This very moment — right now — is our life as we know it, the only thing that is real. Everything before now is gone; everything after now is imaginary. This realization introduces a follow-up question that forces upon us a self-distancing wake-up call: "What relationship do I want with this moment of my life right now?"

These four techniques facilitate the self-distancing required to open and expand The Space Between, where we can take refuge from emotional hijackings and take back control of our unsettled psyches.

Once in the space, then what? Self-distancing broadens to self-interrogation, which builds to self-regulation. How? All through mindfulness.

Mindfulness is an overused, somewhat confusing term with multiple meanings, about which countless books and gurus have given their individual spins. Despite its ubiquity and vagueness, I'm choosing mindfulness as the overarching strategy for dealing with emotional overreaction. Systems thinking confronts the oversimplifying of greedy reductionism; provisional truth battles the overconfidence of certainty addiction; *mindfulness resists the overreaction of emotional hostage-taking.*

What systems thinking is to greedy reductionism, and provisional truth is to certainty addiction, mindfulness is to hostage-taking.

Mindful Self-Regulation

The word *mindfulness* dates back to 1881, when the noun was formed from the more commonly used adjective *mindful* by scholar T.W. Rhys Davids. He was engaged in a multi-year project to translate the Buddha's sermons, written in Pali, into English. He chose *mindfulness* as his translation of the Pali word *sati* (which some academics consider to be better translated as *attention* or *awareness*). In Buddhism, *sati* is a crucial concept: we need to attend to our states of mind as a precondition for seeing reality for what it is and ultimately achieving enlightenment.

The Western use of the word *mindfulness* usually includes "non-judgmental awareness" or "bare awareness with no judgment," attributed to Jon Kabat-Zinn, who created his Mindfulness-Based Stress Reduction program in the late seventies. And there is indeed merit in avoiding judgment of our thoughts and feelings *initially*: to see them clearly, we need to view them dispassionately. But non-judgmental awareness is just the starting point because our ultimate goal is to evaluate the usefulness of the thoughts and emotions that we are experiencing, and evaluation implies judgment. Judgment features in the Buddha's description of "right mindfulness" as holding something in the mind's eye while evaluating its "wholesomeness."

So "mindfulness" comes with many connotations, but I'm using it in its simplest form: *being aware of some aspect of the present moment.* To be mindful is to be attentive to what is happening right now. And there's a lot going on right now — an infinite number of sensations in your body including your breath, thoughts streaming through your mind, emotions bubbling up alongside those thoughts, and the torrent of sights and sounds swirling around you. In an emotional hostage-taking, the particular form of mindfulness that is useful is the one that directs attention to thoughts and feelings as they arise — that aspect of the present moment that is mental. That is why the four self-distancing techniques I've described are all forms of mindfulness that deepen our perception of our thoughts and feelings in a curious but detached way. We simply want to see what is happening in our minds without getting hooked by the actual content of the thoughts and feelings themselves.

But the follow-up is not so neutral, because we need to evaluate the usefulness of what we observe. Are the thoughts and accompanying feelings worthwhile and productive, or are we captive to emotions that are causing needless suffering? This "judgmental" assessment paves the way for us to choose what we want to do with our emotions, since they may be useful to us. Or, if they're not useful, we still need a strategy to deal with them since, even after unhooking from them temporarily, they'll still be knocking on the door, eager to rejoin the party. Deciding what to do with our emotions takes some System 2 thinking — the aid of tools that we don't naturally find ourselves reaching for.

I am using a macro-level umbrella strategy once again, to encompass specific tools (three in particular) that are very powerful for self-regulation. Mindfulness is the umbrella because it's the *sine qua non* of emotional control: only by attending to what's happening inside of us can we access the tools to self-regulate. Unlike the tools for other design flaws, these three are used in a particular order because they build on one another as sequential steps.

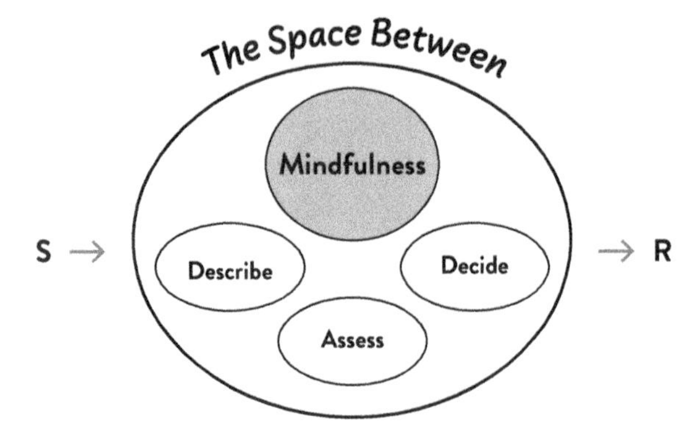

The first step is to *describe* the feeling we are experiencing. The second is to *assess* by "judging" the usefulness of the emotion in the context of whatever triggered it. These two self-interrogatory steps culminate in the self-regulatory last step, which is to *decide* — whether to invest in the emotion or to divest ourselves of it. Each of the three steps incorporates a key question that unlocks the power of the particular tool.

Step #1: Describe (Name the Emotion)

We can't manage negative emotions without acknowledging exactly what we're dealing with. Psychologists call this "affect labelling," and it requires being specific about the feeling by naming it:

Look at me so _______.

The blank needs to be specified, as in angry, frustrated, impatient, anxious, melancholy, and so on. Labelling is a necessary starting point, which is why the most useful way to help *someone else* self-regulate is to validate their feelings by labelling the emotion they are expressing, as in, "I can see why you're so angry," or "I understand why you are feeling hurt."

For identifying our own feelings and filling in the blank, here's a question that originates in Zen Buddhism:

What is this?

It's purposefully vague but useful to ask when an emotion-triggered alarm is set off. Saying, "This is agitation," or "This is intense anger," or "This is hurt" helps externalize the emotion so it is easier to assess.

The Buddha recommended we notice our feelings hundreds of times a day until it becomes second nature to be aware of them. His objective was to encourage perfect equanimity — not a pleasant peacefulness but a literal lack of feeling (which he insisted was a precursor to enlightenment). We don't need to embrace his cosmology to appreciate the wisdom of identifying our emotions as a necessary first step in exercising more control over them. But the Buddha did not stop at mere non-judgmental identification: in addition to awareness (*sati*), he advocated "clear comprehension" (the Pali word *sampajjana*). One of the Buddha's best-known sermons is the *Satipatthana Sutta* (usually translated as "The Foundations of Mindfulness Discourse"), in which he lays out the steps to achieving nirvana. Key to the path is differentiating wholesome from unwholesome states of mind so we can work toward extinguishing the latter. The wise monk must be not only aware of their emotions but also evaluative of them.

Step #2: Assess (Determine if It Matters)

The Buddha targeted unwholesome states of mind (such as the "five hindrances" of desire, anger, lethargy, anxiety, and doubt) as part of his all-encompassing project geared toward permanent liberation from suffering through a deep, meditative understanding of the true nature of reality, leading to release from the painful cycle of rebirths. But for the less ambitious among us (of which I include myself), with the modest hurdle of making our day-to-day lives a bit easier, assessing our emotional states is still the second step of self-interrogation. Assessing our emotional state of mind starts with a question.

The first and all-important question in assessing an emotion is one that is shockingly underused. In my view, it's the most important question anyone can ask themselves when they've been taken hostage by a strong negative emotion:

Does this really matter?

The "this" in the question refers to the situation that triggered the emotion. The question is a shortcut that can reduce the intensity of an emotional reaction by at least half. And for the other half that remains, it can help clarify and deepen our understanding of the causes of our upset.

It's such a powerful question, but one that most of us rarely (if ever) ask ourselves because System 1 decides what matters long before our conscious deliberation kicks in (and even then, System 2 has an uphill battle to override a System 1–generated alarm). *System 1 evaluates the world through the lens of negativity bias, so it errs on the side of assuming a lot of small stuff matters a lot.* Even really small stuff — stuff that is invisible from 10,000 feet; stuff that only Mara could convince us matters.

System 1 is not a good judge of what matters: it assumes a lot of small stuff matters a lot.

In System 1's world, small-time inconveniences and tense interactions are serious threats, instead of petty, irrelevant noise that has no meaningful impact on our lives. There are so many twenty-first-century triggers competing to perturb us, most of which will be instantly forgotten within minutes, if not seconds. But you wouldn't know it from our reactions. "Sayre's law" is named after the political scientist Wallace Stanley Sayre, who shared his perspective of the sniping within university departments with the *Wall Street Journal*, saying, "Academic politics is the most vicious and bitter form of politics, because the stakes are so low." I love this quote because it applies to all of us — it's an indictment of how worked up we can get over inconsequential issues.

Because the question "Does this really matter?" is such an important one and sometimes tricky to give an honest answer to, there are some useful follow-up questions that help us dig deeper. The first is basic:

How much will I care about this one month from now?

A colleague's inconsiderate gesture, being late for an appointment, the waiter bringing the wrong appetizer: if it will be completely forgotten in a month, then it doesn't matter enough to warrant a strong emotional reaction.

When we're really worked up, we need a more probing question to distance ourselves from the heat of the moment:

What will happen if I completely ignore this?

Emotions are designed to motivate action, but a surprising number of times the best course is to do nothing at all: just suck it up, bite your tongue, walk it off, and let the tension subside. Many times, the situation doesn't require action or, more importantly, doesn't lend itself to a productive intervention. Many (many, many) interpersonal conflicts fall into this category, especially within romantic partnerships. System 1 can be itching for a confrontation that serves no productive purpose other than letting off steam that will otherwise dissipate on its own if given a chance. Ignoring the noise is often the best way to stay out of trouble (as per my "shopping lesson"; did I mention that they actually handcuffed me to a chair while they played the CD?).

There is one final aspect to mattering:

Do I have much control?

Even if something really matters, we may still have limited or no control over the situation, as in the traffic jam that makes you late for an important engagement or, more profoundly, when we are unhappy with someone's behaviour but limited in our options to influence them. Important things over which we have limited control require a different response than do the things over which we have influence. Lack of control falls into the "doesn't matter" category of strategies, which I'll get to in Step #3.

If we are legitimately convinced it matters (and we have some control), there is one more step before jumping to a decision point. Our emotional reactions are triggered by first-cut, satisficed interpretations of what's happening, but as I emphasized in chapter 3, there is ALWAYS missing information; the only issue is how relevant the missing information is.

And with complexity, as I emphasized in chapter 5, certainty does not correlate reliably with accuracy. So if the trigger of our emotion really matters, the next question is:

How good of a handle do I have on the facts?

The facts are surprisingly hard to access when we're hostage to emotional overreaction. *My* facts are always at my fingertips, but not necessarily *the* facts. As I pointed out in chapter 5, our cognitive machinery prioritizes *feeling* right over *being* right. System 2 has to work hard to uncover the real facts — not the facts that serve a confirmation bias but the facts that System 1 isn't interested in. Back to the Buddha who believed that we are captive to unwholesome emotions when we misperceive reality: negative emotions often arise from a misinterpretation of facts.

In a heated interpersonal conflict of any kind, we can be pretty sure we don't have a good handle on the facts because System 1 is not proficient at seeking out other people's perspectives for the purpose of changing its mind, especially if it has locked down a self-righteous "I've been wronged" interpretation. System 1 likes to justify strong reactions with its own brand of personal logic, so it takes cognitive discipline to seek out contrary evidence and alternative interpretations — the kind of work that can only happen in the space. In an interpersonal conflict, the best and most obvious tactic for ensuring we've got a good handle on the facts is to repeat our understanding of the other person's perspective and seek their corroboration that we've got it right.

While strong emotional reactions often belie the triviality of the underlying issues, sometimes the emotion is justified. So once the emotion is assessed, the final step is deciding what to do with it. And this is where the Buddha and I part company.

He advised a one-size-fits-all prescription for dealing with emotion: divestiture. He admonished that strong emotion is the product of an unskilled mind; when we truly understand and appreciate the nature of reality, emotion disappears. The Buddha's single prescription works for situations that either don't matter or over which we have negligible control. But for issues that do matter and over which we do have control, there is an alternative path: rather than divesting the emotion, we can invest in it. A very un-Buddhist approach.

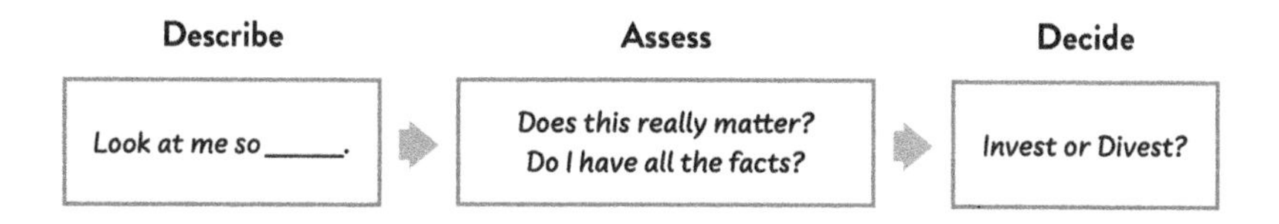

Step #3: Decide (Invest or Divest)

An honest assessment of mattering induces an answer to the all-important final question:

Do I want to invest in this emotion or divest myself of it?

The choice is to invest our energy in the situation (if it matters) or to divest our energy (if it doesn't). We invest by feeding our state of mind with an action plan. We divest by starving our state of mind by letting go and letting be. These are only two options permitted by System 2 in The Space Between.

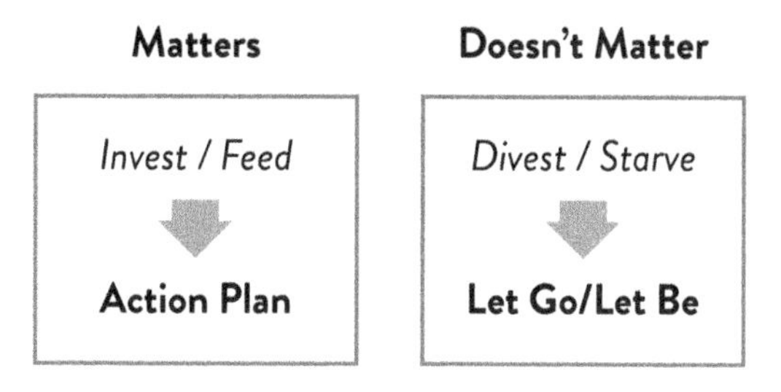

When it doesn't matter, the option to divest our energy is a hard one to execute because System 1's strong emotions motivate us to take action — yelling, lashing out — whatever System 1 commands. But divesting is often the most productive choice we can make despite System 1's bullying. So I'll start with this option: when the best choice is no action, no response.

HOW TO DIVEST: LET GO/LET BE

"Letting go" and "letting be" are often used interchangeably in Western mindfulness practices. It's confusing language but it lends itself to an easy fix: We can *let go* of stubborn negative thoughts; we can *let* stubborn negative emotions *be*.

We can choose to let go of our petty grievances, complaints, frustrations, and irritations when we realize our negative bias is getting the best of us for no productive reason, when the source of our distress doesn't really matter. And rather than struggling with any negative emotions that persist, we can just let them be. We don't have to give in to them, nor do we have to fight them. We can just acknowledge their presence and move on, avoiding the second arrow or "dirty discomfort" that adds to our suffering. Letting be is captured in the Buddha's lighthearted expression "I see you, Mara." I don't know who first came up with the now ubiquitous expression "It is what it is," which first invaded our conversations in the 2000s, but I wish I'd thought of it.

Neither letting go of issues nor letting negative emotions just be comes naturally or easily, because System 1 is tenacious. Both require a System 2 override, starting with another all-important question (the best precursor I know to both letting go and letting be):

Is everything generally okay?

In an emotional hostage-taking, it's too easy to forget that everything *is* okay, which it typically is. When an emotional alarm goes off, we can startle ourselves out of frenzy by answering this question truthfully. Acknowledging that everything is generally okay — nobody is dying, we're not in danger, what matters now probably won't matter much in a month — is a good step toward letting our grievances go and our emotions just be, without the need to act on them. We have many opportunities every day to put whatever is troubling us into perspective so we're less inclined toward catastrophizing (which is a speciality of System 1). One of the best ways to put System 1 in its place is to remind ourselves that most issues are truly not problematic in the medium to long term. "Is everything generally okay?" pairs nicely with "Does this really matter?" (When an emotional alarm goes off, I use the acronym *LMK* as a shortcut reminder, as in "Let Me Know," to remind myself to **L**ook at my emotions, ask myself if it **M**atters, and confirm that all is o**K**ay.)

Going a step further than mere "okay," I invented a game with my former spouse called "What's bad is good." Whenever something looked bad but turned out to be good, we made a point of noting it by invoking the aforementioned expression. It happens more frequently than you'd think: the slow driver in your way that prevented you from getting a speeding ticket further down the road; the restaurant that closed early but led you to a new one that you liked better; the fumbled job interview that redirected you to a more exciting career opportunity; the list is endless if you look for "bads that end up being goods in disguise." (Of course, some goods become bads, but that game is no fun to play and does nothing to offset our negativity bias.)

When we do experience negative emotions, we always have the option to soothe ourselves: *It's okay that I feel this way. I don't have to do anything with this negative feeling and I certainly don't have to add to it by being upset that I have it. I can just be with it as it is, knowing it will pass.* That last bit — knowing that negative emotions pass — is crucial: we can tolerate negative emotions just as we would tolerate a bad cold, until it fades. This insight is so pivotal to emotion management that it's a Need-to-Know.

Need-to-Know: Emotions Fade — All of Them

This may seem so obvious that I hesitate to earmark it as a Need-to-Know. But I'm highlighting it for the same reason I quoted the Buddha in the chapter's epigraph: if you're a living, breathing human being, emotions seem all-consuming in the moment. The last thought anyone has when they are fiercely angry, jealous, anxious, or deeply depressed is *Not to worry — this too will pass.* Even the emotion triggered by catastrophe and trauma fades: the suffering of earthquake victims and quadriplegics has been demonstrated to diminish as they adjust to their circumstances, as does the thrill of lottery winners.[2] In the moment, System 1 overwhelms with emotional flooding, pushing hard on us to do something. But the fact is that we don't have to do anything. The intensity of an emotion decays — it has a half-life just like nuclear material or a drug. Our goal is to shorten the half-life of negative emotions — to quicken the pace of their diminishment so we can escape from them sooner. That's what letting go and letting be are designed to do. To lift a line from the poem "Go to the Limits of Your Longing" by Rainer Maria Rilke: "Just keep going. No feeling is final."

The goal is to shorten the half-life of negative emotions, which fade on their own but not fast enough.

Although he adopted a great deal of sixth-century-BCE Hindu thinking, one of the Buddha's more original ideas was his argument that the notion of "self" is an illusion (one that perpetuates suffering and prevents enlightenment). I'll revisit his skeptical view of self in chapter 10; for now, I want to invoke his description of us as nothing more than a bundle of shifting sensations, thoughts, and feelings. His prescription for suffering was meditation — to bring attention to the fleeting nature of our thoughts and feelings so that we can experience the truth of their (and our) impermanence. I think there is profundity in his recommendation that we acquaint ourselves with the transitory character of our feelings. We are captive to them when we perceive them as monolithic, and when we break this illusion we expedite their decay and recapture our freedom. Being mindful of the fleeting nature of our feelings reinforces the notion that we don't have to act on or even take seriously every emotional impulse we have. Even after System 2 intellectually acknowledges that what ails us in the moment doesn't matter and that everything is generally okay, we still need help to break down the strong negative emotions with which System 1 holds us hostage. Mindfulness-based meditative techniques are the best aids available to do exactly this, and promote the letting go/be process.

Meditative Techniques for Letting Go and Letting Be

The ancient yogic tradition of breath-body focus was intended to unify the individual self with the cosmic Self that pervades the universe. On a more mundane level, meditation can be extremely helpful in letting go and letting be. And, in my humble opinion, it doesn't have to be the consistent, daily sitting practice that most people conjure (although a daily meditation routine is a good way to cement the habit of climbing into The Space Between, making it easier to invoke when needed). I use the phrase *meditative techniques* intentionally, to avoid the resistance that some people have to the off-putting connotations that *sitting meditation* can elicit. That said, the techniques are drawn directly from various Buddhist meditative traditions.

Meditation is the practice of focusing the mind's attention on something, such as the breath, bodily sensations, sights, sounds, tastes, or thoughts and feelings as they arise and float through consciousness. Meditation is the opposite of letting the mind wander or being lost in thought: rather than allowing System 1 to decide what our attention is randomly drawn to, *meditation is the practice of controlling our attentional spotlight, pointing it in a particular direction to bring awareness to something that is happening in the present moment.* What is the difference between meditation and mindfulness? That's a grey zone of wordplay that depends on whom you ask; basically, meditation is an activity or practice with a long monastic history, whereas mindfulness is a psychological state of mind — one that is conducive to meditation. Meditative techniques help us see our thoughts and feelings as objects of consciousness, just as a cloud, a chair, or another person are objects of consciousness; as such, thoughts and feelings are open to the scrutiny that is otherwise not possible when we're completely immersed in them.

Of the many varieties of meditation, the techniques for letting go/be are derived from two dominant forms in the Buddhist tradition: *samatha* and *vipassana*. *Samatha* is focused attention on one particular thing while resisting any distraction from other stimuli. In *samatha*, when our mind wanders, we redirect attention back to the same focal point that we began with, such as the breath or body (or in some cases, a word or phrase, such as a mantra). In contrast, *vipassana* is "open monitoring" meditation, where attention is allowed to shift to any sensation, thought, or feeling as it arises. In *vipassana*, we are not fixating on any particular point of focus; we are merely observing our personal experience as it unfolds, being "mindful" of the shifting nature of that experience.

Samatha is geared toward stillness, which facilitates letting go. *Vipassana* is geared toward insight, which facilitates letting be.

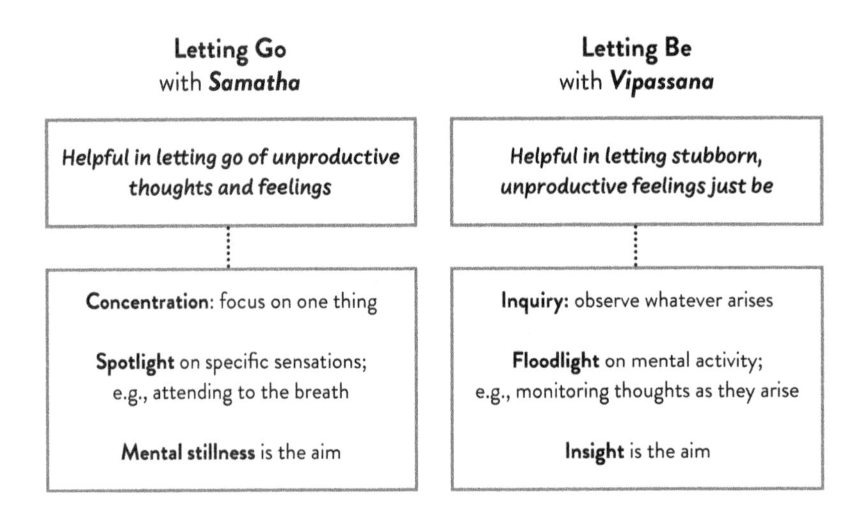

The most common method of *samatha* is focusing on the breath as we inhale and exhale. This can be done anywhere, anytime, for any duration — it doesn't require sitting on a cushion for a specified period (although this is how it's usually practised). As mentioned earlier in this chapter, I find it particularly helpful to sigh on the exhale as a way of releasing tension. (I set my phone to remind me twice a day to take a few deep breaths when the message pops up on the screen.) When our minds are stuck on unproductive thoughts, we need a place to redirect our attention, and our breath is always available — as are the sounds around us, which are diverse and interesting when you pay attention to them. The goal of *samatha* is to let go of mental disturbance by concentrating our attention on a single object.

The aim of *vipassana* is to inquire with a detached curiosity into anything we're thinking or feeling. *Vipassana* is harder, which is why *samatha* is a good way to begin, to achieve a degree of tranquility before moving to the trickier work of watching thoughts float through the mind without engaging them. *Vipassana* is particularly useful in managing difficult and persistent emotions: it allows us to separate from our feelings by exploring them. "Where in my body do I feel my anxiety (e.g., my chest)?" or "How would I describe the physical sensations (e.g., tightness)?" These questions weaken strong emotions by treating them like puzzles to figure out because *inquiry eases emotional intensity. Vipassana* is like a deep massage for the knots in our mind — the hard and tight ruminations and feelings that make our mind stiff and sore.

It is sometimes argued that a sitting meditation builds momentum such that the regular meditator can regain stability much faster than someone who does not formally meditate. That may be true; for me, rather than a formal meditation practice, I prefer fostering a "meditative state of mind" — mindfulness — which enables me to call upon meditative techniques as I need them to let go/let be. One of the hardest lessons of being human is learning to tolerate negative emotions without feeding or acting on them. Meditative techniques empower us to distance ourselves from the emotional states that would otherwise engulf us and to help us see negative emotions for what they really are — fleeting and often damaging distractions that will dissipate if given a chance.

We, by nature, underuse letting go/letting be to divest; however, there are plenty of times when our best choice of handling negative emotion is action. And it's worth repeating — *there are only two options: invest or divest.* Wallowing, stewing, ruminating, self-pitying, and the like are not on offer in The Space Between.

There are only two options for strong negative emotions: invest or divest. Wallowing and self-pity are not on offer in The Space Between.

HOW TO INVEST: CHOOSING TO ACT

If our emotions are well calibrated to a situation that matters, then we can choose to invest in them by formulating an action plan. Note the term *plan*: more often than not, we're better off to plan before acting, especially when our emotions are running hot and we're not capable of productive thought in the moment. System 1 is a notoriously poor judge of urgency — it errs on the side of pushing us to immediate response. By slowing down to think through a plan, we give ourselves the space we need to make smart decisions; for example, by revisiting the all-important question, "Do I really have a good handle on the facts, to the extent that I can convincingly articulate the other person's view?"

So what is the goal of a good plan? It's to do "the next right thing." Which is why the best action plan emerges from this vital, show-stopping question:

What is the next right thing to do?

This question is one of the most powerful ways to focus the mind. The next right thing is what your "Best Self" would do given the facts. It's the action you would take "as if": as if you were not captive to emotional overload; as if you were not influenced by self-righteous certainty that you've been wronged; as if you were your own best friend giving yourself objective advice; as if you were being filmed in real time for all the world to observe and judge; as if your ultimate objective was to do the most mature, thought-through and effective thing; as if you were behaving in perfect concert with your values. I will return to "Best Self" and "as if" in chapter 10. At this point, I want to stress that the "next right thing" question is deeply personal. In fact, I take issue with Viktor Frankl on this point.

Frankl is unequivocal that every problem has only one right solution: "I venture to say that each question has only one answer — the right one!"[3] In Frankl's view, each person must attempt to discover that right answer, even though, "as a finite being, he is not exempt from error." For Frankl, there is a universally "right answer" for every situation (one that presumably God has ordained). I suppose if one had perfect information, including the future outcomes of all possible decisions, one could, in theory, pick the right answer — the single decision that yields the single preferred result. But practically speaking (and if one assumes there is no transcendent moral arbiter), it seems to me too simplistic (i.e., greedily reductionist) to assume there is a definitive, universally shared "next right thing" for every single one of the myriad idiosyncratic tasks of life we face every day. Each of us has unique values that govern our sense of what is "right." Every individual must arrive at an answer that satisfies them in a personal and honest way. While it is far too easy for us to rationalize our behaviour, we usually know deep down whether we are operating as our Best Self or not. Interestingly, we typically have a definitive view of what the right thing to do is for other people! *Doing the next right thing requires the discipline to challenge ourselves in the same way that we challenge others.*

This discipline is available only in The Space Between because the next right thing is rarely what System 1 is pushing for in the moment of an emotional hijacking. We need space to allow System 2 to "play the tape forward" by anticipating the outcomes of our possible responses. If we can take pride in translating our emotions into action that is productive, aligned with our overall objectives and values, and minimizes rather than aggravates suffering for ourselves (and especially for others), then we know we've got a plan that represents the next right thing.

Smaller Bads and Bigger Goods

We may have no control over the thoughts and feelings that automatically arise from the electrical buzzing among our neurons, but we do have the ability to stand back from the noise in our heads to make thoughtful decisions on what we want to do with the raucous goings-on in there. Mindfulness, cultivated by our Observing Self in The Space Between, allows us to do this. The original Buddhist intent of *sati* (mindfulness) was to reveal the profound insight of the Four Noble Truths, which expose our suffering as self-induced and avoidable once we accept that our desires can never be satisfied by the impermanent flux of reality. I am disinclined to join the Buddha in insisting that our desires can never be satisfied, but there is compelling wisdom in the observation that much of our suffering is self-imposed. It is the product of an overheated and unsupervised System 1 emotional system.

The focus of this chapter has been on the self-regulation of negativity bias, but our well-being isn't limited to mitigating negative emotions. Negativity bias not only pushes us to overreact to small, unpleasant events but also minimizes the pleasure we take in small, positive ones. The burgeoning field of positive psychology stresses this latter piece of the emotion-management puzzle — fostering positive emotions. There is pleasure hiding in the crevasses of our daily lives that we overlook, which I will explore in chapter 12. Our challenge in coping with negativity bias is therefore twofold: to minimize the negatives and to magnify the positives; that is, *to make the truly trivial bad stuff matter less and to make the seemingly trivial good stuff matter more.* Design Flaw #3 stems from System 1's proclivity for overreaction and System 2's struggle to contain the hysteria. System 1 is fairly adept at handling the big bads (as in protecting us from danger), as well as reacting appropriately to the big goods (as in enjoying sensual rewards). But it is the *small* bads and the *small* goods that need more of our deliberate attention. We need to override our design both to down-regulate the small bads (by letting go and letting be), and to up-regulate the small goods — the magical everyday moments whose meaningfulness is camouflaged by our impatient and distracted busyness. In short, we need more mindfulness.

One thing to remind yourself every day:
Most things don't matter as much as they seem to in the moment.

One question to ask when you're experiencing a strong negative emotion:
Does this really matter?
(If so, what's the next right thing to do?)

CHAPTER 9

FLAW #4: We Compete with Ourselves

In contrast to the animals, man has cultivated an abundance of contrary drives and impulses within himself. — *Friedrich Nietzsche*

Too many selves to count and too few on the same page.

In the introduction, I reviewed Schopenhauer's extensive list of reasons that other animals have it easier than we do. But he missed a big one.

Nietzsche, influenced by Schopenhauer and writing a half-century after him, was painfully aware of this particular human challenge, as captured in this chapter's epigraph. He described the "contradictory drives [that] swarm within one man" as "the expression of the diseased condition in mankind, in contrast to the animals, in which all existing instincts satisfy very specific tasks."[1] Schopenhauer would have heartily endorsed the description of us as "diseased," even though he overlooked one of our biggest struggles: managing the many conflicting forces within us.

There's nothing like five grams of psilocybin (aka magic mushrooms) and a blindfold to challenge your sense of self. I've only experimented with high-dose psychedelics under the supervision of experienced guides (in the fashion of writer Michael Pollan's book *How to Change Your Mind*). In one intensely hallucinatory episode, my deceased paternal grandmother visited to deliver two messages. The first was that life was one big senseless joke, which she didn't reveal to me when she was alive because she felt I couldn't handle knowing it; but she now insisted on being forgiven for withholding the truth about meaninglessness. The second was that she was making me solely responsible for the well-being of her sons — my father and my uncle. I was surprisingly obstinate in my altered state, refusing to forgive her for hiding the secret of life and protesting that while I loved and would care for them, I couldn't accept *exclusive* responsibility for their welfare because there were too many factors beyond my control. But Grandma Cadsby was uncompromising as she began to vanish, repeating that she was holding me accountable for them and there was nothing I could do to change that.

I had barely recovered from that interaction when my oldest daughter appeared and told me that she knew I didn't love her and nothing I could say would change her mind. I screamed, "You're wrong and you have to believe me that you're wrong. I love you unconditionally and deeply and permanently!" But she wouldn't buy it, and the heated discussion somehow morphed into God telling me I had no choice but to believe in Him. My guide held me tight as I weathered these gut-wrenching storms, including one where I was sucked into the nostrils of a ferocious lion, before turning into a dinosaur, then painfully shedding my reptilian skin to be reborn as a vulnerable, naked human infant.

Psychedelics are a very harsh, unforgiving form of therapy. They force you to confront the contradictions and chaos within your psyche. I felt at war with myself on many levels that were perhaps connected: painful guilt over wanting to avoid sole responsibility for my father and uncle, horror at my daughter's immovable conviction that I didn't love her (maybe because I had not demonstrated sufficient regard for the care of my father and uncle?), and crippling confusion about the leap of faith I needed my daughter to take despite my own resistance to making a spiritual leap of faith. Perhaps it was this inner turmoil that forced me to see myself as a fierce-but-tortured-creature-turned-helpless-baby. Our sense of self is quite shaky if you poke at it with a sharp-enough stick.

Unlike other animals, we are burdened by many conflicting motivations: we want second helpings but also slim physiques; we want accelerated career paths but also more time with family; we want late-night TV but also a good night's sleep; we want to be nurturing parents, generous partners, and all-round good people, but also to release inner tension by impatiently lashing out at those we love when they frustrate us. We are a messy combination of competing desires, and when these conflicting impulses are at war, we suffer.

Other animals have it easier because they follow their instincts. To be human is to be challenged by inner conflict.

Two millennia before Nietzsche's observation about our "contrary impulses," Plato described inner conflict in his chariot allegory, which is based on a tripartite model of the human psyche. The charioteer represents rationality, whose job is to guide the whole psyche toward eternal truth in the heavens. His chariot is powered by two horses. The white horse represents our honour-seeking self, with a strong moral impulse toward righteousness. The black horse represents our desirous self, motivated by our powerful appetites (sex, food, wealth, and so on). The white horse wants to fly toward the heavens, while the black horse wants to remain entrenched in the pleasures of earthly existence. Key for Plato is that the black horse's energy is required to fuel the psyche's journey: prefiguring Sigmund Freud and Carl Jung, Plato believed that a well-functioning psyche harnesses the power of the desirous self but doesn't let it dominate.

Freud picked up Plato's equine analogy, but he envisioned a rider trying to control a single horse. The horse is id — our unconscious but potent instincts and desires, which we are born with and which are the source of our psychic energy. The rider is ego — the part of ourselves we develop after birth when we discover that our instinctual id needs to accommodate the world within which it lives. Ego uses reason and the facts of reality to determine the most effective and socially acceptable ways to satisfy id's demands (such as delaying gratification or suppressing socially unacceptable behaviour). But, again like Plato, Freud's version of the psyche is tripartite: the ego must also contend with the superego, which is our moral compass, largely instilled by our parents, and which weaponizes guilt and shame to get its way. A healthy ego harnesses id's energy while accommodating superego's morality. An underdeveloped ego struggles to reconcile the "murderous id" and the "punishing conscience" of the superego, a task made even more difficult when the id is storing traumatic, repressed memories. A weak ego is vulnerable to breaking down, forming neuroses that disturb psychic stability.

Freud's one-time protégé Carl Jung, who plays a big role in the next chapter, also divides the psyche into three main parts, but his conception is more elaborate. Jung posits an ego (which is everything we are conscious of) and two forms of unconscious: the *personal* (which stores all our individual memories) and the *collective* (which we all share because it developed within, and represents, the history of our species). The collective unconscious houses what Jung described as universal "archetypes," which reside in us at birth as "primordial images" or patterns rooted in ancestral memories. While we all share these various archetypes, their individual form differs from person to person; for example, we all have a shadow archetype, representing the dark parts of our personality that we keep hidden, but my shadow isn't identical to your shadow.

While Plato and Freud emphasized the unifying of our conflicting parts, Jung made it the centrepiece of his work.

Many of Jung's ideas have a basis in Freudian psychology, including and especially Freud's conviction that mental health requires bringing to consciousness the tensions and conflicts that lurk in the unconscious. Similar to Freud's view that a strong ego is key to mental health, Jung was convinced that a strong and fully expressed psychic core is key to unifying the various archetypes in a fully realized individual. Psychic unification was central to Jung's psychology, reflecting the influence not only of Freud but also of the psychologist William James, whose 1902 book *Varieties of Religious Experience* included a chapter entitled "The Divided Self and Its Process of Unification." In it, James writes, "Now in all of us ... does the normal evolution of character chiefly consist in the straightening out and unifying of the inner self," and "a comparative chaos within us ... must end by forming a stable system of functions in the right subordination." (Some scholars have argued that it was James's ideas that eventually lured Jung away from Freud and his psychoanalytic theory.[2])

But Jung's work was not derivative: there is breathtaking originality in his exhaustive exploration of the Platonic-Freudian notion of the splintered psyche. His description of the importance of connecting with our inner self, as we journey through life on a path toward self-realization, preceded and influenced the twentieth-century "self-actualization" movement that flourishes today. Jung elucidated the human struggle as one based on the competing parts of ourselves. We seldom give much thought to the bare fact that we are each the sum of multiple selves. Yet it is an undeniable and problematic aspect of our design. Which is why it's a Need-to-Know.

Need-to-Know #1: We Are Many in One

For pithy, poetic flare, nobody has surpassed American writer Walt Whitman's description of the human psyche in his 1855 poem "Song of Myself": "I am large, I contain multitudes."

But for sheer cleverness and penetrating insight, the French philosopher Michel de Montaigne can't be beat. In his 1580 *Essays* (in essay number 73) he wrote that "there is as much difference between us and ourselves as there is between us and others." This astute insight has been validated by cognitive psychologists over four hundred years later. Research reveals that we shift our personality from moment to moment and situation to situation to such a degree that "within-person variation" is greater than "between-person variation."[3]

Our personalities are extremely variable, in part because they are highly context-dependent: we feel and respond to particular situations; our personality traits are sensitive to the circumstances we find ourselves in. For example, most of us are neither exclusively introverted nor consistently extroverted, but are introverted in some circumstances and extroverted in others.[4] We may be highly extroverted among friends but shy and withdrawn with strangers (or even vice versa). Our personality is anything but monolithic — our traits cover a wide spectrum, even within a single day.[5]

Our "many-in-one" design can be dissected in a variety of ways; what follows are some of the most notable.

Situational Selves: As mentioned, our reactions and behaviours are heavily influenced by situations, stemming in part from the various roles we perceive ourselves to be playing (reflecting "cross-role variability"[6]). A person can be conscientious and organized in their professional role but chaotic and careless in their personal life.

Moral Selves: The earliest work on the inconsistency of our personalities arose from the psychology of situational ethics, pioneered in the late 1920s, where experiments demonstrated that children will be honest in some situations but not in others. The researchers concluded that there was no underlying quality of honesty that was either present or lacking because, for example, a child's proclivity to cheat on a test was driven by the structure of the test itself.[7] There is rarely, if ever, a never-failing trait of honesty in people (even Mother Teresa had her detractors[8]); rather, some situations promote honesty in some people and other situations do not.

Intertemporal Selves: Psychiatrist George Ainslie describes the self as "a population of conflicting reward-getting processes."[9] Conflict arises when rewards accrue over different time periods (e.g., more dessert now versus a svelte physique next summer). The battle between our present and future selves is uniquely human and a cause of much inner strife (a topic I will return to in the next chapter).

Remembering Selves: Psychologist Daniel Kahneman differentiates our "experiencing self" and our "remembering self."[10] His experiments on pain reveal that our remembering self is highly influenced by the intensity and recency of discomfort, which can differ significantly from the self that actually had the experience. For example, a problem with a connecting return flight after a near-perfect vacation forces you to spend an entire evening stuck in an airport; your remembering self will emphasize the horrible journey home even though your experiencing self had a great week away. Kahneman concludes that the "real you" is more your remembering self because it persists in time, even though it distorts the actual past experience.

Social Selves: Jung coined the term *persona* to describe the mask we develop and wear to present ourselves to the world in a way that meets our social objectives. As William James wrote in his classic 1890 book

The Principles of Psychology, "A man has as many social selves as there are individuals who recognize him." We present ourselves in different ways to different people.

We are "multitudes" with protean personalities that fluctuate depending on the situation.

So it seems we are indeed "multitudes." But don't we come into the world with some kind of distinctive psychological traits that are at least partially consistent across similar situations?

Whence Personality?

Once again, it is Jung who was one of the earliest progenitors of personality theory. And again, his influence is still current as the basis of the widely used Myers-Briggs Type Indicator personality test. Jung introduced the concepts and terminology of extroversion and introversion in his 1921 book *Psychological Types*, where he differentiates individuals who get energy from internal self-dialogue from those who get energy from external stimulation. He argued that these two dominant attitudes of extroversion and introversion were expressed in four functions, constituting eight different personality categories — the first modern form of personality typology. Current personality research focuses on traits that lie on a continuum, rather than categorizing people by type. For example, the "Big Five" traits, captured by the acronym *OCEAN*, represent the degree to which a person is Open, Conscientious, Extroverted, Agreeable, and Neurotic: traits that everyone exhibits on a spectrum from low to high, with most of us somewhere in the middle. While our personalities are not fixed over all situations or over time, we certainly have leanings that we carry forward through our lives. Are these leanings genetic — with us from the beginning?

Jung proposed that our dominant orientation of extroversion or introversion is largely with us from birth, and his view has been borne out by behavioural geneticists who believe we are each born with a particular temperament — an emotional way of reacting to the world. But, as I referenced in chapter 3, our personalities are also shaped by innumerable environmental factors, such as our childhood friendships and random events like a chance encounter with a bully or a nurturing teacher. So while research on fourteen million pairs of twins indicates that our personality traits are heritable, some are more heritable than others.[11] Thousands of tiny variations in our DNA predispose us to think, feel, and behave in idiosyncratic ways, but genetic influence is only probabilistic for most traits — DNA is the starting but not ending point. I like the imagery invoked in Stephen Pinker's summation: "Life is a pinball game in which we bounce and graze through a gantlet of chutes and bumpers. Perhaps our history of collisions and near misses explains what made us what we are."[12]

It's no wonder the question "Who is the real me?" bedevils us. Are we the person whom the neighbours would describe as chatty and friendly or the person screaming obscenities at the slow driver when we're late? The extrovert who entertains everyone at the office party after a couple of drinks or the introvert who struggles to make conversation at the park with strangers? It is difficult for us to point to our "real self" but not only because we're always in flux. We are also typically unaware of how contradictory or hypocritical we can be. Seventeenth-century polymath Blaise Pascal, in his book *Pensées*, describes our disjointed personalities bleakly: "We are only falsehood, duplicity, contradiction; we both conceal and disguise ourselves from ourselves." (And his oft-quoted aphorism, "The heart has reasons that reason cannot know.") Two centuries later, Nietzsche opened his book *The Genealogy of Morals* with the declaration, "We are unknown to ourselves," and added that "we are necessarily strangers to ourselves."

Need-to-Know #2: We Are Strangers to Ourselves

In chapter 1, I reviewed how mysterious System 1 can be. Most of its work functions below our conscious awareness, occasionally offering glimpses of what it's up to.

The interesting twist on this cognitive opacity is that our pattern-seeking, meaning-making minds, driven by System 1's disdain for ambiguity, are not satisfied to leave "the heart's reasons" unknown. We fill in the gaps by creating stories to explain the subconscious drives that bubble up to consciousness and don't make sense to us, narratives that infuse logic and coherence into our otherwise mystifying feelings and behaviours. Some cognitive scientists go as far as insisting that when we self-analyze, our observations are pure fabrication. In chapter 5, I pointed out that Nietzsche's psychological insights preceded any academic study of them by many decades. Here is a quote from his *Twilight of the Idols*: "We want to have a reason for feeling this way or that ... [we] become conscious of it only when we have fabricated some kind of explanation for it." The following table captures a sample of contemporary psychologists, a century after Nietzsche, describing how we confabulate reasons to overcome the obscurity of our subconscious motivations.

Timothy Wilson	We are strangers to ourselves because we have no reason to assume that conscious awareness has direct access to the subconscious workings of our brain. We infer our internal states from our behaviour and blindly make up reasons for our actions.[13]
Peter Johansson	"Choice Blindness" is demonstrated by experiments where people are asked to justify choices they haven't actually made (for example, when subjects are asked to explain why they chose a particular kind of jam, even though their jam options were secretly swapped after they stated their preference). People make up arguments for preferences that they don't realize they had previously rejected.[14]
Emily Pronin	The "introspection illusion" describes our proclivity to believe that we have more insight into what motivates us than we really do (while simultaneously believing that others' reports of their own self assessments are unreliable).[15]

There are so many revealing experiments that demonstrate the strangers-to-ourselves phenomenon, but my all-time favourite is courtesy of psychologist Dan Ariely.[16]

Subjects are given a multiple-choice test with the answers to the questions listed at the bottom of each page. Unsurprisingly, most people can't resist looking at the answers before completing the test. The surprising part of this experiment comes in the next phase when a second test that does not include the answers is administered: unsurprisingly, the participants' scores are lower in the second test where there is no opportunity to cheat. The interesting twist in the second test is that participants are asked to predict their scores and are offered a monetary bonus tied to the accuracy of their predictions. Most participants predict scores on the second test that are higher than what they eventually achieve. If they did well in the first test by cheating, they predict they would do just as well in the second test where cheating isn't an option — as if they didn't even know their initial score was inflated by cheating; as if they had two completely independent brains with no communication between them!

Self-deception is a complex psychological process that perhaps evolved as a means of coping with the constant stream of competing impulses within us. We deal with these impulses by suppressing certain desires and beliefs in order to prioritize others. Our talent for self-deception is so advanced that otherwise morally upright individuals can perform horrendous acts without ambivalence. Psychiatrist Robert Jay Lifton examined the harrowing behaviour of Nazi doctors who were assigned to kill Jews in concentration camps. He concluded that they managed internal conflict by splitting themselves into two distinct selves: the "Auschwitz self" (which unflinchingly performed abhorrent duties) and the completely separate "prior self" (which represented the pre-Auschwitz, moral self).[17] The latter was repressed, "reducing expressions of the prior self to odd moments and to contacts with family and friends outside the camp." Ominously, Lifton concludes that "most of what Nazi doctors did would be within the potential capability — at least under certain conditions — of most doctors and of most people." It suits us to be strangers to ourselves occasionally because, to invoke Jack Nicholson in *A Few Good Men,* we "can't handle the truth."

So … combining the above two Need-to-Knows reveals a unique human design flaw. We are an amalgam of conflicting parts and the infighting among these parts is difficult to reconcile because it is at least partially obscured from our conscious awareness. The result is the anxiety and anguish that arises from our fractured psyches.

Feature Becomes Flaw: Functional Flexibility Becomes a Self Divided

There is a community of selves within each of us, a family of diverse personalities that imbues us with enormous depth and dimensionality. Indeed, our multiple-selves design has an important evolutionary benefit: it gives us "functional flexibility" in order to adapt to a variety of situations, including the ability to navigate the complex social demands imposed by different people at different times. Sometimes our best option is passive co-operation; other times it is aggressive intervention. As writer Rita Carter describes it, confronted as we are "with a dizzying rate of cultural change and contradiction, those who have developed a multiple mindscape have an advantage over those who have a one-size-fits-all way of reacting to the world."[18]

But this design feature also plagues us. As primatologist Robert Sapolsky puts it, "We've evolved to be somewhere in between [the] categories that are clear-cut in animals. It makes us a much more malleable and resilient species. It also makes our social lives much more confusing and messy, filled with imperfection and wrong turns."[19] It's not just our social lives that suffer. The multiple energy systems that constitute the human psyche operate somewhat independently, and when they compete, our divided selves catalyze existential angst.

If we have any chance of overcoming this design flaw, there is a conceptual puzzle we must first solve.

We've determined that there is something to the notion of personality, since we're not without some partially innate temperamental leanings. That is a researched, psychology-based conclusion. But what about the more fundamental and intimidating question about the ontological status of self: Is there a real me that defines my essence? If not, then how is a solution to the problem of competing selves even possible?

Is There a "Real" Self Beneath All the Other Selves?

The ancient Hindu concept of self is a good place to start, for two reasons. First, it was the *rejection* of the Hindu self that many scholars consider to be the Buddha's central innovation. Second, it was the *embracing* of the Hindu self that distinguished Jung's thinking. Self was core to Jung's psychology, eventually making its way into the twentieth-century self-help movement.

The contrast between the Buddha and Jung is revealing because it gets to the heart of the competing selves dilemma, especially since Hinduism influenced each of them, but in different ways. Crucial to Hindu philosophy is atman, the Sanskrit term for self (or soul or breath). It is the eternal substance that binds our body and mind but exists before and after them. It is our true, essential self, dwelling within us and migrating from body to body through our many incarnations, until it is liberated through enlightenment. In the yogic tradition of sixth-century BCE Hinduism, liberation of atman is achieved by connecting with this inner self and discovering that it is one with the ultimate and unchangeable spirit that pervades all being — Brahman. When we understand and internalize this profound truth, the karma that fuels the cycle of rebirth is extinguished and our soul is liberated. While Hinduism is the most diverse of all religions, interpreted and practised in a variety of ways, a common concept is atman as the eternal, essential identity within us, distinct from our temporary, earthly body and mind in which it resides. It was this distinction, between eternal self and fleeting non-self, that the Buddha rejected.

BUDDHA'S TAKE ON SELF

The teachings of Siddhartha Gautama (the Buddha, or "awakened one") were memorized and passed down orally by his monk followers for four hundred years before they were written down as discourses (*suttas*) in 29

BCE. Gautama absorbed philosophies from a number of monks with whom he studied, including the common Hindu belief that the culprit behind human suffering is desire, which stems from a misunderstanding of reality. The yogic tradition of the time was directed toward dispelling ignorance through concentrative, meditative practice, which facilitates access to the eternal and unchangeable "Self" (atman) that resides within. This latter point is where Gautama diverged.

He argued that the self is not some central spirit that seeks union with the perfection of Brahman; the self is nothing more than a bundle of shifting sensations, thoughts, and feelings — changing states of existence that arise and vanish as part of the fluid and contingent nature of reality of which we are all part. This contention was not mere hairsplitting: the Buddha did not believe in atman; in fact, he was convinced that believing in a core, permanent "Self" contributes to the illusion that we are separate from the world and therefore fuels the craving that perpetuates suffering and the interminable cycle of rebirths. Where Hindu tradition distinguishes self from non-self, the Buddhist tradition insists there is only non-self: anatman (one of three essential marks of existence, the other two being impermanence and suffering).

The Buddha broke with Hindu tradition by insisting that the self is nothing more than a bundle of shifting mental events that arise and vanish.

The Buddha is sometimes erroneously credited as being the first meditator, but meditation dates back to the pre-Hindu yogic traditions that likely arose from the rituals of ancient shamanism. Like his contemporaries, he believed that enlightenment emerges from a meditative practice. Unlike his contemporaries, he believed the path to enlightenment is through the profound epiphany that we are an indivisible part of a fluctuating, impermanent but unified whole. It's not by unifying with anything outside ourselves that we are freed from suffering and rebirth; it is by coming to know that everything is non-self. As we meditate on the impermanent nature of our moment-by-moment experience, we come to realize that this flow of experience does not *belong* to us: we *are* the flow of change; we are a succession of fluctuating states of existence that is the rising and falling reality that is non-self. By meditating on our immediate experience, we eventually come to see that there is no independent knower behind knowing, no substantive agent behind acting, no enduring experiencer behind experiencing. There is only an ever-changing, interwoven series of arising and fading experiences. Understanding this truth dissolves the illusion of separateness and our suffering ceases. Unlike other animals, we humans are in the enviable position of having the potential for enlightenment because only we are capable of understanding the true nature of suffering.

In his dismissal of a true, deep-down self, the Buddha is in good company. Many philosophers and cognitive scientists argue that our everyday notion of self is just a handy concept that helps us survive, but that the feeling we have of our actual selves "being somewhere behind my face" is just an appearance in our consciousness that lacks any ontological justification.

Bruce Hood	The "self illusion" is created by a brain that needs to consolidate incoming data and respond to it in a coherent way. It's an illusion we cannot live without, no matter how unreal it is.[20]
Daniel Wegner	The "Great Selfini" is the pervasive illusion that we have complete freedom to decide our course of action, unfettered by hidden unconscious drives. We defy causal logic by assuming there is a mysterious, deciding self within us that is completely free of external influences.[21]

The Buddhist view is that there is consciousness and its contents but no distinct, separate self. Thoughts and feelings fall into consciousness, which is merely the recipient of the unconscious processing that generates mental phenomena and deposits it into our awareness. *Conscious awareness does not create thought, it receives it.* Or as Western mindfulness advocates often muse, "Thoughts think themselves," which is to say that thoughts appear in consciousness without any more control by us than sounds present themselves to our ears and sights present themselves to our eyes.

Everything you think or feel jumps from behind the curtain that separates your subconscious synaptic processing from your conscious awareness of the output, but you do not have access to the origin of the mysterious activity behind the curtain. You don't even know what your next thought will be until it emerges from the dark! (Stop reading for a minute and see what thought eventually comes to mind, and what comes to mind after that. Could you have predicted what dropped into your consciousness?) You may feel like you're a knowing self — like a subject in your head behind your face — but there is no fundamental "I" at the centre of all the mental activity, no central self that calls the shots, no conductor orchestrating the cognitive concert, no director overseeing the cerebral drama.

So when we talk about "the deep-down, real me," what exactly are we referring to? It has become fashionable in self-help literature to talk about personal authenticity as "being true to oneself." But this assumes both that there is an underlying true self and that this true self is accessible to our conscious understanding so we know when we are behaving in concordance with it (and therefore being authentic). We may feel we know our true selves because we have an enormous attic full of autobiographical memories, but our self-perceptions are highly selective and highly biased, largely because of "ego-protection,"[22] which skews our ability to judge ourselves honestly. As psychologist Simine Vazire puts it, our self-knowledge is limited by "our own unique biases and tendencies to distort our self-perceptions, such that we do not know our own personalities better, overall, than others know us."[23] We are also subject to "self-serving bias,"[24] which is reflected in our self-reports: when people say they are "acting like my true self," they typically feel that they are being extroverted, agreeable, conscientious, emotionally stable, and intellectual.[25] We think of our true selves in idealized, highly positive, socially desirable ways — perhaps, as psychologist Roy Baumeister hypothesizes, because we put so much emphasis on fostering a desired reputation in order to compete in our socially interconnected world.[26] It's hard to make a logical case for "real me" even though it feels so intuitive that there is one.

Logic and intuition really collide when we contemplate death, bringing the mystery of self into sharp focus. I remember my grandfather's funeral vividly. As a child, I visited my grandparents regularly, spending time in the basement of their home where my grandfather and I would listen to music, paint abstract art, and play board games. When I was fifteen, he tried to take his own life in that same basement. He spent the rest of his life in hospital until he died when I was seventeen. The casket at his funeral was open for family viewing only. As I looked at him, my brain had such difficulty making sense of the waxy and overly groomed body lying in front of me. I was mystified, repeatedly asking myself, "Where is he?" Having been brought up in a secular household, I accepted intellectually that he was nowhere, yet my mind couldn't really believe that. I was convinced that if I could just look him in the eyes, the mystery would somehow be solved, or that I could at least accept that he was gone. I tried to squelch my curiosity but I eventually succumbed and asked my mother if I could open his eyes. She acquiesced. Other relatives turned away in disapproval.

I pushed his eyelids up, but his eyes had rolled back and only the whites were visible. I was searching for him, but he wasn't behind his eyelids. Although my rational mind doesn't believe that there is a heaven waiting for me or another body that will welcome my soul, I still struggle to accept that all my memories and everything I consider to be me will instantly vanish one day. Other than another two or maybe three generations at best, nobody will know I was even here. In the blink of an eye, I will be as unreal as I was before I arrived.

Although there's a strong case against a real self, it's a stretch for most of us to accept the Buddhist view that the cause of suffering is clinging to the illusion of self.

As unreal as we may be before and after, while we're here we do have a sense of who we are — our preferences, beliefs, and values. Before and after our extremely brief appearance as extras in the B movie that is currently playing on planet Earth, there is something about our identity — the character we have been assigned — that feels very real, even if this sense of self is more of a concept than an actual, real entity. David Hume, writing in *A Treatise of Human Nature*, observed that just as members of a government change from time to time but the essential structure of the government stays constant, so an individual "may vary his character and dispositions, as well as his impressions and ideas, without losing his identity." Indeed, without a self-concept, we would have no basis for our choices.

No matter how intellectually compelling the argument may be for Buddha's non-self, most of us are not prepared to accept that the root cause of suffering is the illusion of self. In fact, our suffering often feels as if it stems from the opposite — too precarious a sense of self, confused by too many inner selves warring with each other, hard-pressed to know what we really want or need from others and from life. It often feels as if we need a stronger, dominant self that can reconcile all the conflicting selves and ease the discomfort and dysfunction of our fractured psyches. And this is where Jung comes in.

JUNG'S TAKE ON SELF

Unlike the Buddha, Jung embraced the Hindu notion of atman, making Self (with a capital *S*) the core of his "analytical psychology." *Where the Buddha's rejection of a core self is the gateway to his philosophy, Jung's idolization of Self is the entry point to his.* Jung was strongly influenced by the Hindu notion that connecting with Self and giving it full expression is our life task. He was convinced that Self is very real: it is an inner, divine centre that we are born with; it is the foundation of a mature human psyche because it is the totality of everything that an individual can become. The problem, as Jung saw it, was that Self gets buried. As we develop from birth, our conscious ego helps us adapt to the external world and in so doing, it expands and becomes more prominent within our psyche, squeezing out the other parts — the unconscious aspects that define us. In the second part of our lives, having adapted to the world and therefore being in a stronger position to rein in our ego, we can (and need to) reacquaint ourselves with Self by bringing it into consciousness. Our ultimate maturation as individuals is based on unifying our fragmented selves under the auspices of Self.

Jung owes much debt to Freud's psychoanalytic theories, especially Freud's belief that the key to alleviating mental illness is releasing the blocked energy flows that are submerged in the unconscious as hidden memories and desires, which need to be brought to conscious awareness where they can be confronted and discharged. But while Freud was focused on helping the mentally ill, Jung was more ambitious. For him, bringing the unconscious to consciousness is not just to release the tension of repressed trauma but also to foster the realization of individual destiny. Every single person must get in touch with their Self in order to integrate their "disassociated" parts into a unified whole. If we fail to unify our "splinter psyches," then, according to Jung, we fail to "individuate."

Except for strict Jungian analysts, psychotherapists today do not advocate all of Jung's theories. But conventional psychotherapy is still based on uncovering the obscured inner thoughts that cause dysfunction, based on the Freudian/Jungian foundation that a divided self is an unhappy one. Psychiatrist Irvin Yalom refers to this challenge as "intrapersonal isolation": because "we are isolated from parts of ourselves," the goal of psychotherapy is to "help the individual reclaim these split-off parts of self."[27] It is in this sense that there is something useful about the notion of authenticity: research not only demonstrates that we differentiate our inner self from our public one,[28] but also indicates that our psychological well-being depends on how closely these two match. Feelings of authenticity, even if their legitimacy is suspect, do appear to correlate with higher self-esteem and positive emotions,[29] a greater sense of meaning in life,[30] and greater satisfaction in personal relationships, especially romantic ones.[31] So even if we reject Jung's capital-*S* Self at the core of our psyches, we can still endorse the importance of a healthy self-concept and the research-supported notion that it behooves us to align this self-concept with our behaviours for the benefit of our mental well-being.[32]

Even if we reject Jung's idea of a definitive Self, we can still endorse the notion that well-being depends on a healthy self-concept.

Can we reconcile Jung's Self with the Buddha's non-self? No, but we can combine the best of each to tackle Design Flaw #4.

Shifting from Many to One

The Buddha's philosophy was based on Hindu thinking, but *he was original in rejecting the Hindu notion of self*: non-self is the centrepiece of Buddhist philosophy. Jung's theories were based on Freudian themes, but *he was original in emphasizing the notion of self*, with its Hindu-like quality of collective unconscious: Self is the centrepiece of Jungian psychology.

Gautama and Jung represent two extremes on the spectrum of solutions to the competing selves design flaw. The Buddhist remedy is to wake up to the fact that we are ever-fluctuating parts of a unified whole; there is no real division within self (or, for that matter, between self and other) because there is only non-self, the realization of which liberates us from suffering. At the other end is the Jungian solution to connect with our inner Self and let it direct the integrative process among our many selves, in order to mature into fully realized individuals. If taken metaphorically rather than literally, both men offered deep insights into the essence of human nature. The Buddha captures a fundamental aspect of our being as fluctuating and always transitioning: the notion of self is a mental construct, an image of ourselves that doesn't necessarily correspond to anything separate from our experiences and memories. Jung offers a profound and uplifting vision: not only are we capable of evolving as individuals, but personal maturation is our ultimate purpose.

So the puzzle that I indicated needed to be addressed to fix the flaw — whether there is a "real me" — doesn't lend itself to a tidy solution; however, we've got something to work with to confront the flaw of competing selves. We each operate with a self-concept, which, although somewhat unstable, is fundamental to our functioning as independent agents, and appears to play a significant role in our mental health. This concept of self is, as the Buddha argued, a mental construct, but it is a real, non-illusory construct that, as Jung argued, is the basis of our opportunity to mature.

Both the Buddha and Jung believed that unifying our psyches was a means to an end. The Buddha's fourth noble truth (which lays out the eight-fold path) is geared toward the cessation of suffering and ultimately enlightenment. Jung's process of individuation is geared toward improved mental health and ultimately self-realization. Combining the best of both thinkers reveals a fundamental principle for human well-being: *a healthy self-concept requires the integration of a fractured psyche.*

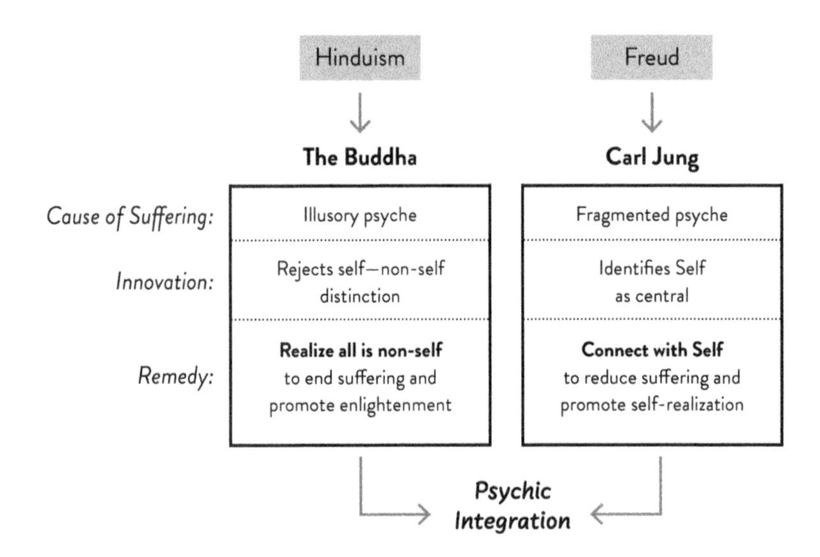

William James wrote that when contemplating the "rivalry and conflict of the different selves … I am often confronted by the necessity of standing by one of my empirical selves and relinquishing the rest."[33] He makes it sound easy. Indeed, sometimes we do simply "stand by" one of the selves. At other times, when the stakes are high and the conflict is acute, our competing selves are not easily reconciled and our conflicting goals and desires produce real psychic disturbance, not only in the moment but also in the future when we suffer painful regret over our choices. Other animals have it easier because they follow their instincts; to be human is to be challenged by inner conflict.

Psychologists have worked hard since Jung to research and explore ways of integrating our competing selves. But Jung is a good jumping-off point in the next chapter for solving Design Flaw #4. We can sidestep Jung's controversial assumption of a deep-down true self by focusing on our *sense* of self, which is exactly that — a *self-concept* that is always shifting and evolving. The key question for psychic integration is not "Who is the real me?" The key question is "Who is the me I aspire to be?" The answer emerges from the existentialist-inspired notion of Best Self — conceived and brought to life, of course, in The Space Between.

One thing to know about the human mind:
It is designed to be "functionally flexible" such that we are many in one.

One thing to know about reality:
"Self" is more concept than reality, but a crucial concept for well-being.

CHAPTER 10

FIX #4: Being at One with Ourselves

We are like onions with many skins, and we have to peel ourselves again and again in order to get at the real core. — Carl Jung

To negotiate successfully, Best Self needs a competent mediator.

Freud was fifty-seven and Jung thirty-eight when they had the falling-out that ended their six-year collaboration and friendship. Freud thought Jung's notion of a collective unconscious was unscientific mysticism. Jung thought Freud's description of the unconscious as the repository of repressed sexual tensions was far too narrow. (Their criticisms of each other are echoed by most psychologists today.) But they shared many foundational principles for the simple reason that Freud built the edifice upon which Jung developed his own theories. Freud invented the "talking cure" (or, more accurately, co-invented it with his initial collaborator Josef Breuer), convinced that psychic disturbance arises from our divided nature and that the solution lies in bringing the unconscious into consciousness through dialogue, thereby bringing balance to our otherwise disassociated selves.

Freud's ideas ripple through Jung's work, but it is Jung who is one of the heroes of this chapter because, standing on the shoulders of Friedrich Nietzsche, William James, and Sigmund Freud, he pioneered the notion of self-realization, which later morphed into "self-actualization" with the advent of humanistic psychology. Jung believed that it takes a lifetime to explore and give full expression to our potential for being mature, "individuated" persons, who have unified their multiple selves. Jung invented the notion of mid-life crisis because he was convinced that it was at this point in every individual's development that they come to a fork in the road and either transition toward full realization of themselves, or get stuck, unable to successfully integrate their various selves.

The Buddha is another hero of this chapter. Integration requires two main steps that are analogous to the first two steps in the Buddha's Noble Eightfold Path to the cessation of suffering: right vision and right intention. We have to see things clearly and then resolve to behave in ways that reflect this clear vision. We have to define our aspirations and then live in accordance with them; we must articulate our values and then discipline ourselves to manifest those values; we must clarify a view of our Best Self and then cultivate that view. The two tasks of integration are, therefore, to *define* Best Self and to *prioritize* Best Self.

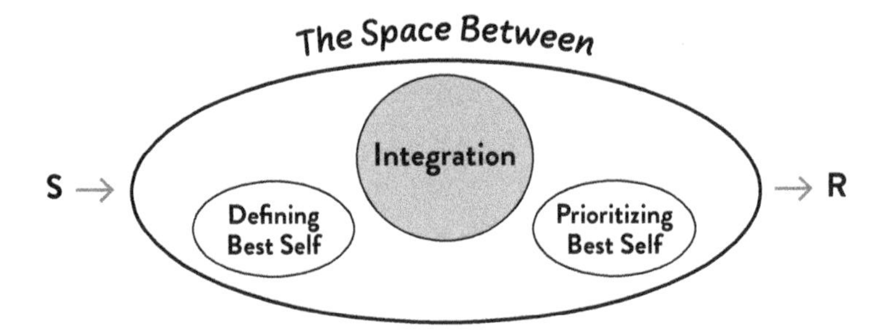

Defining Best Self is not as elusive as Jung's view that we need to listen to Self, nor is it as pointless as the Buddha's view that self is illusory. Self-concept is what we're working with and what we shape inside the space.

Tool #1: Defining Best Self

Best Self is the self we aspire to be. This is the self that, for most of us, eats and drinks in moderation, exercises regularly, gets sufficient sleep, controls its temper, is ambitious and productive, nurtures loved ones, treats everyone respectfully, and enjoys the moment. To top off that intimidating list, and in the spirit of Jung, Best Self expresses the fullness of our personal individuality.

Best Self is the self we aspire to be, however we define that for ourselves.

In Freud's early writing, he used the term *ego-ideal* to describe the image we develop of our ideal self (but that term morphed in his later work into his concept of the superego). Jung never used the term *Best Self*, but the idea was implicit in his description of the archetypal Self that embodies the full individuality within each of us. Jung had a very specific conception of the role of Self in orchestrating psychic integration, a process he referred to as "individuation."

JUNGIAN BEST SELF

Jung's starting point is that we are each incomplete and therefore suffer psychic distress from imbalances among our splintered psychic parts. For example, we may have overdeveloped social personalities that we rely on too heavily for our sense of identity, or we may have deeply repressed aspects of ourselves that we are afraid to confront. The process of individuation sets us on the path to becoming complete — a unified human being whose various selves are balanced and integrated. Individuation is our "coming to selfhood" as fully realized individuals.

As per this chapter's epigraph, Jung describes each of us as onions that need to be peeled over and over again in order to arrive at our core Self.[1] A first step in this peeling process is confronting our persona archetype — the personality we present to others. According to Jung, we begin to develop our personas as children learning how to conform to society's norms and expectations. We refine our personas as we age, taking on roles such as lover, manager, and parent. Jung believed that many of us identify too strongly with the masks we construct and wear and the roles we play, putting ourselves at risk of disassociating from our innate (i.e., non-constructed) Self. To give full expression to Self, we must risk others' disapproval by refining or even recreating our persona so it is more tightly connected to who we really are.

The second archetype that must be confronted is the shadow. Whereas the persona is the person we want others to see, the shadow is our dark side that we hide from the world and often from our own consciousness. The shadow represents all the inferior qualities that we don't like, including impulses such as lust, greed, jealousy, rage, cowardice, and other urges that are hard to accept in ourselves (but that we are quick to notice in others!). The shadow lurks in our unconscious but reveals itself through strong, explosive emotion. Just as we need a persona (to operate in pubic), the shadow is also essential because without it, our persona would dominate, rendering us captive to an overdeveloped concern for how others view us. Our shadow gives us depth and dimensionality. As a universal archetype exerting immense power over our emotions and behaviours, we have no choice but to learn to live with it productively. The less conscious we are of our own shadow, the "blacker and denser" it is; the more we repress it, the more turmoil it wreaks in the form of debilitating neuroses. Unlike our constructed persona that we can recreate, our shadow requires that we give it a voice by bringing it into consciousness. Rather than deny our "shadowy" parts, we must accept them as inevitable and with us from womb to tomb. (This concept is reflected in Acceptance and Commitment Therapy, or "ACT" for short, which is geared toward accepting unwanted feelings and thoughts while not allowing them to determine our behaviour.[2])

According to Jung, we're at risk of disassociating from Self by overidentifying with our constructed persona and by ignoring our inner shadow.

There are other archetypes to wrestle with, but the most important archetype of all is Self — that which remains after all the skins of the onion have been peeled back. Self is deeply buried within us and the central archetype of the psyche, the unifying force around which all other archetypes orbit. It is the entirety of who we are, reflecting all aspects of ourselves (both conscious and unconscious), including an impulse for self-realization; it is the source of our individual potential; it is "our life's goal"; it is the "completest expression of that fateful combination we call individuality."[3] Everything we are and are capable of becoming as unique individuals is contained in Self.

Key to the individuation process is recognizing that Self is much bigger than ego: who we are is much bigger than our conscious sense of our identity. While ego, as defined by Jung, is the centre of our consciousness, it is *not* the centre of our psyche. In the first half of our lives, our conscious ego develops to cope with the world. As we busily adapt to external realities, our ego becomes more solid and defends itself against challenge or change. In Jung's schema, ego comes to think of itself as the totality of who we are, and it doesn't want to surrender power to other aspects of our psyche that are submerged below consciousness but yearn for self-expression. When a stubborn ego resists the expression of unconscious selves, these energies become more forceful in pushing to be heard, resulting in neuroses such as depression, anxiety, and obsessions.

In the second half of our lives, having adapted to the world, we begin to acknowledge the various archetypes lingering below the surface of our awareness. We can then integrate these various selves by bringing them into consciousness, thereby expanding Self into consciousness such that ego more accurately reflects the totality of who we are. To become whole, complete and at peace, we must fulfill Self's destiny to unite our fragmentary selves on the path to "becoming an 'in-dividual'" and "'coming to selfhood' or 'self-realization.'"[4] Individuation can be difficult because it's hard to accept that our conscious sense of our self is not nearly the totality of who we are: "Everything good is costly, and the development of personality is one of the most costly of all things."[5]

Jung's view of bringing the unconscious to consciousness in order to release stifled energy systems and relieve neurotic symptoms has its roots in Freud. But Jung's innovation was his notion that by tapping into the full power of the core Self, embracing all elements of the psyche, a person can move toward their full potential of "incomparable uniqueness." If we do not individuate successfully, our psychic development is obstructed and we never fully mature; we never reach completion. While perhaps a bit romantic, Jung's Hindu-like image of a destiny-bound Self residing within each of us is a majestic, compelling vision of the need for psychic integration.

Jung's innovation was his notion that by embracing all aspects of our psyche, we can move toward our potential as fully mature and unique individuals.

But how exactly are we supposed to "individuate"? According to Jung, we integrate our psyches by listening to Self. But Self cannot communicate with consciousness except via symbols and images. Influenced by Freud, Jung believed that dreams provide clues for our attempts at excavating unconscious energies. Freud was not hesitant to interpret his patients' dreams and was convinced that much of dream symbolism is sexual in nature and reasonably straightforward to categorize. But Jung believed that the analyst should only assist the patient as they interpret their own dreams because the symbolism used by Self is unique to each individual — it is not confined to sexual tension but open to creative understandings. (Jung's second method for listening to Self was "active imagination," by which he meant letting our minds relax by adopting a meditative stance and allowing images to float up from the unconscious.)

Best Self, in the Jungian sense, represents the wholeness of our distinctive, integrated selves. Jung's solution to the conflicting-selves problem was to tap into the psychic energy of Self, which is within us and seeking full expression, not metaphorically but literally. On this point, he was at odds with the existentialist philosophers. Jung and the existentialists shared a common idolization of individuality and the necessity of avoiding self-deception to realize one's full potential. But where Jung emphasized *self-discovery* (listening to Self), the existentialists highlighted *self-creation* (owning our choices).

EXISTENTIALIST BEST SELF

The first existentialist, Søren Kierkegaard, writing a half-century before Jung in *The Sickness Unto Death*, emphasized the importance of being faithful to "the self which one truly is" rather than conforming to the herd mentality of the masses. Prefiguring Jung, he wrote about the anxiety that comes with accepting our freedom to become fully mature individuals. Even more striking are some key ideas of Friedrich Nietzsche, writing a few decades before Jung. Here are some highlights of Nietzsche's thinking that should sound familiar in the context of Jung's psychology:

- Each of us is irreducible multiplicity — the sum of many drives that are largely prehistoric; if we ignore these deeper, dark energies, they will turn against us.
- But this "abundance of contrary drives and impulses" (from *Will to Power*) means that "our instincts now run back all over the place; we ourselves are a kind of chaos" (from *Beyond Good and Evil*).
- To bring wholeness to ourselves, we must harmonize these competing drives with an "organizing idea" (from *Ecce Homo*) or "ruling passion" (from *Untimely Meditations*), which resides at the centre of the psyche as the master drive.
- We must be on the lookout for this master drive as it gradually reveals itself, so we can allow it to unify all of our drives in the pursuit of a single heroic goal, such that one "becomes what one is" (from *Ecce Homo*).

These ideas are clearly represented in Jung's thinking (and Jung refers to Nietzsche in his writing). But where Jung conceived of Self as the pole star of our personal evolution, Nietzsche didn't believe in a separate self per se: he thought that we are each a chaotic collection of competing drives and only the strong-willed person (the "overman") transcends traditional values by harnessing the universal "will to power" that resides in each of us. This power enables us to overcome the feeble and submissive parts of ourselves, especially the stifling "herd instinct of obedience" that society uses to tame us. Nietzschean Best Self reflects an individual's ability to liberate a ruling passion through creative determination to make and own the choices in their life. This theme of creative self-overcoming is quintessentially existentialist, and contrasts with Jung's view of Self as a given, fixed entity — a contrast revealed very pointedly in the philosophy of Martin Heidegger.

In his 1927 book *Being and Time*, Heidegger emphasized personal authenticity or "ownness," by which he meant owning oneself — being one's own person, owning one's choices, taking responsibility for oneself. We are inauthentic (not owning ourselves) when we are entwined in activities without reflecting on them, mindlessly conforming to social norms by acquiescing to "the dictatorship of the One," by which Heidegger meant public opinion. Humans are unique beings because we can stand outside our lives and resolutely move forward with choices we own rather than passively accepting a "falling into life," where we follow the grooves we have been socialized into, "tranquillizing" ourselves with "average everydayness." Unlike other animals, we can pull back from our busyness to contemplate the eventuality of our death, motivating us to take ownership of our decisions. Without naming it, Heidegger was endorsing The Space Between, because it is within this calm space that we enliven Heidegger's version of Best Self — the self that authors its own story rather than settling for the story written by the momentum of a busy life.

For Heidegger, there is no deeply buried Jungian Self that guides us; in fact, exactly the opposite: we experience anxiety precisely because our conscience calls on us to make choices but doesn't instruct us on what choices to make. The notion of an unconscious Self that directs our choices is anathema to existentialist philosophy because such a thing would deprive us of freedom and responsibility for our decisions. Informed by the eventuality of our death, we must proceed resolutely "with the sober anxiety which brings us face to face with our individualized ability to be." Heideggerian Best Self is absolutely free in every moment.

Jean-Paul Sartre, in his 1943 book *Being and Nothingness*, echoed Heidegger's themes (and book title) with his description of "bad faith," which is to live without acknowledging responsibility for our choices and simply accepting oneself as a fixed essence with no freedom to self-create. In Sartre's view, we are each faced with the challenge of "transcending our facticity," by making choices in the situations we find ourselves in rather than being defined and trapped by these situations. Sartre's Best Self is always self-creating through its lifelong journey: "Man is nothing other than his own project."[6]

So we have two contrasting descriptions of Best Self: the existentialist version (something *to create* for ourselves) and the Jungian version (something *to discover* within ourselves). I think both versions have merit and are therefore worth reconciling.

CONNECTING WITH BEST SELF

We may be nothing more than a collection of fluctuating selves loosely enveloped by an amorphous self-concept. But that doesn't prevent us from conceiving of a Best Self that we can hold out as our personal ideal. In fact, defining Best Self is integral to integration. Psychologist Scott Barry Kaufman sums it up nicely when he writes that the relevant question to ask ourselves is not "Who am I really?" or "How can I become myself?" The better question, according to Kaufman, is "Which potentialities within me do I most wish to spend my limited time cultivating, developing, and actualizing in this world?"[7] Kaufman captures a nice blend of Jungian and existential Best Self, which are reconciled when Best Self is conceived as an act of creation in every moment, representing deeply held personal values and goals that guide our choices.

The question Kaufman poses is future-oriented, which is crucial because it is an antidote to our tendency to define ourselves by our history rather than by our ambition. According to psychologist Benjamin Hardy, our self-concept is typically defined by the stories we tell about our past and not about the aspirational person we strive to become.[8] The trick is to flip this from a backward-looking self-identify to a forward-looking one — a Best Self we can aspire to be in every future moment. This is a Best Self that can only be defined individually because it is deeply personal: it is the self that we would prefer to be the dominant one in any given situation. Best Self is the self that we envision taking pride in when we look back from the future to the present; it is the self that guides us in answering a crucial question:

How will "future me" evaluate the choices I make right now?

This question, more than any other, defines Best Self for each of us: it forces us to look inside (per Jung) before freely choosing our actions (per the existentialists). This question helps us answer the key question from chapter 8 to escape an emotional hostage crisis:

What is the next right thing to do?

The next right thing is the one that Future Self will be proud of. Will my Future Self be more impressed that I fired off an angry email in response to a criticism or that I waited to cool off and think through a productive response that will de-escalate the conflict? Will my Future Self be pleased that I ate two chocolate bars in a row because I was feeling sluggish? Will my Future Self congratulate me tomorrow morning if I stay up late watching a crappy movie? The next right thing is defined by Future Self's watchful eye. I invoke these two questions daily when I need them to define and concretize my Best Self. And I've found the two questions to be crucial in fostering the best relationships I'm capable of, romantic and otherwise (but especially romantic).

But defining Best Self is only the first of two battles to win in the war among competing selves. The second is prioritizing Best Self over other selves, who have their own agenda. This second battle is even harder because in it we're playing two roles simultaneously — general and soldier (in fact, many soldiers, most of whom have little interest in obeying a general). And who is the general? Who is issuing the order to prioritize Best Self?

Returning to Hume's analogy in *A Treatise of Human Nature*: "I cannot compare the soul more properly to any thing than to a republic or commonwealth, in which the several members are united by the reciprocal ties of government and subordination." Good analogy, except for one hole: in a republic or commonwealth there's a head of state, so who is the head of our psyche? Who is the monarch or president whose responsibility it is to put Best Self's interests ahead of all others'? Or take another analogy, this one with a Jungian flavour to it, courtesy of psychologist David Lester: "Just as family members are embedded in the large family system, multiple selves are embedded in the mind."[9] Lester suggests that a well-functioning person must take account of each self, just as "family members learn rules for relating to one another." (Internal Family Systems, or "IFS," is a therapy based on the notion that a family of different selves resides in each of us.[10]) But in a family, the parents exert authority over the children, so who are the parents of our psyche?

If there is no core Jungian Self and merely a wobbly self-concept, and if the key to well-being depends on our power to integrate competing selves by preventing them from thwarting Best Self, whose job is that? Who's in charge?

Tool #2: Prioritizing Best Self

For Freud, ego should be in charge, captive neither to the id's explosive demands nor the superego's harsh criticisms. For Jung, Self should be in charge, guiding the integration process. We may want Best Self to be in charge, but the self that is *actually* in charge is the self with the most power at any given point in time — the strongest self of the many that are competing for dominance.

The self in charge at any point in time is the one with the most power, which is only sporadically Best Self.

Best Self is often not the most forceful since there are other selves that are much stronger. Why? Because System 1–generated selves seek payoffs that are short-term, if not instantaneous, whereas System 2–conceived Best Self has interests that lie in the future, and often in the distant future. This imbalance of power makes negotiating with ourselves very challenging. And that is exactly what it is — a negotiation.

Need-to-Know: We Bargain Across Time

Psychologists Richard Thaler and Hersh Shefrin propose that within each of us is a "planner" who prioritizes long-term rewards, and multiple "doers" who are "completely selfish" in focusing on rewards that are immediately available.[11] Put another way, our long-term interests are the purview of our Future Self, who bears the brunt of our bad decisions or benefits from our good ones. Competing with Future Self are the various present selves, who may be vaguely aware of the long-term implications of their motivations but aren't interested in compromising. Conflict arises and we are confronted with the uniquely human challenge of negotiating with ourselves across time in an epic intertemporal clash.

Here is what's interesting about this negotiation: *Future Self is not present for the transaction, so it negotiates through its proxy — Best Self.*

Best Self represents Future Self's interests by considering the long-term consequences of decisions. And Best Self has its work cut out for it because the bargaining is unfairly skewed in favour of our immediate desires: even after suffering the regret of eating too much, drinking too much, or watching too much TV, we find ourselves repeating these behaviours again and again. As psychologist Angela Duckworth describes it, "Our default response is to do things that feel good right away, even if we have enough life experience to anticipate regretting doing so after the fact."[12] Why? Because "response tendencies for most temptations tend to dominate those for rival long-term goals." Why? Because, as psychologist Mark Leary points out, "The self did not evolve to exert the amount of control that we require of it in modern life."[13] Prior to the agricultural revolution, "life was lived mostly day to day with no long-term goals," but as we transitioned to agriculture we moved from an "immediate-return environment ... to a delayed-return environment." We are not well designed for delayed returns. Psychiatrist George Ainslie uses the term *hyperbolic discounting* to describe how rapidly and steeply the strength of our preferences changes with delays in receiving rewards: we value immediate rewards highly, but the value we put on those same rewards deteriorates quickly if they are delayed.[14] (We don't discount future rewards at a constant exponential rate but in an exaggerated hyperbolic way.) The Need-to-Know is that we are constantly engaged in an intertemporal negotiation between strong present rewards and weaker future rewards. This contest would be a losing proposition for Future Self if all it could rely on was Best Self to battle on its behalf. Fortunately, Future Self has other means of support.

Comparative psychologists note that "whereas other animals can wait no longer than a minute or two for a larger reward, humans can delay immediate gratification indefinitely."[15] We have, it seems, some choice in who is in charge; we don't have to default to the self with the strongest pull in a given moment. Unlike other animals, we can call upon a mediator to take charge of all the competing selves. That mediator is System 2 metacognition, aka Observing Self. When Observing Self is mediating, it can account for Best Self's interests by levelling the playing field.

There is a mediator available to look out for Best Self's interests: System 2 metacognition, aka Observing Self.

How do we prioritize Best Self, empowering us to do what we want when we don't want to do it? By putting Observing Self in charge. This metacognitive self is the one we want as the general among soldiers, the de facto head of state among citizens, the parent of the children. Metacognition turns the spotlight of attention inward on our own thinking and feeling, giving Observing Self the broadest possible perspective of any self. Observing Self mediates by correcting the power imbalance between Best Self and other selves.

PUTTING OBSERVING SELF IN CHARGE

A number of metacognitive tactics are at Observing Self's disposal to bolster Best Self's negotiating power; I've narrowed the list to the three I think are most effective.

But before we can invoke these three tactics, we have to first get Observing Self to the party by climbing into The Space Between. Only in the space are we capable of the clarity of mind required to both envision Best Self and actualize it. Only there can we see how dysfunctional some of our other selves can be. Only there can we fully engage System 2 metacognition because only there can we remove ourselves from the "hotness" of current emotions and find refuge in the "coolness" of standing at a distance. Only in this cool space can we mobilize Observing

Self's expansive perspective and ask the crucial question, "What will my Future Self think of my current decisions?" and, in the spirit of Viktor Frankl, "What does life expect of me right now?" Without the benefit of The Space Between, other selves, powered by the immediacy of their desires, have a huge advantage over Best Self, whose longer-term interests are less pressing.

We open the space by self distancing with a few deep breaths. We expand this space by fully awakening Observing Self — taking stock of the tension between our competing desires. Then, inside the enlarged space, Observing Self can conduct a fair negotiation.

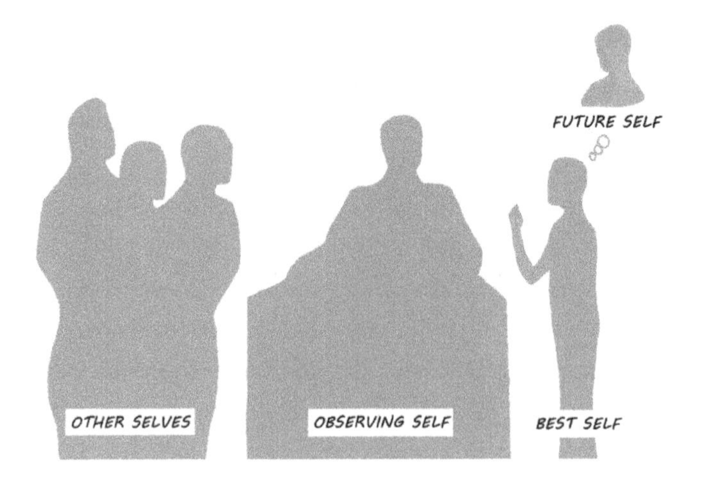

How often do we instinctively step back and observe the negotiation as it is happening, in a detached enough way to give Best Self a fighting chance? It doesn't come naturally to us because System 1 does not take kindly to being asked to slow down or suppress its appetites. So not often enough.

Once on the scene, Observing Self can avail itself of three tactics to support Best Self.

TACTIC #1: CONTESTING HOT STATES WITH PRE-COMMITMENTS

Nietzsche coined the term *will to power*, which he defined in grand terms as a central force that motivates living things to exert their power in the world. We've come to think of *willpower* more narrowly, as the force we exert on ourselves to resist strong inner urges. But willpower is not a reliable resistance strategy because we habitually overestimate our ability to control our impulses and withstand temptation. Overconfidence in willpower ("restraint bias"[16]) leads us to put ourselves in precarious situations, such as buying a tub of ice cream "just for the occasional dessert" or turning on the TV before bed "for just a few minutes." The problem is that our "hot" impulses are hard to recall when we are in "cold" states, meaning we underestimate how powerful our impulses are when we aren't immediately experiencing them. This lack of imagination (i.e., "empathy gap"[17]) makes it difficult for us to imagine how we will feel in the future when we're in a different emotional state than our current one. The plan we make the night before to get up early to exercise doesn't take into account how, the next morning, we'll give anything for just twenty more minutes of sleep. (As an aside, the empathy gap also makes it difficult for us to empathize with others when they are in a hot state and we are in a cold state, as in, "What is he all worked up about?" and "Why is she so stressed out over something so trivial?") Added to the empathy gap is the reduction in our decision-making autonomy when we are tired, hungry, or overwhelmed ("ego depletion"[18]). The verdict is in: self-control is a finite and constrained resource.[19] Because we perpetually underestimate the pressure of our hot states when we're not in them, *willpower is overrated.*

Best Self needs stronger reinforcement than mere willpower because we badly underestimate the power of hot states when we're not in them.

Rather than let cold-state, future-focused Best Self duke it out with hot-state, present-focused competing selves, Observing Self can engage reinforcement strategies. The consensus of psychologists is that "the path to better self-regulation lies not in increasing self-control but in removing the temptations available in our environments."[20] As Duckworth puts it, *situational* strategies (which manipulate circumstances to minimize struggle) are much more effective than *intrapsychic* strategies (which rely on one self battling another).[21] How do you resist temptation at an all-you-can-eat buffet? Don't go to one. How do you avoid racking up credit card debt? Cut up your card. How do you avoid staying up late watching crappy TV? Set the sleep function to turn off at 11:00 p.m.; better yet, listen to some soothing music instead. How do you improve your diet? Don't buy tubs of ice cream "to keep for guests." These obvious examples are all situational manipulations that Observing Self uses to eliminate temptation in advance: they are pre-commitments that take into account the weakness of willpower.

The term *pre-commitment* was originated by the economist Robert Strotz.[22] He introduced the concept with an excerpt from *The Odyssey* in which Ulysses instructs his sailing crew to tie him up to a mast so that he can't give in to the deadly temptation of the singing sirens to jump off the ship and swim to them. Observing Self knows our vulnerabilities and establishes pre-commitments to ensure that Best Self's choices reign supreme. *Pre-commitments help our cold-state decisions endure by inoculating them from future hot-state desires.*

Sometimes we can't simply eliminate temptation altogether, so we have to weaken competing selves in advance with pre-commitments that must be very specific. Vague pre-commitments are vulnerable to rationalizations that goad us into the boxing ring to face muscular competitors who are eager to pummel our weak willpower. Planning to lose ten pounds this month is too general a goal and, therefore, at high risk of failure, compared with the specific goal of avoiding all sugar-related treats and alcohol for one month. Resolving to write a book this year is not nearly as promising as an explicit pledge to spend one hour after dinner every day working on a draft. Unambiguous pre-commitments reduce the friction that Best Self has to overcome in its quest to dominate other selves.

Those hot-state selves are forceful enough to contort System 2 thinking to support their agenda, as in "I'll have a second helping now and diet tomorrow," or "I deserve a lazy day of Netflix binging and will get back on task when I'm refreshed." We excel at finding loopholes and justifying exceptions to rules — including our own rules. Rationalization is the enemy of Best Self. As Robert Sapolsky points out, "The road to hell is paved with rationalizations."[23] Exceptions need to be managed.

TACTIC #2: MANAGING EXCEPTIONS WITH GOOD HABITS

We are highly skilled cheaters because we rationalize that one-off exceptions have no bearing on our future decisions. But this is delusional. George Ainslie draws a contrast between choices that are legitimate exceptions and choices that are precedent-setting.[24] We typically assume we are engaging in the former when in fact we are establishing the latter. The empathy gap encourages us to assume that rule-breaking today will not impact Best Self's ability to dominate in the future, but this is not true: *exceptions are precedents for future rule-breaking because they establish patterns.*

This insight is crucial: *current choices influence future choices.* We self-signal with our choices in a way that shapes our self-concept and hardens our self-identity (for example, coming to see oneself as a person who can't resist sweets, or can't keep a romantic commitment, or is always late). When we indulge in exceptions to pre-commitments by rationalizing them, we make it easier to indulge in future exceptions, which solidifies bad habits. It is because our choices in the moment are predictors of our future behaviour that exceptions today erode the likelihood of Best Self flourishing tomorrow. And why "100% is easier than 98%," according to management professor Clayton Christensen, who argues that breaking our personal rules "just this once" may not feel life-changing because the marginal cost of cheating seems very small, but the full cost of our decisions can be enormous when we understand them as precedent-setting: "If you have justified [an exception] once, there's nothing to stop you doing it again."[25]

Our current choices influence our future choices: habits make our decisions for us.

Rather than relying on the feeble tenacity of willpower to resist exceptions, we need to make it easier to follow a preselected path. And that is precisely what good habits do. Habits that conform to our vision of Best Self are plows that cut paths to our desired futures. How? Habits foster automaticity — they literally sculpt our neurocircuitry so that we follow pre-established pathways. Habits reduce optionality: their automaticity means we default more easily to the familiar paths that our energy-preserving minds favour. Habits reduce "decision fatigue" by diminishing the calories required to think through trade-offs and resist undesired temptations. Habits make the decisions for us. Automaticity, of course, cuts both ways: good habits are allies by reinforcing desired behaviours; bad habits are enemies by reinforcing undesirable ones.

Author James Clear encourages the building of "identity-based habits," which focus on who we wish to become.[26] If you decide in advance that you are the type of person who exercises every other morning, or who never raises their voice, or who always reads for thirty minutes after dinner, then the identity-based habits that correspond to these self-descriptions solidify the self-concept you are trying to sustain. A Best Self virtuous cycle translates your chosen identity into habitual behaviour, which reinforces your identity. Much better than the reverse, where you default to System 1, impulse-driven behaviours in which a Worst Self vicious cycle builds a self-identity that perpetuates bad habits. When my Best Self is struggling to prevail, I find it very helpful to say to myself, *I am the kind of person who pauses before he responds angrily to provocation, I am the kind of person who stops eating before he is overfull, I am the kind of person who always prioritizes his kids when they need him.* I have broken more than one bad habit with the simple words, *I am not the kind of person who _____.*

Good habits invest power in Best Self by exploiting automaticity. But neither pre-commitments nor good habits guarantee that Best Self triumphs. We are still prone to veering off our chosen paths when we're tired, hungry, stressed, and especially when our emotions are running hot. We still need an "In Emergency, Break Glass" tactic. This last tactic is an extension of the identity-based habits strategy and can be summed up in two words: *as if.*

TACTIC #3: BEHAVING "AS IF"

When neither pre-commitments nor habits are enough to stop us from inching toward rationalizing an exception, we need a "last resort" to protect Best Self. Psychologist Alfred Adler developed the "acting as if" technique to encourage behaviours that don't come naturally but fit the kind of person we aspire to be. If all else fails, we still have the option to act "as if." Say I'm furious at my partner and itching to ignite an imbroglio: I can jump headfirst into the space and invoke the two magic words that remind me to behave *as if* I'm someone who does not intensify conflict when they feel incensed; I walk away to cool off. Or I'm feeling languid, lonely, and longing to lounge in bed, but I choose to play the role of someone who is not so lethargic, *as if* I can handle my low points by calling a friend or going for a walk. "As if" is a good way to pump the brakes on urges that are inconsistent with Best Self.

"As if" is our last and best resort to stay on our preselected paths.

In fact, "as if" isn't just for emergencies. It's a useful way to envision how Best Self behaves when it's unencumbered. Four centuries ago, long before psychologists began to research how habits are cultivated, Shakespeare offered his typically shrewd insight into human nature; in this case, how "as if" can jump-start good habits. Hamlet, disapproving of his mother's romance with his uncle, admonishes her, "Assume a virtue if you have it not." And continues to lecture her in act 3, scene 4, on how to use precedent-setting behaviour to form good habits: even if she isn't virtuous, she can abstain from sex that evening, making it easier the next night to abstain and easier still the night after that. Habits, explains Hamlet, can change our natural instincts for the better or for the worse. "As if" can jump-start a good habit in the absence of any better inducement.

Navigating the River of Our Best-Self Choices

Who are we? Neither fleeting illusions in the Buddhist sense, nor durable Selves as Jung would have it. We are somewhere in between — more fluid than solid. The river of our identity ebbs and flows. A river has no "inner core," but it can move with great force. When we climb into The Space Between and let distractions fade into the background, Observing Self imbues us with a greater degree of freedom than our non-observing selves — the freedom to create and cultivate Best Self. In the space, we can exercise control over the various mental states that we float through, skillfully navigating a lifelong stream of consciousness that eventually empties into an ocean of we-know-not-what.

One thing to remind yourself every day:
Best Self is always on standby, waiting to be invoked.

One question to ask when you're feeling conflicted:
Am I giving Observing Self enough space to prioritize Best Self?

CHAPTER 11

FLAW #5: We Misdirect Our Need for Meaning

If I were ... a cat among animals, this life would have a meaning, or rather this problem would not arise, for I should belong to this world. – Albert Camus

Wrestling with the wrong problem; asking the wrong question.

Camus's point above is that other animals don't struggle with the problem of meaning because they "belong here" insofar as they don't consider the alternative. Or as philosopher Thomas Nagel put it: "A mouse … is not absurd because he lacks the capacities for self-consciousness and self-transcendence that would enable him to see that he is only a mouse."[1] We, on the other hand, are prone to feeling that something is fundamentally wrong with our situation, that our existence feels oddly contingent or precarious or peculiar.

I vividly recall the first time I was visited by the question of meaning — although "visited" is too gentle a description. Studying at home for a grade 9 French test, I was sitting on my bedroom floor, textbook in hand and notes sprawled around me. While conjugating verbs, I was suddenly enveloped by a crushing sense that there was absolutely no value in what I was doing or would ever do. I stared at my book, sapped of all motivation. It seemed painfully clear that my deeds didn't matter, I didn't matter, and there was nothing I could do to change these raw facts.

I was bewildered by my relatives chatting in the living room. Did they not see the pointlessness of everything as clearly as I now did? They were adults, after all, so they should have already figured this out. Why weren't they overcome with near-paralysis by the realization that nothing mattered? What was propelling them through the gruelling tedium of day-to-day existence?

At that point in my life, I wasn't familiar with French existentialist philosopher Albert Camus's essay *The Myth of Sisyphus*, which begins, "There is but one truly serious philosophical problem, and that is suicide. Judging whether life is or is not worth living amounts to answering the fundamental question of philosophy." Although I wasn't suicidal, Camus's opening salvo captures the essence of the dilemma that overcame me that night. (Camus's cat and Nagel's mouse really are spared the human quandary, according to psychiatrist Antonio Preti: "Naturalists have not identified suicide in nonhuman species in field situations, despite intensive study of thousands of animal species."[2])

On that evening, I had two new struggles to contend with: an almost-debilitating dismay about the universe's indifference to my existence, and the confusion and odd feeling of alienation that arose from my perception that nobody else seemed to see this "truth." I somehow found my way back to a bit of lacklustre studying, but from that moment on, a lifelong, twofold quest arose: to discover an antidote to my pessimism and to figure out why the human condition perturbed me more than it appeared to plague others.

Four decades later, the answers have crystallized for me, in large part from absorbing the wisdom of philosophers and psychologists who have grappled with the problem — key ideas that fourteen-year-old me would have benefitted from and middle-aged me relies on every single day. The next chapter has more of a psychology focus, as the basis of the fix. This chapter is more philosophy-based because philosophers have written eloquently about their struggle with the conundrum labelled "the meaning of life." To define the fifth design flaw, I've chosen five writers who have distinctive and contrasting takes on the problem and how to solve it:

	Proposed Solution:
Leo Tolstoy (1828–1910)	*Religion*
Albert Camus (1913–1960)	*Rebellion*
Arthur Schopenhauer (1788–1860)	*Resignation*
The Buddha (circa 500 BCE)	*Release*
Viktor Frankl (1905–1997)	*Rising Up*

I'll start with someone who posed the exact questions I asked myself that fateful night of studying. Although I would not have found his solution satisfying.

Tolstoy: Religion

A decade after the publication of *War and Peace*, Russian novelist Leo Tolstoy plummeted into a depression, described in his book *A Confession*: "Sooner or later my affairs, whatever they may be, will be forgotten, and I shall not exist. Then why go on making any effort? … How can man fail to see this? And how go on living? That is what is surprising!"

A Confession is as detailed a personal exploration of the struggle to find meaning as you will find anywhere. With searing candour Tolstoy reveals that he initially decided the only rational response to the "stupid and evil joke" of life was suicide. But he was unable to kill himself — a "weakness" that "was disgusting and painful" to him. At the same time, he marvelled at the number of people who were unhampered by the questions that plagued him.

Tolstoy muddled along, waiting for "something to happen," when it eventually struck him that his quest for meaning was misguided: "Rational knowledge denies the meaning of life, but the huge masses of people acknowledge meaning through an irrational knowledge. And this irrational knowledge is faith." Arriving at his conclusion with great fanfare, Tolstoy attached his finite life to an infinite being: "What meaning is there which is not destroyed by death? Union with the infinite God, paradise." (Interestingly, he couldn't find coherence in the God that he'd been brought up to worship in the Orthodox Christian Church, so he opted instead for faith in an ambiguously defined God that for him was more emotional than biblical.)

Putting aside Tolstoy's contentious conclusion, there is considerable merit in his view that the problem of meaning cannot be addressed as a purely intellectual puzzle to solve. It took me many years to realize that the most powerful elements of meaning are accessed in ways that aren't governed exclusively by reason. Each of us must develop our own response to the problem, a point I will revisit at the end of this chapter when I share my own grand conclusion, albeit with less definitiveness and flourish than Tolstoy.

Tolstoy was on to something: the problem of meaning cannot be categorized as merely an intellectual puzzle to solve.

I may have unwittingly channelled Tolstoy as a young teenager because the solution he arrived at was the first one I explored when I befriended Warren, a devout Jehovah's Witness. But unlike Tolstoy, and despite the admirably persistent and patient efforts of Warren (which I described in chapter 6), I was incapable of making that irrational leap of faith. I was stranded — at least for a few years, until I studied philosophy in university, the existentialists in particular.

Writing sixty years after Tolstoy, Camus tackled the same problem but took a different route to solving it.

Camus: Rebellion

Rational explanation is built into our consciousness as a monolithic need, wrote French philosopher Albert Camus, who describes it in *The Myth of Sisyphus* as "this desire for unity, this longing to solve, this need for clarity and cohesion." But he insists that the world is fundamentally devoid of eternal truths or clarity of purpose (or if it has meaning and purpose, they are unknowable to us). The result of this clash? "The absurd is born of this confrontation between the human need and the unreasonable silence of the world." When rational humans try to make sense of an irrational universe, absurdity arises. His objective in the essay is to explore three options for coping with the unavoidable absurdity of the human condition: suicide, faith in God, or perhaps an alternative.

Camus rejects suicide on the grounds that it merely succumbs to absurdity by surrendering our free will, relinquishing the choice we have to confront meaninglessness. We mustn't avoid the problem, which is why he's equally dismissive of faith in anything otherworldly. Faith is a false promise and "philosophical suicide"; appealing to the beyond, according to Camus, avoids the problem in the same way suicide does.

He concludes that the only viable response to the absurdity of our situation is to accept it with dignity and fortitude. We must live defiantly, neither succumbing to absurdity nor trying to eliminate it with a contrived belief system. The only legitimate response to meaninglessness is to live passionately, intensely, to seek out a variety of experiences, living life to its fullest, all the while maintaining awareness of how pointless it all is. To rebel against absurdity is to live with it and despite it: "That revolt is the certainty of crushing fate, without the resignation that ought to accompany it." Our revolt against absurdity "challenges the world anew every second."

Both Tolstoy and Camus start with the grim evaluation of our inability to make sense of our situation, and then leap to triumphant, but very different solutions.

Reading Camus is inspiring, but after the glow of rebellion has been fired up, an emptiness lingers. What he says has intuitive appeal and makes for a great pep talk but isn't particularly satisfying or energizing the day after. It's asking a lot of a person to find the strength and courage to relish how pointless life is.

Both Tolstoy and Camus start with reason's inability to make sense of an irrational world, but then each jumps to a very different resolution. This move from desperation to triumph is common among thinkers who tackle the problem, with one very notable exception — a philosopher who starts with the same depressing premise and then doubles down on his pessimism. Who else could it be, other than …

Schopenhauer: Resignation

Writing in the early nineteenth century, Arthur Schopenhauer had an influence on Tolstoy, who even mentioned him by name in *Anna Karenina*.

Schopenhauer believed that ultimate reality is characterized by a relentless force or energy (which he labelled "Will"), which underlies all existence but has no particular purpose or point. There is nothing profound for us to discover about our lives; there is only the relentless drive of Will that pushes us to nowhere other than our eventual death. As he describes in his essay "On the Vanity of Existence," we are trapped by the incessant striving that this force bestows upon us: "Man is a compound of needs which are hard to satisfy … their satisfaction achieves nothing but a painless condition in which he is only given over to boredom." So each of us "swings like a pendulum to and fro between pain and boredom."

I was struck by this description: most of us in the modern world tend to oscillate between being slightly hyper and anxious on the one hand and slightly lethargic and melancholic on the other. We spend much of our time in these two extreme states. What was Schopenhauer's proposed solution to the human dilemma in a godless universe where we are captive to the blind, interminable force that manifests itself in all being?

He conceded the possibility of distracting ourselves from meaninglessness, but in typical fashion he thought this option was extremely limited: only when we are immersed in art can we enjoy a momentary reprieve from suffering. He rejected suicide on the grounds that it merely succumbs to Will rather than opposing it through resistance. The only authentic response available to us is to continually deny the impulses that Will exerts on us. We can mitigate our misery by living simple lives, resisting our

Will-driven desires rather than giving in to them. Where Camus advocated embracing meaninglessness in order to live defiantly and passionately, Schopenhauer advocated defiance by resigning ourselves to a miserable existence where our only recourse is to curb the desires and ambitions that aggravate our suffering.

It's tempting to reject Schopenhauer's dire worldview as cartoonish. But his writing is deep and penetrating. Eighty years before Sigmund Freud's description of the unconscious, Schopenhauer postulated that we are driven by forces that we don't fully understand, including painful ideas that we repress. And he is certainly not alone in his admonition that we must renounce our desires. If Schopenhauer's counsel sounds vaguely Buddhist, it's because he had an affinity for Hinduism and Buddhism, both of which he studied. In fact, as I immersed myself in the study of Buddhism, I came to view Schopenhauer's philosophy as actually less pessimistic than the Buddha's in one fundamental respect.

The Buddha: Release

According to Siddhartha Gautama's cosmology, which was highly influenced by the Hindu beliefs of his time, those who haven't yet been enlightened (i.e., you, me, and the other 99.99 percent of us) are destined to endure suffering through an infinite series of torturous rebirths — and not necessarily in a comparatively comfortable human form. Schopenhauer, at least, provided some comfort in his view that the whole miserable horror show ends with death.

Schopenhauer's depressing philosophy is actually less pessimistic than the Buddha's in one fundamental respect — no infinite series of rebirths.

To be fair, the Buddha's grander vision is ultimately more optimistic: not only do we have the opportunity to eliminate the angst in our current lives, but the benefit of being human is that it provides an opportunity to break free from the cycle of painful rebirths by killing the seeds of karma that otherwise mature into more suffering in future lives. Angst arises from craving: yearning for something that is not contained in the present moment. We can release ourselves from craving and attachment by meditating deeply on our present experience — the flux of our ever-changing sensations and thoughts that represent the only true reality. So for the Buddha, the question of the meaning of life is nonsensical, because when we see reality for what it is — a unified, constant flux that we are inseparably part of — all questions of meaning disappear. When we realize that our suffering is triggered by an illusory sense that our desires can be satisfied, all we are left with is our immediate experience. This epiphany releases us from yearning and paves the way for Nirvana — the extinguishing of the flame that reignites rebirth and repeated suffering.

Leaving aside the mystical elements of the Hindu cosmology that the Buddha inherited (karma, rebirth, etc.), there is something soothing about his insistence that the only meaning available to us is our immediate experience. Yet there is also something quite stark about his philosophy. Is it truly in our best interest to abandon the richness of our multi-faceted goals and desires? Striving is a recipe for suffering, according to the Buddha, but I could never fully embrace the notion that my ambitions and pleasures were all based on a fundamental misunderstanding of reality, and that all that mattered was contained in the present moment.

In striking contrast, the Austrian psychiatrist (and Holocaust survivor) Viktor Frankl insisted that a meaningful life requires the tension of meaning-seeking. In fact, it's just this anxiety — the kind that the Buddha seeks to release us from — that Frankl urges each person to endure, even seek out, in order to discover personal meaning.

Whereas the Buddha advocated the abandonment of yearning, Frankl was convinced that we need to seek out the tension of striving.

Most who read Frankl's work, including his seminal *Man's Search for Meaning*, are immediately taken with his view of the human condition. Initially, I was not one of them.

Frankl: Rise Up

Frankl begins at a familiar starting point, that any form of ultimate, non-personal meaning is beyond the intellectual capacities of human beings. From there he veers from the above thinkers, arguing that meaning must be pursued in personal terms: every individual must define their own meaning. It's the pursuit of a meaningful task that inoculates us from feeling that our lives are empty and futile. What is a meaningful task? It's one that suits the particular situation; it is the right response to each unique dilemma. How do we know what's right? We don't. But by focusing our effort on responding to every challenge in the best way possible, we create meaning in every moment. "We need to stop asking about the meaning of life, and instead to think of ourselves as those who were being questioned by life — daily and hourly."[3] He advocated that we must take responsibility "to fulfill the tasks which [life] constantly sets for each individual." Very much contrary to the Buddha's prescription to renounce earthly ambitions, Frankl argues that mundane goals infuse an individual's life with meaning. Striving weakens the feeling of emptiness and futility that we are vulnerable to. A degree of anxiety is the price we pay for setting challenges for ourselves, a healthy tension that arises from establishing goals that give us reason to persevere.

When I first read Frankl, I was distracted by the theological undertones of his ideas. Similar to Tolstoy, he believed in a transcendent "super-meaning" that is only accessible by faith. The theological underpinnings of his beliefs are sometimes cryptic and ambiguous; his insistence that there is only one answer to each of life's challenges and that our responsibility is to work to discover that answer was too rigid and mystical for me. But I was enchanted with his emphasis on the uniqueness of each individual life such that there is no one-size-fits-all solution to the question of meaning. Expunged of its theological undertones, his writing is profound: "Life ultimately means taking responsibility to find the right answer to its problems and to fulfil the tasks which it constantly sets for each individual."[4] Where Camus urges us to bravely accept existential despair, Frankl is more nuanced and more practical in his prescription — to search out the meaning that resides in every challenge we confront.

Another element of Frankl's work struck me: he differentiates two forms of meaning that most thinkers conflate. Frankl explicitly separates transcendental, non-rational "super-meaning" from the personal meaning we can pursue in the tasks of our everyday lives. The former meaning applies to the human condition in general, which resides outside of ourselves and relates to questions about why any of us are here and what our purpose is. The latter meaning is the one we can experience when we're absorbed in pursuing our individual goals. This distinction between transcendental and personal meaning is crucial: how we conceive of life in general is not the same as how we find meaning in our individual lives. The two meanings can overlap, as they do for many religious people. But the point is that they don't have to overlap; they aren't identical and treating them as the same confuses the issue because one of them is not rationally solvable and one of them is.

To make sense of the human-meaning dilemma, *we need to be clear about which of the two forms of meaning we are addressing*, since each leads to a different path. It so happens that we default to ruminating about the form of meaning that is the wrong one to be fussing about.

Feature Becomes Flaw: Sense-Making Becomes a Misguided Search for Meaning

Tolstoy was on the right track in *A Confession* when he insisted that a rational answer is not possible to the question of how to make sense of the apparent meaninglessness of life. He stayed on track when he wrote that "a reply can only be obtained by a different statement of the question." But then he took a wrong turn — "and only when the relation of the finite to the infinite is included in the question." He called for the reframing of the question (good move) in a way that must include reference to something infinite (oops). The problem with his particular reframe is that it may satisfy people who have faith in an infinite God, but it won't satisfy those who don't and are unable to argue themselves into it the way Tolstoy did. By failing to distinguish Frankl's two kinds of meaning (transcendent and personal), Tolstoy's solution (exclusively transcendent) has limited applicability.

The transcendent form of meaning that our minds search for leads either to a purely non-rational and mystical conclusion (God, Spirit, Being, Unity, Wholeness, Dao, etc.) or, for non-believers, to a complete dead end. So if your sense-making brain prompts you to pursue transcendent meaning, but you are hard-pressed to make a Tolstoyan leap to "the Infinite," then you've got nowhere to go ... except maybe insane, as per Voltaire's novel *Candide*: "'But to what end,' Candide muses, 'was the world formed?' Martin replies: 'To make us mad.'" Or, less poignantly but more specifically, Camus in his essay *The Myth of Sisyphus*: "The absurd is lucid reason noting its limits." Or, more vividly, psychologist William James: "We may be in the universe as dogs and cats are in our libraries, seeing the books and hearing the conversation, but having no inkling of the meaning of it all."[5] You may remember "mysterianism" from chapter 6 (Krishnamurti's parable about the devil rejoicing at our attempt to put the puzzle of reality together). This is the philosophical position that our limited cognitive capacities have not evolved (and may never evolve) to the point of understanding the whole picture, much as Job was admonished by God for presuming to have the capacity to understand His unknowable mysteries. But unlike the Job-God discussion, our cognitive limits do not necessarily imply that there is a grand meaning out there that we can't get our little, earthbound heads around, because that implication assumes there is a form of intelligible meaning to tap into, if only we had better mental apparatus to work with (just as James's dogs would appreciate the library if their brains were bigger). Instead, our limits could simply indicate that our relentless pursuit to make sense of things is a survival-enhancing design feature that morphs into a design flaw when extended to the question of our place in the universe. Remember in chapter 3 how I emphasized how greedy we are? Well, we are greedy for meaning that is unavailable to us, not because we're a few neurons short of a full load, but because our default notion of meaning is ill conceived.

We're greedy for universal meaning, not because we're a few neurons short of a full load, but because our notion of meaning is ill conceived.

The flaw is what philosophers call a "category mistake" — treating the universe's mystery as if it were in the same category as a word puzzle. In the same vein, the Austrian philosopher Ludwig Wittgenstein argued that language can be deceiving because it can be used to pose questions that appear intelligible but are essentially nonsensical. And because words can have multiple meanings in different contexts, language gets us in trouble when we employ words or expressions in a context that is different from their original usage (when we mix up our "language games"). When we pose a question about transcendent meaning like "What is the meaning of life?" language is tricking us because "meaning" belongs to a different category than "existence"; it does not apply to an all-encompassing description of life in the universe. (The error is more obvious when the question is formulated this way: "What is the meaning of the quantum mechanical wave function that defines the universe?") "What does it all mean?" may sound intelligible — the mouth noises collide with my ear in a way that sounds coherent. But it is a flawed question posed by a flawed brain that is overextending one of its design features. It's the wrong problem to wrestle with, no matter how desperate we are for "meaning" in a twenty-first-century world where religious and social communities are eroding (Facebook, Instagram, and Twitter being poor substitutes).

"What does it all mean?" is a flawed question posed by a flawed brain overextending one of its design features.

To fix the flaw, we need to differentiate transcendental from personal meaning so that we can explore the latter: the search for personal meaning is the right problem to address and it points to the right question to ask. So back we go to Tolstoy's insight before he veered off toward metaphysics, that there is perhaps a better way to ask the question about meaning. Contemporary psychologists have worked hard to define the problem more coherently and reframe the question in a practical way that doesn't require us to take the road of theism but also doesn't force us into an intellectual dead end.

Shifting from Philosophy to Psychology

When I was overcome by angst while studying French, I was bewildered that others didn't seem plagued by the same feeling of hopelessness. I wondered if my distress was unique. Do we all hunger for meaning in the same way? Research reveals that some people suffer meaning crises more deeply than others, and some don't have a high need for meaning at all. A good portion of the population (35 percent in the sample studied in one case[6]) don't perceive much meaning in their lives but aren't bothered by the lack of it: they still enjoy a level of satisfaction in the life they lead. For some, a sense of meaning is a profound and deeply felt need; for others, it's fully satisfied by their theistic beliefs; and for others, the question doesn't haunt them at all.

It's probably safe to assume that all of the philosophers I have highlighted in this chapter had a high need for meaning. Each had insight into the topic, and combined, their perspectives point toward a fix for the flaw of overextending our sense-making design feature. We must reconceptualize the problem of meaning by converting it from an intellectual puzzle to a psychological challenge.

Tolstoy: meaning is not an intellectual riddle to be solved rationally

Camus: our cognitive limits require bravery and defiance

Schopenhauer: meaninglessness is a natural state with only temporary reprieve

Buddha: meaning only exists in the profundity of the present moment

Frankl: personal meaning arises from striving

Meaning is a persistent psychological challenge for which we need specific strategies.

By framing meaning as a particular mental state, we can leave transcendent meaning aside by acknowledging that the "meaning of life" question does not lend itself to an intelligible and universal (non-theistic) solution. And we can reframe the question about meaning based on a different starting assumption: *meaning is not an intellectual riddle to solve, but a feeling to be generated.* That is, *meaning isn't an answer; it's a psychological state.* It's an emotional experience — one that contributes to human well-being. The question, therefore, is not "What is the meaning of life?" The right question is "How does one generate the feeling of meaningfulness?"

Meaning isn't a riddle to solve; it's a feeling to generate. The question isn't "What?" but "How?"

The next chapter answers the question "How?" But first, what is "the feeling of meaningfulness"? What does the meaning feeling *feel* like?

The feeling of meaningfulness is a positive state of well-being that arises when we are deeply absorbed in the activities of our lives. It is a feeling of engagement, engrossment, fulfillment, and, at its peak, self-realization. It is different than what we think of as happiness in the form of pleasure. The distinction between meaning and happiness goes back to the Greek philosophers, notably Aristotle, who wrote that pleasure (*hedonia*) should be secondary to living well or flourishing (*eudaimonia*).

The psychological literature today still uses these Greek terms to describe the two experiences. Devouring a delicious meal feels good in a different way than raising a family. Being amused by a sitcom is a different emotional experience than working toward a degree or mastering a golf swing. The hedonic feelings of pleasure are distinct from the eudaimonic feelings of meaning.

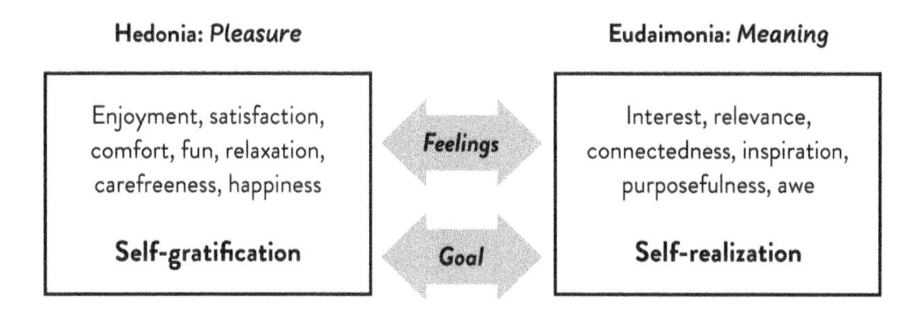

The point of contrasting pleasure and meaning is that the latter can be quite unpleasant: learning to play an instrument, mediating a difficult conflict, or starting your own business can be frustrating and anxiety-provoking. But making progress on tough challenges and enduring struggles can also feel rewarding: *meaning is a positive state of mind even when it is accompanied by disquiet.* The strategies that generate the feeling of meaning are not specifically geared toward short-term pleasure, but they don't exclude it either, since there is some overlap between the two. Meaning is different than pleasure, but the two are not opposites.

Nor is the opposite of meaning indifference. Its opposite is the horrible feeling of meaninglessness: when we're floating above our lives, wondering what the point is; when studying French verbs seems pointless but no more pointless than everything else we're doing. German philosopher Martin Heidegger, in his book *Being and Time*, does a masterful job of describing meaninglessness as feeling "not-at-home," a feeling of displacement from our familiar routines and connections with other people. We usually operate within a familiar context of activities and relationships in a world that feels more or less orderly. But we are vulnerable to suddenly encountering "nothingness" according to Heidegger, when we perceive ordinary things as strange, pointless, and disorienting; when we are confronted by the frightening truth that nothing reinforces our reason for being and that underlying our reality is only "groundless floating"; when we realize that our routine lives are underpinned by nothing other than "it's what one does." We suffer when, as Camus described in this chapter's epigraph, we feel we don't belong to this world. It is this feeling of meaning*less*ness that we can forestall with tactics that engender the feeling of meaning*ful*ness.

Contemporary psychologists have championed some helpful meaning-generating tools, which are accessed in The Space Between and which fall under the rubric of a broader System 2 strategy. When we focus on fostering personal meaning, we open up a near-infinite number of individual solutions. So maybe Tolstoy wasn't far off when he invoked "the infinite" to resolve the struggle with meaning. He just invoked the wrong kind of infinite.

One thing to know about the human mind:
It is designed to search for meaning
(and look for problems when it is not occupied).

One thing to know about reality:
The universe does not offer up
the kind of answers we want or expect.

CHAPTER 12

FIX #5: Pursuing the Meaning Feeling

When things matter, they don't need meaning to matter!
— Irvin Yalom

Engagement is the only reliable inoculation against meaninglessness.

As a teenager struggling with meaninglessness, I would have sneered at the above seemingly trite observation by the noted American psychiatrist. Later in life, I got it. Although I would phrase the point differently: *When things matter, they feel meaningful.* When we aren't questioning the purpose and value of our lives but are just busy living, our projects and relationships matter to us. Which is why Yalom's solution to meaninglessness is to engage "in any of the infinite array of life's activities."[1] When we are engaged with life, we aren't indulging the depressing cosmic view of ourselves as frenetic little ants. According to Yalom, and here I can't improve on his wording, "Engagement does not logically refute the lethal questions raised by the galactic perspective but it causes these questions not to matter." Engagement dissolves the problem of meaning. As philosopher Ludwig Wittgenstein wrote, also somewhat cryptically on a first reading, "The solution of the problem of life is seen in the vanishing of the problem."[2] Meaninglessness vanishes when we are absorbed in an activity, especially when we're immersed in what positive psychologists call "flow," where we are in a groove of deep concentration. This form of engagement is characterized by what psychologist Robert White labelled "effectance" — a feeling of competence as we interact with the world and experience a sense of effectiveness and control in what we're doing.[3]

Yalom believes that the desire to engage with life is present in all of us and that a key goal of the therapist is to remove the obstacles that prevent people from achieving this engagement. Both Yalom and Camus have unbridled enthusiasm for a life lived with maximum freedom and passion, but Yalom aims to vanquish absurdity, whereas Camus insists that we maintain top-of-mind awareness of just how meaningless our lives are. Camus's heroism is a bit romantic: most of us would find it unnatural and unhelpful to revel in the burden of our absurd existence. Most of us would prefer the Yalom route of releasing ourselves from meaninglessness. And we have two very different paths to choose from to do exactly that.

We can give up our earthly desires and ambitions, as the Buddha and Schopenhauer advised, narrowing the gap between what we aspire to and what is available to us. Alternatively, we can take the opposite approach and plunge ourselves into the personal projects that absorb our attention, which is what Yalom prescribes.

For most of us, the latter solution of engagement is more inspiring than the former, which is too stark and, in the case of the Buddha, depends on a particular mystical worldview that hinges on being reborn into a better life or, ideally, not being reborn at all. The Yalom solution, which builds on the insights of Viktor Frankl, is more promising.

Getting Engaged

Voltaire's novel *Candide* concludes with the following oft-quoted line from the eponymous main character, who has travelled the world, witnessing horrors and enduring misfortune: "Let us tend to our garden." He and his entourage have decided that the focused, demanding, and non-reflective life of the farmer is the best kind of life because it avoids the inevitability of living "either in convulsions of misery or in the lethargy of boredom," as described by one of Candide's more pessimistic companions, Martin. Martin ultimately agrees with Candide: "Let's work without speculating; it's the only way of rendering life bearable." By engaging with the work of the garden, the problem of meaninglessness vanishes (as per Wittgenstein).

Engagement is the solution to meaninglessness. But even Yalom's version of the engage-with-life solution provides no guarantee that we can produce the feeling of meaning on demand. The best we can do is put the pieces in place to maximize *the opportunity* to feel meaning.

While engagement is the solution, it can't be created on demand — the best we can do is pursue opportunities to feel meaning.

Having reframed meaning as a psychological experience, we can now ask how to engender this particular state of mind: How do we create the opportunity for meaning? How do we foster the kind of engagement that produces feelings of meaningfulness?

And of course, the answers to these questions are more fully available in The Space Between, where System 2's Observing Self can take us to places that System 1 doesn't venture. Engagement is the macro-strategy, supported by two main tools.

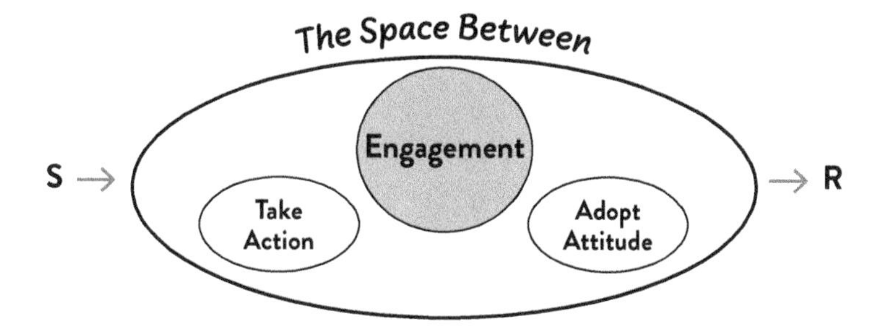

American psychotherapist Eric Maisel argues that it behooves us to seek out "a rich mix of meaning opportunities" so we're not captive to just one method of creating meaning for ourselves.[4] And he counsels us to schedule into our days the activities that are likely to generate a feeling of meaning, thereby reducing the tempting "meaning substitute activities" that feed our languor and even depression, such as watching too much TV, drinking too much, or overeating. He identifies two fundamental methods of generating meaning: action and attitude.

Tool #1: Action — Choosing What to Do

Maisel's view is that one of our main jobs as humans is to become meaning-making experts. The first and key way to make meaning is action. When we feel our lives are meaningless, "the door to meaning is closed but not locked. Taking action opens the door."[5] Action protects us against feelings of meaninglessness. Each of us is tasked with figuring out which activities provide the highest chance of meaning for ourselves — what gives us the highest probability of generating feelings of meaningfulness. These meaning-enhancing activities are deeply personal: whatever engages me might leave you feeling cold.

Psychologist Abraham Maslow popularized the term *self-actualization* as the fulfillment of an individual's potential to be the complete expression of themselves. He argued, in the spirit of Frankl (and Jung before Frankl), that each individual must pursue their own distinct path to growing and evolving as a unique human being, which is a lifelong process of striving to be the best form of self that each of us is capable of being: the best artist, the best parent, the best teacher, the best carpenter, or the best of whatever actualizes a particular person. The feeling of meaning arises from activities that represent Best Self; however, each individual defines "best" for themselves.

As should be obvious by this point, I'm one of those people who have a high need for meaning. Which is to say I crave the feeling of meaningfulness. Which is to say I'm vulnerable to feelings of meaninglessness. I take Maisel's wisdom very seriously: every night I plan the meaning opportunities for the following day. I realize that very rarely will an entire day be meaning-filled, but scheduling at least a few activities that engage me deeply keeps the eerie sense of meaninglessness from creeping into my consciousness. If a day looks like it will be short of meaning-inducing opportunities, I schedule an hour of abstract painting or writing, a meal with a friend, a trip to a gallery, or simply a walk somewhere new. But I don't rely exclusively on scheduling meaning for myself. I am alert throughout the day for meaning-making opportunities as they present themselves.

I can't schedule myself to help an elderly man pick out the best bananas at the grocery store, but I can jump to support him when I notice he's struggling and use the opportunity to make a connection, even if just momentarily. These mini meaning-making moments continually present themselves if you have a meaning-making mindset. That's not to say that meaning has to be altruistic. We're all wired differently, and the high that some people get from doing good deeds isn't universal because, as psychologist Scott Barry Kaufman puts it, "There is no one way to live."[6] There are many non-altruistic activities that have meaning-making potential, such as cooking an elaborate meal, taking a painting class, or reading an absorbing book.

So engagement is boosted by both planning for and taking advantage of meaning-making activities every single day. But action is just one tool of engagement. There is a subtler meaning-making opportunity available to us in places where we might not expect — where System 1 rarely finds meaning. For a guy who needs a lot of meaning, this second method turned out to be a gold mine once I discovered it. We can generate meaning by adopting a specific attitude — by *being* in a particular way.

Tool #2: Attitude — Choosing How to Be

Our choice of attitude is one of the greatest freedoms available to us as human beings. This freedom is the centrepiece of existential philosophy, exemplified by Sartre's rallying cry "existence precedes essence," by which he insisted that we are born without the constraints of an essence but free to choose *how* we want to be.

We can choose to practise being calm in a long lineup, or to be a good listener to a friend in need, or to be appreciative of a sunny day. We can choose to adopt an attitude of forgiveness and generosity in circumstances where we would otherwise lean toward resentment or selfishness. As discussed in chapter 8, we can choose to "do the right thing," however we define that for ourselves, including the choice to let go of our negative thoughts and feelings. Our choices are meaning-making because we are exercising System 2's power to be in a way that differs from System 1's default way of being. The annoyingly long lineup or harsh word from our partner instantly becomes an opportunity to create feelings of meaningfulness as we practise some new moves. (Again, remember chapter 8 — the "lucky me opportunities" that pop up throughout the day.) Just as our meaning-making activities are highly personal, our attitude choices also need to be customized to suit our individual values and objectives. And because System 1 has no interest in "new moves" or "finding meaning in the moment," we can reset ourselves and engage System 2 with a very brief *samatha* meditation (described in chapter 8). By focusing on a few of our breaths, in and out, we can climb into The Space Between and prime Observing Self to consider our options for a meaning-making attitude shift.

There is a way of being, a particular attitude shift, which lends itself to enormous meaning, but which most of us neglect because we don't even know it's quietly waiting for us, almost invisibly, in The Space Between. It's an attitude that other animals default to naturally by virtue of not being burdened with overly intricate brains. Schopenhauer homed in on this point when he described other animals: "Brutes show real wisdom when compared with us — I mean their quiet, placid enjoyment of the present moment."[7] But rather than the negative spin that Schopenhauer took, we can use this comparison with other animals as an opportunity for ourselves, because the cognitive complexity that sometimes plagues us also offers a degree of control over our attention that no other animal shares. We can place our mind's focus where we want it to be. In The Space Between, our Observing Self can choose to indulge in the "placid enjoyment of the present moment" just as other animals do by default. We can invest meaning in virtually any moment by focusing our attention on what is happening: the brilliant colours and intricate textures of what our eyes take in, the fascinating and constantly changing cacophony that resonates within our ears, the myriad tastes as we eat, or the elaborate sensations as we walk — any or all of the majesty that surrounds us in any given moment.

This form of meaning-making is an extension of *vipassana* meditation (also described in chapter 8). But rather than inquiring into our immediate experience as a means of assessing negative emotions, we can use the same technique to "just be" with the amazing things that are happening around us. We can meditate on the "meaning" that is swirling around us in every waking moment. This attitude of appreciative awareness for what is happening right now is as powerful as it is underutilized, because System 1 was not designed to exploit it. But in The Space Between, System 2's Observing Self helps immerse us in the present moment with an attitude of complete openness to whatever is happening. Only System 2 is capable of acknowledging that the present moment is all that is real (past and future are only mental phenomena); only System 2 can choose what kind of relationship it wants to have with life in the present. This refocusing of our attention to the present moment is especially useful when feelings of meaninglessness strike (in addition to anxiousness, impatience, melancholy, or any negative affect). We can simply exercise our right to move our attention to the best place it can be when these negative emotions arise and persist — to the ampleness of the moment, to all of the activity bundled in the present, to a spot where "just being" is all that is required. Thereby creating feelings of meaningfulness in an instant (and in *the* instant).

In The Space Between, Observing Self can invest meaning in any moment, simply by focusing on what is currently happening.

I wish as a younger man I had understood how captivating the present moment can be if you just pay attention to it. It's not in our nature to step out of the busyness or the boredom of our daily routines to appreciate what is happening around us; our minds usually want to be elsewhere than right here right now. But with a bit of regular practice, stepping out can become a regular feature of our lives. I know, because I went from never taking in the fullness of the moment to doing it multiple times a day in an effort to stave off feelings of meaninglessness. By experiencing everything that is happening in the present to the fullest extent possible, we create meaning from exercising control over our attitude, leveraging our freedom and thereby bolstering our sense of agency and power — all in the most unlikely and dullest of circumstances. The secular Buddhist writer Stephen Batchelor points out that our search for meaning "beyond the mundane clutter of daily existence" is like a fish looking for water, because meaning surrounds us all the time, if only we are able to see it.[8] We need to awaken to the fact that we are swimming in meaning. Batchelor captures the spirit of this shift in attitude by stressing, "The mystical does not transcend the world but saturates it," and "The world is excessive: every blade of grass, every ray of sun, every falling leaf is excessive."[9]

We tend to think of the big, scheduled events as the ones that are meaningful and make life worth living. These planned ones may indeed be the peaches in the still-life paintings of our lives. But Maisel points out that even if we live "for the sake of the peach," we can nonetheless imbue the less interesting parts of our life painting with meaning.[10] He describes how Picasso explained his painting philosophy as all-encompassing: if he is painting a peach, the rest of the painting gets as much of his attention as the peach itself. Maisel's point is that both the meaningful and non-meaningful have important places in our lives, since the peach is defined in large part by the non-peach parts. The less meaningful parts don't invalidate the meaningful ones; in fact, they highlight them. A meaningful day contains pockets of meaning, and the rest of it is important in the way that background is important to foreground. It is the totality that defines a well-crafted life.

While the peach-painting analogy is clever, it is impossible to welcome *all* of the non-peach parts of our lives with equanimity. Sure, we can search out the meaning that hides within non-peach moments, but some of these are hard to tolerate. Much of our daily routine is riddled with non-peach frustration and disappointment, where meaninglessness is ready to impinge, where background can overtake foreground. As Camus so poignantly pointed out, "At any street corner the feeling of absurdity can strike a man in the face."[11] I also like how science writer Jesse Bering describes happiness, with a Schopenhauerian tone: "It defines not a permanent state of being but slippery moments of non-worry."[12]

So in addition to proactively creating feelings of meaning by taking action and choosing attitudes, we need to cope with unavoidable feelings of meaninglessness.

Muddling Through Meaninglessness

One option is to simply ignore meaninglessness. Before landing on faith as a solution for himself, Tolstoy struggled and failed with this approach: "Once I had discovered the truth I could not close my eyes to it." He merely stumbled through as best as he could, waiting for "something to happen."[13] The Irish writer Samuel Beckett tackles Tolstoy's "stumble through" option in his play *Waiting for Godot*. When one character insists, "I can't continue," his colleague retorts, "That's what you think." Beckett returns to this idea again in his novel *The Unnamable*, which closes with "I can't go on. I'll go on." Beckett offers no solution to the problem of waiting for something meaningful to happen. He simply observes that we persist, without meaning, because we have no other choice. The same sentiment is captured by Nietzsche is his typically pithy and poetic way: "There comes for every man an hour in which he asks himself in wonderment 'How is one able to live? And yet one does live!'"[14]

But feelings of meaninglessness are hard to ignore. Meaninglessness is one of the hardest pills that we humans have to swallow. (In fact, I would say it's the hardest of the "red pills" of reality, to invoke a metaphor from *The Matrix*.) For those of us who don't embrace theism, who lack a universal, transcendent meaning to appeal to, we are stuck with the not-particularly-edifying view that the universe doesn't care about us. Yet we are designed to yearn for transcendent, comfort-inducing meaning. As Jung put it, "As far as we can discern, the sole purpose of human existence is to kindle a light of meaning in the darkness of mere being."[15] We are not designed to live free of existential anxiety; our goofy minds wander and race and ruminate, and search for a sense of purpose in our lives that gives us at least a modicum of reassurance that some of what we do actually matters.

Because action and attitude cannot completely inoculate us from the feeling of meaninglessness, our last defence, when it arises, is climbing into The Space Between where we can acknowledge that meaninglessness is a part of being human and the feeling comes and goes but rarely persists indefinitely. Coping with bouts of meaninglessness is an inevitable predicament for a peculiar animal with an overdeveloped brain that can pose questions about its place in the universe that it can't answer.

In The Space Between, we can tolerate meaninglessness as a feeling that comes and goes and a natural part of being human.

Remember Abraham Kaplan's distinction, in chapter 4, between problems that can be solved and predicaments that can only be coped with? Predicaments are perpetual dilemmas that ebb and flow but never get fully resolved — they can be mitigated but never eliminated. So it is with our quest to create meaning, because *meaning is a psychological state, and like any feeling, it will come and go* (remember chapter 8: the fundamentally fleeting nature of all feelings). Life itself is neither meaningful nor meaningless — *it just is.* Meaning is psychological, and engagement is how we generate the feeling of it: by pursuing activities that engage our spirit and by fostering productive attitudes toward being. So while we can reduce the frequency and intensity of the feeling of meaninglessness, we have to tolerate a degree of it in the same way that we have to tolerate degrees of many negative feelings. As per chapter 8, if we can't let meaninglessness go, we have to just let it be, without inviting "the second arrow" to poison us by overreacting. Some human suffering is, to use a term that has unfortunately come up before in this chapter, *unavoidable.*

The dual challenges of creating meaning and tolerating meaninglessness are the relentless tasks of being human. As psychologist Carl Rogers put it, "The good life is a process, not a state of being."[16] Looking back at myself as a young teenager suffering through the conundrum of meaninglessness, I'm sympathetic to Jung's observation that the "most important problems of life … can never be solved, only outgrown."[17] I can't say I'm anywhere close to outgrowing the important problems, including and especially the challenge of meaning. But as I age, I'm coming to peace with their insolubility. Which I suppose is exactly what Jung meant.

One thing to remind yourself every day:
I need to plan for some meaning today.

One question to ask when you're experiencing meaninglessness:
What are my best opportunities for engagement right now?

CONCLUSION

We're Still in Beta

The problem of man's existence, then, is unique in the whole of nature; he has fallen out of nature, as it were, and is still in it; he is partly divine, partly animal; partly infinite, partly finite. – Erich Fromm

Predicaments require subtle manoeuvres.

About six million years ago, as we were stumbling our way down an inconceivably long evolutionary path in the African jungle, we came upon a fork in the road not unlike the one described in Robert Frost's brilliant poem "The Road Not Taken," which concludes:

Two roads diverged in a wood, and I –
I took the one less traveled by,
And that has made all the difference.

At that point in our history, we chose a road *never before* travelled, and it has indeed made all the difference.

Our ancestors' brains at that time were the same size as the brains of all great apes, housing around thirty billion neurons (which is roughly the same as today's orangutan, gorilla, and chimpanzee brains).[1] But at the fork in the road, some great apes diverged from the well-travelled path of living in the trees; in fact, natural selection nudged them right out of the woods.

Natural selection "chose" to invest more caloric energy into building a bigger brain for these intrepid travellers, compared with the other great apes, who maintained larger and more muscular bodies. For the first 4.5 million years, changes were slow and subtle among these travellers, and then, over the subsequent 1.5 million years, their brain size and neuronal count more than doubled, taking an astonishing diversion from the path of other apes:[2]

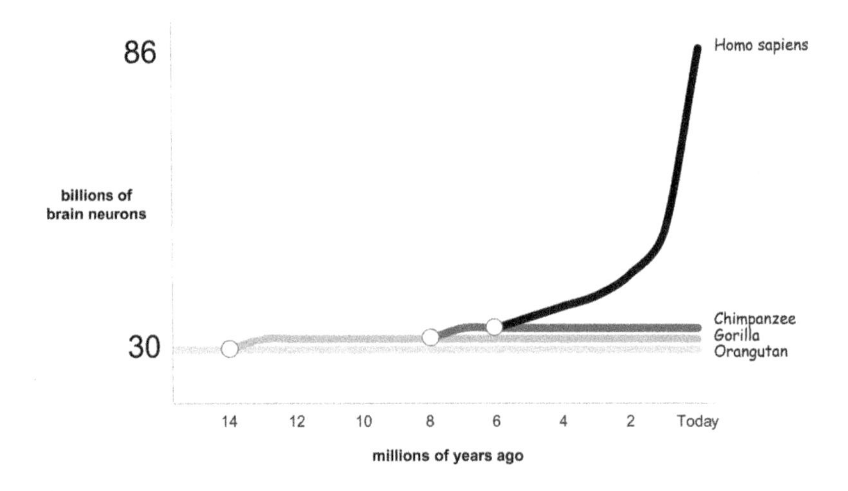

There are only so many hours in a day to forage for food, so there are a limited number of calories that can be ingested and used for metabolic functioning and growth. This energy restriction forces a trade-off between brains and brawn: brains are heavy energy users, which makes it difficult to build an unusually big brain while simultaneously building a big, strong body. An animal needs a good-enough brain to find food, protect itself, and reproduce, but beyond these basics there is more environmental pressure to grow bigger and stronger bodies because those investments more readily increase the odds of survival. The great apes grew to the size and muscular strength their energy intake could maintain with the brains they had. But at the fork, the earliest protohumans began to divert energy from growing their bodies to growing their brains, to the point that our brains today take about 30 percent of our total energy expenditure compared to other great apes, whose brains use about 15 percent (they invest more energy into muscle development and digestion).[3]

How did this fork arise in the first place? Why did our ancestors venture down the unusual path of diverting energy to bigger brains?

As with any complex system, multiple interacting factors contributed, but anthropologists generally agree on the most significant contributor to the formation of that fork: bipedalism.

All great apes, as occasional bipeds, can stand on their hind legs. So we already had a "running start." As climate fluctuation caused the African jungles to recede and vast plains to expand, some adventurous tree-loving apes slowly adapted to living on the ground, presumably in search of food and shelter. Their legs grew longer, and they gradually improved their ability to stand and walk on two feet. It took a few million years for them to become habitual bipeds, but if there's a single factor that represents the evolutionary fork in the road, it's the ability to continuously walk on two feet, because of the numerous advantages that bipedalism proffers. You can see food and predators farther in the horizon; you can run faster and longer than other primates (less of your body is exposed to the hot sun so you don't overheat as quickly); and with your forelimbs freed up, you can carry food in your hands over a distance for later consumption. But wait, there's more.

Our erect posture allowed us to evolve a lower larynx and a freer vocal tract, conditions for the eventual development of verbal language, which dramatically increased the complexity of our communication and therefore the speed and quantity of knowledge-sharing with each other. Our free forelimbs allowed us to evolve hands that are extraordinarily nimble and dexterous; these new hands were critical in the creation of stone tools that enhanced our ability to both hunt and cut up animal meat, bolstering a protein-rich diet that provided us even more caloric energy. So bipedalism ultimately enabled us to extract more energy from our environment while at the same time reducing our energy needs: cut-up meat requires less digestive effort, and walking on two feet requires about one-quarter of the energy required to walk on all four.[4] Bipedalism rewarded us with surplus energy.

Bipedalism was the gift that kept on giving.

But why was this newly acquired energy invested into brain development rather than into bigger bodies? There is a consensus answer to this question, but it is speculative. The incremental pressure for bigger brains over bigger bodies was probably related to the increased social complexity that developed as we became better hunters. Hunting big game requires a great deal of intra-group co-operation. As we banded together to track down prey, smarts became more important than brawn, both for developing co-operative hunting strategies and for coping with the nuances of complex social living (such as managing conflict, outsmarting competitors, and wooing mates). Hunting-gathering takes more intelligence than basic food picking and eating, which other great apes rely on (and which absorbs much of their time, leaving little freedom for more cognitively complex tasks).

A virtuous cycle of reinforcing factors fuelled our brain growth, but bipedalism was undeniably monumental in prodding us down a divergent path to a point where, just over one million years ago, we suddenly transitioned from gradually growing brains to rapidly growing brains. What was the trigger for this huge step up? We learned how to control fire; in particular, we learned how to cook with our dexterous hands. Cooking marks the point in the chart where human brain growth shoots straight up.

Bipedalism + Cooking =

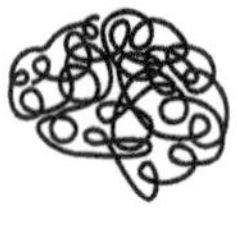

Cooked food is already partially broken down when ingested, so it not only takes less digestive energy to absorb but also allows our gut to absorb more nutrients before it is excreted (which is why human feces have less residual nutrients than other animals').[5] Just as bipedalism generated both an energy supply increase and an energy demand decrease, cooking also produced a twofold energy boost — higher nutrient absorption and lower digestive effort. The energy breakthrough that cooking facilitated launched an exponential step-up in the growth and complexity of the human brain, expediting our exponential cognitive development. Our mental complexity feeds on itself because of our unique ability to share learnings: we accumulate and pass on cultural knowledge from one generation to the next, continually upgrading our knowledge and skills. It's debatable but unlikely that any other species is capable of even rudimentary forms of cumulative, intergenerational learning. Unlike other animals, we are still learning and discovering, and "complexifying" our world and our lives.

So six million years after our ancestors took the unusual primate route of bipedalism, here we are: neuron-packed brains bouncing atop a pair of feet, with some reproductive organs in between to keep the evolutionary odyssey moving forward.

But it hasn't been a complete success story.

A Huge Brain Aloft Two Feet

I opened chapter 1 with the observation that the list of our bodily imperfections is a long one, and the brain is no exception. As their posture straightened, our ancestors' spines became much curvier than those of other apes, specifically, the lumbar part of our lower back. This curvature creates occasional or chronic lower back pain for an estimated 80 percent of humans today — especially those who spend a lot of time sitting in desk chairs. Not to mention the uncomfortable strain the female lower back is subject to during pregnancy. This same curvature also compromises the cartilage between our vertebrae, pushing them out of place, creating the uniquely human problem of "slipped disc" herniation. But that's just the beginning. Quadrupeds spread the strain of running and jumping across four limbs, whereas we overwork our knees and ankles, which are both prone to injury, as are our ligaments (especially our ACL, which is prone to tearing). But wait, there's more. To walk upright, our hips and pelvis had to become quite narrow, forcing the female birth canal to become distorted and difficult for a fetus's big-brained head to get through. Unlike other animals, female humans need assistance in giving birth, and it's only thanks to modern obstetrics that infant mortality has decreased in the past century from 10 percent to less than 0.5 percent in most developed countries.[6]

Our bodies are highly imperfect. Same goes for our brains.

Natural selection can only work with the materials it has, so it took a long time for us to become bipedal, and our bodies are still adjusting. Here's the key point: *the evolution of our imperfect bodies is precisely parallel to the development of our big, complex, and patently imperfect brains.* And just as we are generally ignorant of the drawbacks of bipedalism, even though most of us suffer varying degrees of back pain, we also tend to be oblivious to the specific design flaws of the human brain, even though we suffer varying degrees of psychological torment from them. We don't see our backs and brains for what they are — still in the development stage.

Beta, Buddha, and Bringing It All Together

The epigraph that opens this chapter is a quote from psychologist Erich Fromm's book *The Sane Society*, which captures the spirit of the human condition: "He has fallen out of nature, as it were, and is still in it." With his inimitable flare, Nietzsche, in *Thus Spoke Zarathustra*, captures the same dilemma: "Man is a rope stretched between the animal and the Overman — a rope over an abyss." Both writers emphasize that we are still evolving from our roots as primates. Our "half-in, half-out" condition makes it hard to be human because our brain, and more specifically the human mind that emerges from this brain, is still in the beta testing stage.Which is to say that some features of our cognitive software have yet to be ironed out — flaws that cause us incremental difficulty and suffering, especially in a twenty-first-century setting for which System 1 is not well adapted. (Come to think of it, maybe our fancy brains are still only in the preliminary alpha testing stage!)

In this book, I identified five of our most problematic cognitive design flaws: five battles that constitute the war with ourselves. For each flaw, I offered a high-level coping strategy that encompassed specific tools to confront these human peculiarities. The war with ourselves occupies us every day to varying degrees. We struggle because we don't appreciate the sources of our suffering (how design features become design flaws) and because, even when we become aware, the solutions don't come easily or naturally to us. But The Space Between is always waiting to be opened. And standing by in that space is Observing Self, willing and able to help implement tactics for overcoming the design flaws that cause us to suffer. Within that magical space lies the precious human freedom of cognitive control.

Only a self-important and preposterously arrogant faux-intellectual would have the audacity to revise the Buddha's Four Noble Truths. An even more egregious egotist would imagine engaging in a discussion that attempts to educate the Buddha. With that caveat out of the way, here are my proposed tweaks to his ancient wisdom:

Buddha: The first noble truth is that there is suffering.

Ted: No argument from me.

Buddha: The second noble truth is that there is a cause of suffering: our craving, desire, and attachment to things, which stem from our ignorance of the true nature of reality.

Ted: I agree that we often misperceive reality and that is a source of suffering. If, by craving or attachment, you mean we want things from the world that it doesn't offer, I agree. We desire simplicity, certainty, clarity, predictability, and meaningfulness.

Buddha: We misperceive reality as something that is fixed and outside ourselves — something that can satisfy our cravings. But reality is forever in flux, inseparable from us, and therefore cannot satisfy our desires. The illusion fuels our insatiable cravings and so we suffer. The third noble truth is that the cessation of suffering is possible. Our liberation is dependent upon renouncing craving.

Ted: "Cessation" is too ambitious. We can't completely escape our cognitive design — the best we can aim for is mitigating the suffering that we subject ourselves to. We can't realistically renounce our desires; we just need to temper our demands of the universe by understanding it better.

Buddha: The renunciation of misplaced desire comes naturally once we break the illusion of a separate, unchangeable world. Only then can suffering cease, because only then can we be liberated from the infinite cycle of painful rebirths that karma traps us in.

Ted: Uhhh ... that's a lot of metaphysics to ascribe to suffering. I'm just aiming for mitigation in one lifetime, not eternal liberation. So let's agree that much of our suffering stems from not seeing things as they really are.

Buddha: The fourth noble truth is the eightfold path leading to the renunciation of craving and therefore suffering: right view, right intention, right speech —

Ted: I have a "fivefold path" of my own — a path for each design flaw. Each of these five paths have ancillary paths, which are the tools —

Buddha: Sounds like a lot of paths. It's not that complicated: we simply need to correct the illusion of ourselves as separate from an unchanging world. By meditating on our immediate experience, aware of all that arises in a given moment, we can see reality more clearly.

Ted: I think the solution to suffering is more complicated than eliminating a single illusion. But yes, meditating is one way to insert The Space Between. The trick is to step out of our System 1–generated thoughts and feelings by taking refuge in this space, where System 2–generated strategies and tools can overcome our faulty ways of thinking and reacting.

Buddha: Good luck with that.

I'm not a Buddhist for the simple reason that I don't buy into Buddhist cosmology (karma, rebirth, etc.). But I'm sympathetic to many Buddhist ideas; in fact, I'm inspired by them. There is good reason that Gautama Buddha has been called the very first psychologist: he diagnosed human suffering, scrutinized the nature of the human mind and its vulnerabilities, and prescribed methods for equanimity. Many centuries before human metacognition was defined and studied, Gautama explored what it meant to look inward and study mental patterns as they arise and fall.

The core idea at the heart of this book is the Buddhist-inspired notion that *our ultimate freedom lies in our unique metacognitive ability to self-distance, which opens up a whole world of cognitive control that is otherwise unavailable.* Much of our suffering is self-inflicted, originating from the goofy way our minds work. When design features become flaws, we need paths to guide us through the forest of our cognitive deficiencies. Paths that are only available in The Space Between.

We need The Space Between to make being human easier. We need the space to take refuge from the private machinations and fantasies unfolding in the drama that is always playing in our heads. We need the space to be smarter — a place to broaden our perspective beyond

THE WAR PLAN

Problem:

Feature ⟶ Flaw

System 1 dominates when it shouldn't

Solution:

Fix in The Space Between

System 2 metacognition can override System 1

5 BATTLE PLANS

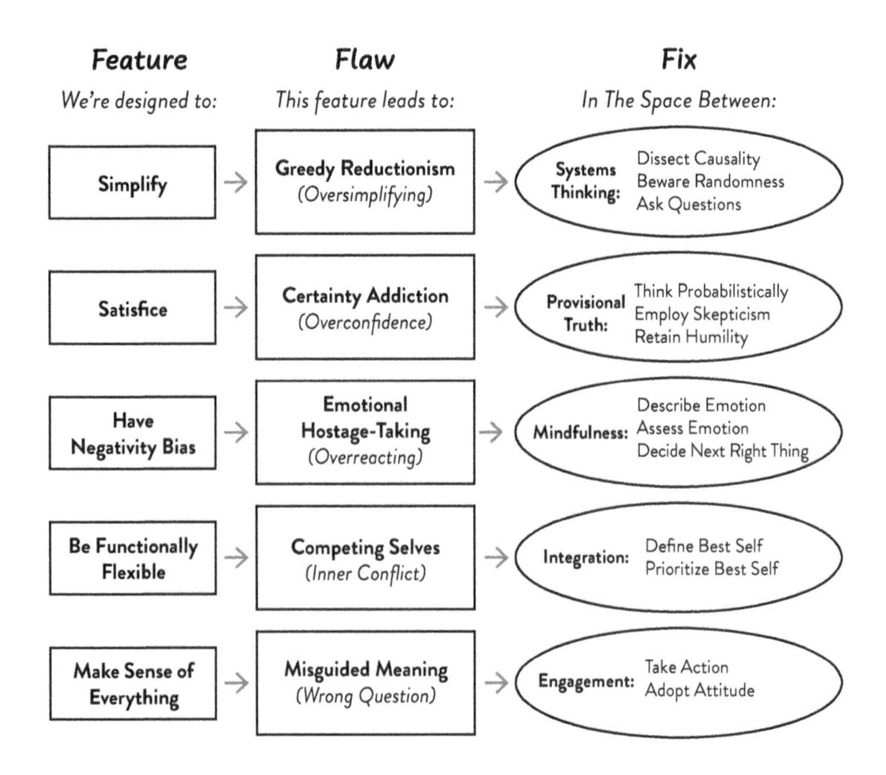

the severely skewed personal lens through which we interpret absolutely everything. To describe our individual take on reality as "subjective" or "biased" doesn't do justice to how shockingly confined our personal worldview truly is. Our acute myopia feeds our tendency to be astoundingly self-centred, self-focused, self-absorbed, and self-righteous. Which is why we not only need the space for perspective, we also need each other — desperately — for all the obvious reasons but also for the less obvious reason that without the benefit of others' vantage points, our individual views are stunningly narrow.

Subtle Manoeuvres and the Wisdom of Plants

Research indicates that 83 percent of us, at some point in our lives, will experience "the psychiatric symptoms and resulting functional impairment necessary to meet criteria for the diagnosis of a mental disorder."[7] But unique human suffering, as any good existentialist would point out, is the price of unique human freedom, the cost of having more control over the world and ourselves than any other animal. Freedom, apparently, comes with a heavy psychological toll (which is why Sartre, in *Being and Nothingness*, describes us as "condemned to be free"). Not only is the price of freedom high, but the prize itself doesn't come easily. Our best System 2 thinking, which allows us to step out of the clutches of System 1 and its instant responses, resides in a place that is always available but is hard to get to, because System 1 resists relinquishing its power and discourages us from retreating to The Space Between, where our profoundest freedom awaits.

German novelist Franz Kafka, writing to his lover, noted that "if a pleasant, straightforward life is not possible then one must try to wriggle through by subtle manoeuvres."[8] In this book I have addressed some of the manoeuvres for navigating the complex challenges of being human, most of which are neither intuitive nor obvious because life's challenges themselves are not the "straightforward" kind that Kafka, you, and I might prefer. The human condition is less a problem to solve than it is a predicament to manage, if you recall Abraham Kaplan's distinction, described in chapters 4 and 12. We can only cope with predicaments in the best way possible, because they don't lend themselves to clear, definitive solutions. Hence, the need for "subtle manoeuvres."

I think Nietzsche captures the essence of the human struggle brilliantly in an unpublished notebook where he addresses the question of how a person can manage to keep living despite horrendous obstacles and a lack of universal meaning: "He begins to understand that he possesses an inventiveness of the same kind as he admires in plants, which climb and wind and finally gain some light and a patch of soil and thus create for themselves their share of joy on inhospitable ground."[9] Like persistent plants, we push through inhospitality in search of the firm grounding of certainty and the warmth of meaning. (Perhaps Nietzsche was inspired by Voltaire's *Candide*, whose protagonist, as I indicated in chapter 12, solves the mystery of a good life with, "Let us tend to our garden.")

I suspect most of us would be bored if being human was too straightforward and didn't require subtle manoeuvres. Other animals may have it easier, but they can't possibly be having as much fun.

(Can they?)

Notes

Introduction | Other Animals Have It Easier

1 John A. Chiles et al., *Clinical Manual for the Assessment and Treatment of Suicidal Patients*, 2nd ed. (Washington, DC: American Psychiatric Association, 2019).
2 R. Harris, "Embracing Your Demons: An Overview of Acceptance and Commitment Therapy," *Psychotherapy in Australia* 12 (2006): 70.
3 Nassim Nicholas Taleb, *The Black Swan: The Impact of the Highly Improbable* (New York: Random House, 2010).
4 H.G. Wells, *The Last Books of H.G. Wells: The Happy Turning and Mind at the End of Its Tether* (New York: Monkfish, 2006).
5 Nassim Nicholas Taleb and Mark Blyth, "The Black Swan of Cairo: How Suppressing Volatility Makes the World Less Predictable and More Dangerous," *Foreign Affairs* 90, no. 3 (May/June 2011).

Chapter 1 | Big Cognitive Problem

1 Daniel Kahneman, *Thinking, Fast and Slow* (Toronto: Doubleday Canada, 2011).
2 Benjamin Libet, *Mind Time: The Temporal Factor in Consciousness* (Cambridge, MA: Harvard University Press, 2005).
3 David Eagleman, *Incognito: The Secret Lives of the Brain* (Toronto: Penguin Canada, 2012).

4 Jonathan Haidt, *The Happiness Hypothesis: Finding Modern Truth in Ancient Wisdom* (New York: Basic Books, 2006).
5 Steven Pinker, *The Blank Slate: The Modern Denial of Human Nature* (New York: Penguin, 2003).
6 Owen Flanagan, *Consciousness Reconsidered* (Cambridge, MA: MIT Press, 1993).
7 Daniel M. Wegner, *The Illusion of Conscious Will*, 1st ed. (Cambridge, MA: MIT Press, 2003).
8 Kahneman, *Thinking, Fast and Slow.*

Chapter 2 | Huge Metacognitive Solution

1 Charles Darwin, *The Descent of Man* (London: Penguin Classics, 2004).
2 Stephen R. Covey, foreword to *Prisoners of Our Thoughts: Viktor Frankl's Principles for Discovering Meaning in Life and Work*, 2nd ed., by Alex Pattakos and Elaine Dundon (Oakland, CA: Berrett-Koehler, 2010).

Chapter 3 | Flaw #1: We're Greedy Reductionists

1 Robert Wright, *Why Buddhism Is True: The Science and Philosophy of Meditation and Enlightenment* (New York: Simon and Schuster, 2018).
2 Aldous Huxley, *The Doors of Perception* (New York: Harper Perennial, 2009).
3 Huxley, *The Doors of Perception.*
4 Daniel C. Dennett, *Darwin's Dangerous Idea: Evolution and the Meanings of Life* (New York: Simon and Schuster, 1996).
5 Amos Tversky and Daniel Kahneman, "Availability: A Heuristic for Judging Frequency and Probability," *Cognitive Psychology* 5, no. 2 (1973): 207–32.
6 Virgil, *Georgics*, trans. Peter Fallon (Oxford: Oxford University Press, 2009).
7 Michael S. Gazzaniga, *Who's in Charge?: Free Will and the Science of the Brain* (New York: Ecco, 2011).

Chapter 4 | Fix #1: Reining in Reductionism

1 Peter M. Senge, *The Fifth Discipline: The Art and Practice of the Learning Organization*, rev. ed. (New York: Crown Business, 2006).
2 Arthur De Vany, *Hollywood Economics: How Extreme Uncertainty Shapes the Film Industry* (New York: Routledge, 2003).
3 Michael J. Mauboussin, *The Success Equation: Untangling Skill and Luck in Business, Sports, and Investing* (Boston: Harvard Business Review Press, 2012).
4 Philip M. Rosenzweig, *The Halo Effect: ... and the Eight Other Business Delusions That Deceive Managers* (New York: Free Press, 2009); Michael E. Raynor, Mumtaz Ahmed, and Andrew D. Henderson, *A Random Search for Excellence: Why "Great" Company Research Delivers Fables and Not Facts* (Westlake, TX: Deloitte University Press, 2009).
5 Charles D. Ellis, *Winning the Loser's Game: Timeless Strategies for Successful Investing*, 7th ed. (New York: McGraw-Hill, 2017).
6 Nassim Nicholas Taleb, *Antifragile: Things That Gain from Disorder* (New York: Random House, 2012).
7 Martin Heidegger, *The Question Concerning Technology and Other Essays* (New York: Harper Perennial, 1982).
8 Voltaire, *Letters Concerning the English Nation* (Oxford: Oxford University Press, 1994).
9 Paul B. Baltes and Ursula M. Staudinger, "Wisdom: A Metaheuristic (Pragmatic) to Orchestrate Mind and Virtue Toward Excellence," *American Psychologist* 55, no. 1 (2000): 122–36.
10 Karl Popper, *All Life Is Problem Solving* (New York: Routledge, 2001).
11 Thomas Sowell, *Basic Economics: A Common Sense Guide to the Economy*, 4th ed. (New York: Basic Books, 2010).
12 Richard Farson, *Management of the Absurd: Paradoxes in Leadership* (New York: Free Press, 1997).
13 Carl Jung, commentary to *The Secret of the Golden Flower: A Chinese Book of Life*, trans. Richard Wilhelm (Boston: Mariner Books, 1970).

Chapter 5 | Flaw #2: We're Addicted to Certainty

1 Shane Frederick, "Cognitive Reflection and Decision Making," *Journal of Economic Perspectives* 19, no. 4 (2005): 25–42.
2 Keith E. Stanovich, "Distinguishing the Reflective, Algorithmic, and Autonomous Minds: Is It Time for a Tri-Process Theory?," in *In Two Minds: Dual Processes and Beyond*, ed. Jonathan Evans and Keith Franklish (Oxford: Oxford University Press, 2008).
3 H.A. Simon, "Rational Choice and the Structure of the Environment," *Psychological Review* 63, no. 2 (1956): 129–38.
4 Barry Schwartz et al., "Maximizing Versus Satisficing," *Journal of Personality and Social Psychology* 83, no. 5 (2002): 1178–97.
5 Kahneman, *Thinking, Fast and Slow.*
6 Robert A. Burton, *On Being Certain: Believing You Are Right Even When You're Not* (New York: St. Martin's, 2009).
7 Irvin D. Yalom, *Existential Psychotherapy* (New York: Basic Books, 1980).
8 Leonid Rozenblit and Frank Keil, "The Misunderstood Limits of Folk Science: An Illusion of Explanatory Depth," *Cognitive Science* 26, no. 5 (2002): 521–62.
9 David Dunning and Justin Kruger, "Unskilled and Unaware of It: How Difficulties in Recognizing One's Own Incompetence Lead to Inflated Self-Assessments," *Journal of Personality and Social Psychology* 77, no. 6 (1999): 1121–34.
10 Darwin, *The Descent of Man.*
11 Kahneman, *Thinking, Fast and Slow.*
12 Burton, *On Being Certain.*
13 Friedrich Nietzsche, *Twilight of the Idols* (Indianapolis: Hackett Publishing, 1997).

Chapter 6 | Fix #2: Breaking Our Addiction

1 Friedrich Nietzsche, *Human, All Too Human: A Book for Free Spirits* (Cambridge, UK: Cambridge University Press, 1996).

2 Friedrich Nietzsche, *On Truth and Lies in a Nonmoral Sense* (Scotts Valley, CA: CreateSpace, 2015).
3 Friedrich Nietzsche, *Nietzsche: Writings From the Late Notebooks* (Cambridge, UK: Cambridge University Press, 2003).
4 J. Krishnamurti, *Truth Is a Pathless Land* (Louisville, CO: Sounds True, 2003), audio CD, 2:30:00.
5 Pinker, *The Blank Slate.*
6 Iain McGilchrist, *The Master and His Emissary: The Divided Brain and the Making of the Western World*, rev. ed. (London: Yale University Press, 2009).
7 Stephen Jay Gould, *Hen's Teeth and Horse's Toes: Further Reflections in Natural History* (New York: Penguin, 1984).
8 Antonio Damasio, *Descartes' Error: Emotion, Reason, and the Human Brain* (New York: Penguin, 2005).
9 Philip E. Tetlock and Dan Gardner, *Superforecasting: The Art and Science of Prediction* (New York: Crown, 2015).
10 John P.A. Ioannidis, "Why Most Published Research Findings Are False," *PLOS Medicine* 2, no. 8 (2005): 696–701.
11 John R. Lott and David Mustard, "Crime, Deterrence, and Right-to-Carry Concealed Handguns," *Journal of Legal Studies* 26, no. 1 (1997): 1–68.
12 Abhay Aneja, John J. Donohue, and Alexandria Zhang, "The Impact of Right-to-Carry Laws and the NRC Report," *American Law and Economics Review* 13, no. 2 (2011): 565–632.
13 Hillel J. Einhorn and Robin M. Hogarth, "Prediction, Diagnosis, and Causal Thinking in Forecasting," *Journal of Forecasting* 1, no. 1 (1982): 23–36.
14 Nassim Nicholas Taleb, *Fooled by Randomness: The Hidden Role of Chance in Life and in the Markets*, 2nd ed. (New York: Random House, 2005).
15 Taleb, *Fooled by Randomness.*
16 Chris Argyris, "Double Loop Learning in Organizations," *Harvard Business Review* 55 (September 1977).
17 Tetlock and Gardner, *Superforecasting.*
18 Philip E. Tetlock, *Expert Political Judgment: How Good Is It? How Can We Know?* (Princeton, NJ: Princeton University Press, 2006).

19 McGilchrist, *The Master and His Emissary.*
20 Taleb, *Antifragile.*

Chapter 7 | Flaw #3: We Hold Ourselves Emotionally Hostage

1 Arthur Schopenhauer, *On the Suffering of the World* (New York: Penguin, 2004).
2 Robert M. Sapolsky, *Why Zebras Don't Get Ulcers*, 3rd ed. (New York: Henry Holt, 2004).
3 Stephen Batchelor, *Buddhism Without Beliefs: A Contemporary Guide to Awakening* (New York: Riverhead Books, 1998).
4 Matthew Killingsworth and Daniel Gilbert, "A Wandering Mind Is an Unhappy Mind," *Science* 330 (2010): 932.
5 Frank Wilczek, *Fundamentals: Ten Keys to Reality* (New York: Penguin Press, 2021).
6 Michael Lewis, *The Undoing Project: A Friendship That Changed Our Minds* (New York: W.W. Norton, 2017).
7 Harris, "Embracing Your Demons."
8 Schopenhauer, *On the Suffering of the World.*
9 Daniel Kahneman and Amos Tversky, "Prospect Theory: An Analysis of Decision Under Risk," *Econometrica* 47, no. 2 (1979): 263–92.
10 Alison Ledgerwood, "A Simple Trick to Improve Positive Thinking," TEDxUCDavis, May 2013, video, 9:59, ted.com/talks/alison_ledgerwood_a_simple_trick_to_improve_positive_thinking.
11 Alison Ledgerwood and Amber E. Boydstun, "Sticky Prospects: Loss Frames Are Cognitively Stickier Than Gain Frames," *Journal of Experimental Psychology: General* 143, no. 1 (2014): 376–85.
12 John Gottman, *Why Marriages Succeed or Fail* (New York: Simon and Schuster, 2012).
13 Nina Strohminger, Joshua Knobe, and George Newman, "The True Self: A Psychological Concept Distinct From the Self," *Perspectives on Psychological Science* 12, no. 4 (2017): 551–60.
14 Roy F. Baumeister and John Tierney, *Willpower: Rediscovering the Greatest Human Strength* (New York: Penguin, 2012); Barbara L.

Fredrickson, *Positivity: Top-Notch Research Reveals the 3-to-1 Ratio That Will Change Your Life* (New York: Harmony, 2009); Roy F. Baumeister et al., "Bad Is Stronger Than Good," *Review of General Psychology* 5, no. 4 (2001): 323–70.

15 Robert W. Schrauf and Julia Sanchez, "The Preponderance of Negative Emotion Words in the Emotion Lexicon: A Cross-Generational and Cross-Linguistic Study," *Journal of Multilingual and Multicultural Development* 25, no. 2–3 (2004): 266–84.

16 Kent C. Berridge, "Comparing the Emotional Brains of Humans and Other Animals," in *Handbook of Affective Sciences*, ed. R.J. Davidson, K.R. Scherer, and H.H. Goldsmith (Oxford: Oxford University Press, 2003), 25–51.

Chapter 8 | Fix #3: Freeing the Hostage

1 David Hume, *An Enquiry Concerning Human Understanding* (Oxford: Oxford University Press, 2008).

2 Daniel Gilbert, *Stumbling on Happiness* (New York: Vintage, 2007).

3 Viktor E. Frankl, *Psychotherapy and Existentialism* (New York: Simon and Schuster, 1967).

Chapter 9 | Flaw #4: We Compete with Ourselves

1 Friedrich Nietzsche, *The Will to Power*, trans. Anthony M. Ludovici (New York: Sterling, 2016).

2 Walter Melo and Pedro Henrique Costa de Resende, "The Impact of James's Varieties of Religious Experience on Jung's Work," *History of Psychology* 23, no. 1 (2020): 62–76.

3 William Fleeson, "Moving Personality Beyond the Person-Situation Debate: The Challenge and the Opportunity of Within-Person Variability," *Current Directions in Psychological Science* 13, no. 2 (2004): 83–87.

4 William Fleeson, "Situation-Based Contingencies Underlying Trait-Content Manifestation in Behavior," *Journal of Personality* 75, no. 4 (2007): 825–61.

5 William Fleeson, "Toward a Structure- and Process-Integrated View of Personality: Traits as Density Distribution of States," *Journal of Personality and Social Psychology* 80, no. 6 (2001): 1011–27.
6 Kennon Sheldon et al., "Trait Self and True Self: Cross-Role Variation in the Big-Five Personality Traits and Its Relations with Psychological Authenticity and Subjective Well-Being," *Journal of Personality and Social Psychology* 73, no. 6 (1997): 1380–93.
7 Hugh Hartshorne et al., *Studies in the Nature of Character* (New York: Macmillan, 1928).
8 Christopher Hitchens, *The Missionary Position: Mother Teresa in Theory and Practice* (Toronto: McClelland and Stewart, 2012).
9 George Ainslie, *Breakdown of Will* (Cambridge, UK: Cambridge University Press, 2001).
10 Kahneman, *Thinking, Fast and Slow.*
11 Tinca J.C. Polderman et al, "Meta-Analysis of the Heritability of Human Traits Based on Fifty Years of Twin Studies," *Nature Genetics* 47, no. 7 (2015): 702–9.
12 Pinker, *The Blank Slate.*
13 Timothy D. Wilson, *Strangers to Ourselves: Discovering the Adaptive Unconscious* (Cambridge, MA: Belknap, 2004).
14 Lars Hall et al., "Magic at the Marketplace: Choice Blindness for the Taste of Jam and the Smell of Tea," *Cognition* 117, no. 1 (2010): 54–61.
15 Emily Pronin, "The Introspection Illusion," in *Advances in Experimental Social Psychology*, ed. Mark P. Zanna (Amsterdam: Academic Press, 2009), 1–67.
16 Nina Mazar and Dan Ariely, "Dishonesty in Everyday Life and Its Policy Implications," *Journal of Public Policy and Marketing* 25 (2006): 117–26.
17 Robert Jay Lifton, *The Nazi Doctors: Medical Killing and the Psychology of Genocide*, 2nd ed. (New York: Basic Books, 2017).
18 Rita Carter, *Multiplicity: The New Science of Personality, Identity, and the Self* (Boston: Little, Brown, 2008).
19 Robert Sapolsky, *Behave: The Biology of Humans at Our Best and Worst* (New York: Penguin, 2017).
20 Bruce Hood, *The Self Illusion: How the Social Brain Creates Identity* (Oxford: Oxford University Press, 2013).

21 Daniel M. Wegner, "Self Is Magic," in *Are We Free?: Psychology and Free Will*, ed. John Baer, James C. Kaufman, and Roy F. Baumeister (Oxford: Oxford University Press, 2008).
22 Simine Vazire, "Who Knows What About a Person? The Self-Other Knowledge Asymmetry (SOKA) Model," *Journal of Personality and Social Psychology* 98, no. 2 (2010): 281–300.
23 Simine Vazire and Erika N. Carlson, "Self-Knowledge of Personality: Do People Know Themselves?," *Social and Personality Psychology Compass* 4, no. 8 (2010): 605–20.
24 Thomas Shelley Duval and Paul J. Silvia, "Self-Awareness, Probability of Improvement, and the Self-Serving Bias," *Journal of Personality and Social Psychology* 82, no. 1 (2002): 49–61.
25 William Fleeson and Joshua Wilt, "The Relevance of Big Five Trait Content in Behavior to Subjective Authenticity: Do High Levels of Within-Person Behavioral Variability Undermine or Enable Authenticity Achievement?," *Journal of Personality* 78, no. 4 (2010): 1353–82.
26 Roy F. Baumeister, "Stalking the True Self Through the Jungles of Authenticity: Problems, Contradictions, Inconsistencies, Disturbing Findings — and a Possible Way Forward," *Review of General Psychology* 23, no. 1 (2019): 143–54.
27 Yalom, *Existential Psychotherapy.*
28 Andrew G. Christy, Rebecca J. Schlegel, and Andrei Cimpian, "Why Do People Believe in a 'True Self'? The Role of Essentialist Reasoning About Personal Identity and the Self," *Journal of Personality and Social Psychology* 117, no. 2 (2019): 386–416.
29 Michael H. Kernis and Brian M. Goldman, "A Multicomponent Conceptualization of Authenticity: Theory and Research," *Advances in Experimental Social Psychology* 38 (2006): 283–357.
30 Rebecca J. Schlegel et al., "Feeling Like You Know Who You Are: Perceived True Self-Knowledge and Meaning in Life," *Personality and Social Psychology Bulletin* 37, no. 6 (2011): 745–56.
31 Robert E. Wickham, "Perceived Authenticity in Romantic Partners," *Journal of Experimental Social Psychology* 49, no. 5 (2013): 878–87.
32 Djurdja Grijak, "Authenticity as a Predictor of Mental Health," *Klinička Psihologija* 10, no. 1–2 (2017): 23–34.

33 William James, *The Principles of Psychology*, 2 vols. (Pantianos Classics, 2018).

Chapter 10 | Fix #4: Being at One with Ourselves

1 Carl Jung, *Visions: Notes of the Seminar Given in 1930–1934*, ed. Claire Douglas (Princeton: Princeton University Press, 1997).
2 Steven C. Hayes, Kirk D. Strosahl, and Kelly G. Wilson, *Acceptance and Commitment Therapy, 2nd ed.* (New York: Guilford, 2016).
3 Carl Jung, *Two Essays on Analytical Psychology* (Eastford, CT: Martino Fine Books, 2014).
4 Jung, *Two Essays on Analytical Psychology.*
5 Jung, commentary to *The Secret of the Golden Flower.*
6 Jean-Paul Sartre, *Existentialism Is a Humanism* (London: Yale University Press, 2007).
7 Scott Barry Kaufman, *Transcend: The New Science of Self-Actualization* (New York: TarcherPerigee, 2020).
8 Benjamin Hardy, *Personality Isn't Permanent: Break Free from Self-Limiting Beliefs and Rewrite Your Story* (New York: Portfolio, 2020).
9 David Lester, *A Multiple Self Theory of Personality* (Hauppauge, NY: Nova Science, 2010).
10 Richard C. Schwartz and Martha Sweezy, *Internal Family Systems Therapy,* 2nd ed. (New York: Guilford, 2019).
11 Richard H. Thaler and H.M. Shefrin, "An Economic Theory of Self-Control," *Journal of Political Economy* 89, no. 2 (1981): 392–406.
12 Angela L. Duckworth, Tamar Szabó Gendler, and James J. Gross, "Situational Strategies for Self-Control," *Perspectives on Psychological Science* 11, no. 1 (2016): 35–55.
13 Mark R. Leary, *The Curse of the Self: Self-Awareness, Egotism, and the Quality of Human Life* (Oxford: Oxford University Press, 2007).
14 Ainslie, *Breakdown of Will.*
15 Jason P. Mitchell et al., "Medial Prefrontal Cortex Predicts Intertemporal Choice," *Journal of Cognitive Neuroscience* 23, no. 4 (2011): 857–66.

16 Loran F. Nordgren, Frenk van Harreveld, and Joop van der Pligt, "The Restraint Bias: How the Illusion of Self-Restraint Promotes Impulsive Behavior," *Psychological Science* 20, no. 12 (2009): 1523–28.
17 George Loewenstein, "Out of Control: Visceral Influences on Behavior," *Organizational Behavior and Human Decision Processes* 65, no. 3 (1996): 272–92.
18 Roy F. Baumeister and Kathleen D. Vohs, "Self-Regulation, Ego Depletion, and Motivation," *Social and Personality Psychology Compass* 1, no. 1 (2007): 115–28.
19 Roy F. Baumeister, Kathleen D. Vohs, and Dianne M. Tice, "The Strength Model of Self-Control," *Current Directions in Psychological Science* 16, no. 6 (2007): 351–55.
20 Marina Milyavskaya and Michael Inzlicht, "What's So Great About Self-Control? Examining the Importance of Effortful Self-Control and Temptation in Predicting Real-Life Depletion and Goal Attainment," *Social Psychological and Personality Science* 8, no. 6 (2017): 603–11.
21 Duckworth, Gendler, and Gross, "Situational Strategies for Self-Control."
22 R.H. Strotz, "Myopia and Inconsistency in Dynamic Utility Maximization," *Review of Economic Studies* 23, no. 3 (1955–56): 165–80.
23 Sapolsky, *Behave.*
24 Ainslie, *Breakdown of Will.*
25 Clayton M. Christensen, James Allworth, and Karen Dillion, *How Will You Measure Your Life?* (New York: HarperCollins, 2012).
26 James Clear, *Atomic Habits: An Easy and Proven Way to Build Good Habits and Break Bad Ones* (New York: Avery, 2018).

Chapter 11 | Flaw #5: We Misdirect Our Need for Meaning

1 Thomas Nagel, "The Absurd," *Journal of Philosophy* 68, no. 20 (1971): 716–27.
2 Antonio Preti, "Suicide Among Animals: A Review of Evidence," *Psychological Reports* 101, no. 3 (2007): 831–48.
3 Viktor Frankl, *Man's Search for Meaning* (Boston: Beacon, 2006).

4 Frankl, *Man's Search for Meaning.*
5 William James, *A Pluralistic Universe* (Scotts Valley, CA: CreateSpace, 2015).
6 Tatjana Schnell, "Existential Indifference: Another Quality of Meaning in Life," *Journal of Humanistic Psychology* 50, no. 3 (2010): 351–73.

Chapter 12 | Fix #5: Pursuing the Meaning Feeling

1 Yalom, *Existential Psychotherapy.*
2 Ludwig Wittgenstein, *Tractatus Logico-Philosophicus* (New York: Cosimo Classics, 2007).
3 Robert W. White, "Motivation Reconsidered: The Concept of Competence," *Psychological Review* 66, no. 5 (1959): 297–333.
4 Eric Maisel, *Life Purpose Boot Camp: The 8-Week Breakthrough Plan for Creating a Meaningful Life* (Novato, CA: New World Library, 2014).
5 Eric Maisel, *The Van Gogh Blues: The Creative Person's Path Through Depression* (Novato, CA: New World Library, 2007).
6 Scott Barry Kaufman, "There Is No One Way to Live a Good Life," *Scientific American* (blog), Sepember 21, 2017, blogs.scientificamerican.com /beautiful-minds/there-is-no-one-way-to-live-a-good-life.
7 Arthur Schopenhauer, *On the Suffering of the World* (New York: Penguin, 2004).
8 Stephen Batchelor, *Living with the Devil: A Meditation on Good and Evil* (New York: Riverhead Books, 2005).
9 Stephen Batchelor, *After Buddhism: Rethinking the Dharma for a Secular Age* (London: Yale University Press, 2017).
10 Maisel, *The Van Gogh Blues.*
11 Albert Camus, *The Myth of Sisyphus* (New York: Vintage, 2018).
12 Jesse Bering, *Suicidal: Why We Kill Ourselves* (Chicago: University of Chicago Press, 2018).
13 Leo Tolstoy, *A Confession* (Garden City, NY: Dover, 2005).
14 Quoted in Graham Parkes, *Composing the Soul: Reaches of Nietzsche's Psychology* (Chicago: University of Chicago Press, 1994).

15 Carl Jung, *Memories, Dreams, Reflections*, ed. Aniela Jaffé, trans. Richard Winston and Clara Winston (New York: Vintage, 1989).
16 Carl Rogers, *On Becoming a Person: A Therapist's View of Psychotherapy* (Boston: Houghton Mifflin, 1961).
17 Jung, commentary to *The Secret of the Golden Flower.*

Conclusion | We're Still in Beta

1 Suzana Herculano-Houzel, *The Human Advantage: A New Understanding of How Our Brain Became Remarkable* (Cambridge, MA: MIT Press, 2017).
2 Suzana Herculano-Houzel and Jon H. Kaas, "Gorilla and Orangutan Brains Conform to the Primate Cellular Scaling Rules: Implications for Human Evolution," *Brain Behavior and Evolution* 77, no. 1 (2011): 33–44.
3 Herculano-Houzel, *The Human Advantage.*
4 Daniel Lieberman, *The Story of the Human Body: Evolution, Health, and Disease* (New York: Pantheon, 2013).
5 Richard Wrangham, *Catching Fire: How Cooking Made Us Human* (New York: Basic Books, 2010).
6 Nathan H. Lents, *Human Errors: A Panorama of Our Glitches, from Pointless Bones to Broken Genes* (New York: Houghton Mifflin Harcourt, 2018).
7 Jonathan D. Schaefer et al., "Enduring Mental Health: Prevalence and Prediction," *Journal of Abnormal Psychology* 126, no. 2 (2017): 212–24.
8 Franz Kafka, *The Diaries of Franz Kafka, 1910–1923* (New York: Schocken, 1988).
9 Quoted in Parkes, *Composing the Soul.*

Index

About the Author

Ted Cadsby is a corporate director with experience on a number of for-profit and non-profit boards. As the former executive vice president of Retail Distribution at the Canadian Imperial Bank of Commerce (CIBC), he led eighteen thousand employees in Canada and internationally. He has also been president and CEO of CIBC Securities Inc., chairman of CIBC Trust Corp., and chairman of CIBC Private Investment Counsel Inc.

Ted is the bestselling author of three books, most recently *Closing the Mind Gap: Making Smarter Decisions in a Hyper-Complex World*. He has written numerous articles for various publications, including the *Globe and Mail* and *Harvard Business Review*. Ted advises, teaches, and speaks on decision-making in complex environments, leadership, and group discussion effectiveness. He is a business advisor to the Ted Rogers School of Management Leadership Centre at Ryerson University, where he is also the co-lead of its executive leadership program, Effective Leadership in Complex Times.

Ted graduated as the medalist in philosophy from Queen's University, completed his MBA at the Ivey Business School, and holds the Chartered Financial Analyst designation from the CFA Institute and the ICD.D designation from the Institute of Corporate Directors.